AROUSED
by
BOOKS

AROUSED by BOOKS

by
Anatole Broyard

Random House
New York

These essays originally appeared in *The New York Times*; some have been revised and some expanded.

Library of Congress Cataloging in Publication Data

Broyard, Anatole.
Aroused by books.

A collection of the author's book reviews which originally appeared in the New York Times from 1971–1973.

1. Books—Reviews. I. New York times. II. Title.
Z1035.A1B72.   028.1   74-8271
ISBN 0-394-49104-1

Manufactured in the United States of America

9 8 7 6 5 4 3 2

First Edition

Contents

vi   Contents

AROUSED
by
BOOKS

Introduction

The books discussed in this collection had such a powerful effect on me that I would like to pass the experience along. I feel that every time I open a book, I risk my life—my conception of my life—and having survived some three hundred such experiences in the past three years, I think I can safely recommend the adventure. In fact, books may be our best cure for what Baudelaire called the quotidian frenzy. Recently, there has been a rash of true stories about people who threw up everything and went to live in the woods to get away from it all. I have found that getting *into* it all is a far better defense against the onslaught of our age. When you know what you're up against, you feel better about it. In some cases, you may even want to press closer.

It may sound as if I'm talking exclusively about nonfiction books—state of the union analysis of the American soul—but I believe that fiction, poetry, books on art, *any* kind of book can have an equal effect. Every work of the imagination offers another view of life, an invitation to spend a few days inside somebody else's emotions. And if the book is any good, you won't escape unscathed.

I chose to reprint about one third of the pieces I wrote in 1971–1973. These books, I felt, were good enough—or, in some cases, bad enough—to deserve your attention. Most of them are still available and still pertinent, so I consider this volume a series of passionate suggestions as well as a collection of short essays in criticism.

I don't agree with the notion that you can't write literary or cultural criticism in less than five thousand words. Of course, a longer essay has certain advantages, but I've read many in the quarterlies that I should have liked to see reduced, and I suspect that the shorter reviews in the back pages of these magazines are more closely read than any other part. In any case, a man who turns out a hundred pieces a year will discover that he is really writing a number of long essays, in short, self-contained installments, on his favorite themes.

Here are just a few of the subjects I find myself continually coming back to, each time from the fresh vantage point of a different book: changes in technique, sensibility and subject matter in the novel and the short story; the tone, texture and quality of American life; the advance, by women writers, into areas of experience that they themselves used to regard as a no-woman's-land; the struggle for survival of certain emotions we once subsumed under the general heading of love; the agony of formal education; the attempt to domesticate the idea of death; the groping toward something resembling a faith to replace all the faiths we've broken or lost; the contemporary impulse to confess all in writing or rewriting history; the nostalgia for undefeated personality in biographical works; the seduction of art by the promiscuity of theory; the attempt of some of the young to secede from our species; the gallant rear-guard action of their elders.

Some of the books I reviewed gave me a palpable physical thrill, like goose pimples or a bristling of the hairs on the nape of my neck. Others brought me to the brink of apoplexy. Taken all together, they present a view of people and their predicaments that reminds me of the x-ray picture of herself that Clavdia Chauchat gave to Hans Castorp to commemorate their one night of love. It showed, simultaneously, the shape, the structure and the sickness that he had embraced with so much feeling.

I had intended simply to reprint here what I wrote about these books in *The New York Times*, but in rereading the original reviews I was seized all over again to such an extent that I expanded many of them. Some grew to two or three times their published length; others were increased by several hundred words. In this amplifying, I relied on the compulsively extensive notes I had taken while reading and on the fact that the reviews brought the books vividly to mind. Sometimes I went back to the books themselves. In writing for the paper, I frequently found that I had more to say on a subject after I had filled my allotted space, and I saw no reason not to take advantage of this second chance.

These essays were written so close to one another in time that arranging them in chronological order did not strike me as useful. Grouping them by subject matter also seemed arbitrary, for two reasons: people don't normally read in any such sequence; and a good book is, in a sense, about almost everything. What I have done instead is to arrange the selections in an order that best sets them off against each other, so that each book may strike with the freshness of impact I felt when I first read it.

People often ask who chooses the books to be reviewed: My colleague, Christopher Lehmann-Haupt, and I choose them. Because we have different personalities and try to accommodate those differences, we are each able, more often than not, to write about those books that are closest to our feelings. Our employers generally encourage us—with only an occasional resort to irony —in our efforts.

If I were to perorate over the past few years, I might be tempted to say that they were among the least flattering in this nation's history—except for the books that they produced. I suppose the quality of its literature says something about the health or resilience of a culture. I have tended to exclude here those works that took too easy advantage of our indigenous absurdities, that were rather like hit-and-run affairs or one-night stands at the expense of unwary readers. Instead, I've gravitated toward books that betrayed at least an ambivalent affection for our faltering institutions and their victims. In my experience, authors who lack even the most grudging feeling of attachment for the country they live in are as arrested in their development as people who proudly proclaim that they hate their mothers and fathers.

Powerlessness Corrupts

I was once fond of listening to a radio program that, I believe, was called *Negro Church of the Air*. It consisted of a spirited sermon and gospel singing. During the sermon, there was a man other than the preacher who seconded his statements by crying out, after a particularly telling one, something like "That's right!" or "I know it's the truth!" I always wanted to be that other man. Lest anybody misunderstand me and suppose that I was indulging a taste for the picturesque, I want to make it plain that I envied, and thrilled to, his conviction—his sense of having heard and grasped the truth.

This is the only way I can think of to tell you how I felt in reading Rollo May's *Power and Innocence*. When he says "powerlessness corrupts," I want to shout, "That's right!" When he says, "I cannot recall a time during the last four decades when there was so *much* talk about the individual's capacities and potentialities and so *little* actual confidence" in them, I want to cry, "I know it's the truth!" Like the preacher on *Negro Church of the Air*, Dr. May has a gift for gut truths. He says a hundred things I've been unconsciously hoping to hear from someone who could assert them with authority. He takes the vague, generalized anxieties of American life and dissects them into clear, concrete particulars.

Writing about power, Dr. May points out that most of us misunderstand both the nature of the thing itself and its uses. Our fear of it amounts almost to a neurotic obsession, because we insist on thinking of power only in its negative forms, in terms of aggressors and victims. We have not yet learned that it is not power but its opposite—impotence—that leads to violence. Our sentimental habit of seeing power and love as opposites, he finds absurd, for you must have the power to be before you can even attempt to love. Without an element of self-assertion, lovers would disappear into each other like vanishing cream. To bypass self-affirmation, as so many of us do, is to risk jumping into

7

aggression and violence. Nor, he adds, can we expect our individuality to develop automatically. We must choose it, pursue it and persist in articulating it.

One of our favorite ways of avoiding power and its attendant responsibilities is the assumption of innocence—or, more often, pseudo-innocence. America's whole history is one of "innocence," the author reminds us. We all left decadent and exhausted countries to come to the Garden of Eden, where we have driven away not only the snakes but the original inhabitants as well. Real innocence is childlike, pseudo-innocence is childish, or as some psychoanalysts would say, infantile. Most, but not all, of our counterculture innocence Dr. May considers pseudo, living in the limbo between a dying Establishment and an unborn alternative.

When a society is in profound transition like ours, language is the first thing to disintegrate. And when language is corrupted, people lose faith in what they hear and begin to hit one another. Dr. May puts it very succinctly: "Violence and communication are mutually exclusive." Our despair of expressing what we feel —even what we *are*—explains the trend to action therapies and nonverbal communication. And though one of the commonest symptoms of our lonely silence is a yearning for the solace of immediate intimacy, this, too, is hopeless, for "intimacy requires a history." Man, says the author, is a symbol-making creature, and he needs a sustaining symbolism before he can experience love or intimacy. In what may be an aside to the Women's Liberation movement, the doctor adds that, if our old symbols of love and sex seem dead, they should be mourned rather than denied.

If the medium is truly the message, communication as we once knew it is a thing of the past, and we are like people in a dream, wandering in a foreign country where we can neither feel nor sense anything of what is going on. In *Power and Innocence*, obscenity is regarded as a halfway stage in the disintegration of language—a hurling of words like stones at one another.

The appeal of violence, according to the author, lies in the fact that it represents "a uniting of the self in action." To those who never even felt they had a self, it is like a religious call. The "ecstasy of violence" is the only ecstasy of which such people are capable. They will light up the void with fires, fill the silence with vituperation. For these reasons, the goal has shifted in too many rebellions from a desire for reform to an addiction to the ecstasy of violence.

Dr. May distinguishes between the rebel and the revolutionary by remarking that the "rebel's mind meets other minds." He and society need each other as dialectical dancing partners. If we want to help underdeveloped countries in their rebellions toward self-expression, we would do better to send them not money or arms, but poets, as Frantz Fanon suggested, to show them how they too might articulate a dialectics of their own.

Coming back to innocence, Dr. May finds that it lacks not only responsibility, but spirituality, what Wordsworth described as the "deeper music of humanity." It begs the question, just as so much of our morality does. "Trying to be good all the time will make one not into an ethical giant, but into a prig," because the moral life is an equilibrium between good and evil. Before we can improve the human condition, we must first *recognize* it. Dr. May even dares to attack one of our most untouchable sacred cows: the notion that growth can be only good. Growth is a quantity, he reminds us, not a quality, just as progress is movement, not always toward perfection.

These are mere skimmings, just a taste of the author's auscultation of the American anatomy. And though he answers many of the questions he raises, some of them will have to wait their turn. For these, he refers us to Rilke, who said: "*Live* the questions now. Perhaps you will then . . . live along some distant day into the answer."

Woman as a Groaning Board

I looked into four new novels by women writers and found that they are all about divorce. It is not unreasonable, I think, to talk about a trend, one that may have begun way back with Joan Didion's *Play It as It Lays* and worked its way up through Lois Gould's *Such Good Friends* and Sandra Hochman's *Walking Papers*. The "divorce" in Lois Gould's book was brought about by the death of the husband, but their relationship had the same tone—it was reeling for the same sort of reasons—as the others.

What it seems to come down to is that the husbands in these books simply don't offer enough. Some are sexually inadequate, either in quantity or quality; some don't "communicate"; some are bores. Almost all of them have lost whatever romantic connotations they may have had. Once upon a time these men would not have been sued for divorce: the wives would have put up with them as the price of marriage. A short ten years ago, only the leisure classes or movie stars divorced for such personal reasons.

On the evidence of these new novels many women seem to be discovering a new kind of hunger in themselves—or acting on one they have long repressed. I'm tempted to call this hunger existential, or something equally portentous. It's as if these female protagonists were waking from a long uneasy sleep to a cold gray morning. They're saying I am; I want; I need; I will. They're ready to bet their lives on what they feel, to risk security in exchange for adventure or disappointment. Even disappointment is better than boredom.

In a way, it's as if women have suddenly realized their full market value, understood that they can drive a better bargain. The homes they nurtured, the meals they put on the table, have become secondary to their personalities and their bodies. I'm your home, I'm your supper, they're saying to their men. I'm the groaning board: gorge yourself on me.

Security is almost an ironical word today: it doesn't carry the weight it once did. Live as if you were going to die at any moment, the existentialists advise us: as if you were going to *age* at any moment, some of these women would say. They're forever examining their faces, skins, necks, breasts, bellies, buttocks, thighs, for intimations of mortality. I want it now, they cry, not altogether sure what "it" is.

In the beginning, it often seemed to be sex. The frisson of infidelity, the novelty of unsanctified intercourse, the first flood of enthusiasm a new lover offers. In one of these books, two of the heroine's early infidelities are accomplished under water—one in a swimming pool, another in the ocean—a circumstance that may be taken as a measure of her determination to find new paths to satisfaction, or at least to eschew the old.

This was in Shelley List's book, which seemed the most convincing, most deeply felt and least trendy of those I looked into. In *Did You Love Daddy When I Was Born?* Rachel marries Fred, just what the doctor used to order because he is a doctor, and handsome besides. But he's a lecher too, or at least toward anyone but his wife. And his talk runs to tennis, money and who's-sleeping-with-whom. As if to underline the irrationality of it all, he is unfaithful to her with women who are not half as attractive or interesting as she is.

John, her first man after her separation, teaches her how to make love—as Fred never did—and then, after introducing her to herself and her potentialities, leaves her to contemplate them while he dallies with his other mistress or tries to write his novel. As Rachel says, she is about ninety-ninth on his list of priorities. It is one of the first lessons in her new freedom: everyone else is free too, free to feel something other than what she feels. Like a miser counting his gold, Rachel takes stock of her new awareness and wonders what to do with it.

She has discovered that John doesn't need her. Perhaps only men who marry them need women. The love instructors, the poets of the bedroom, the great communicators, are often divorcés with no wish to remarry. John has fought for his freedom too, and it doesn't exactly mesh with Rachel's. What she wants is a paradox: to be "free" with John every day, and exclusively. But he knows that, in a world vibrating with divorced or available women, he can have his cake and eat it too. In fact, it may be his egocentrism that makes him so satisfying in and out of bed. It concentrates him, like a gourmet or connoisseur, on what he is doing.

Mrs. List's conclusion offers cold comfort. Her heroine has discovered what she wants: by being herself, she wants to be the best of everything to someone else. The irony is that the kind of man who will fill this bill is either already married, or rare as a unicorn. But, in spite of the odds against her, Rachel is honest: she doesn't pretend to be sufficient unto herself, independent of all outside response, like some of the more militant of the liberated women. She has revised the equation, but the symbols—man and woman—are still the basis of it.

The feeling I took away from this book was that of a crisis in our evolution, one that goes deeper into the blood and bones of our society than most of us realize. No one has yet suggested a popular solution, but since neither sex can go on standing on one foot forever, something is fated to change. Right now, more and more women are telling it like it is in these bittersweet love letters. Perhaps we can look forward to a reciprocal genre in men's novels, when they feel that women are ready to read them with open hearts and minds.

Daddy and the Dog Trainer

"Later, he will be a grotesque, but now he is beauty in its richest, most fleeting sense." This is Josh Greenfeld, a writer in his forties, looking at his autistic son Noah, who is three years old and who will probably always be three years old. When Noah's father wrote this line, he was neither exaggerating nor being sentimental. I received a picture with my copy of the book and the child *is* beautiful—not only in the ordinary way of a boy who just happens to be good-looking, but in another, unearthly way as well. He has that look of inner-directed innocence or purity of heart that you see on the faces of angels in Renaissance paintings.

He looks like that because he *is* pure, in a sense: he is not touched by anything in this world. Everything he feels, everything he is, comes from inside himself. That's what autism means. It means being locked in the confines of the self, being one's own entire world. Sometimes Noah's world makes him jump, laugh and whoop with mysterious enthusiasm. At other times it stuns him into a frozen silence or wild, absolute crying.

Mr. Greenfeld and his Japanese wife, Foumi, have tried every form of treatment they could find for Noah. He has been to doctors of every persuasion, several kinds of schools; he has taken various vitamins, even chiropractic treatments. He has been to see the country's most successful specialists in the field of his disorder, and they have told his father that the very best he and his wife can hope for is something approaching ten percent of normal development. The most that can be conceived for Noah is that he will be conditioned to a robot, who, under careful and constant supervision, will barely meet the minimal standards of social behavior. Noah was so far from this definition that it seemed to his father like some impossible, luminous dream. And so gratefully did he accept this heartbreaking hope that he even went to consult a famous dog trainer, on the ground that if his son could be helped, any technique was acceptable.

Before Noah was born, Mr. Greenfeld had always supposed—

like most of us—that this rich, technological society of ours would have a tremendous range of treatment for children like his. One thinks of all the appeals for different disabilities to which one responds—yet the Greenfelds scoured the country from coast to coast and were not even able to get a convincing diagnosis of their son's condition. The most successful therapy—the operant-conditioning program at the University of California at Los Angeles, headed by Dr. O. Ivar Lovaas—pragmatically tried to improve the patient simply on the basis of what the therapy team could see.

Through a program of carefully patterned reward and punishment, they attempted to push and/or pull retarded children out of their passive withdrawal so that they would enter the real world and begin to respond to it. As one of the consequences of this treatment, Noah's father was no longer able to kiss or hug him simply because he loved him: if the treatment was to work, affection had to be a reward for a problem solved. Though, under the circumstances, Noah's father had always hugged and kissed him more than most fathers do, Noah had never hugged or kissed back. This was one of the things that made it so difficult for the author and his wife: there was no "feedback" to refuel them in their endless nursing of their son.

Their marriage began to suffer. Mr. Greenfeld could not write and his wife could not paint. They were too exhausted and too preoccupied. Noah kept them awake most nights—he hardly ever seemed to sleep—and they walked around in a red-eyed daze. Noah became physically too heavy for his eighty-four-pound mother to lift, spiritually more than his father could bear. And then, because in some mystical sense a child is always the fruit, the symbol, of a marriage, each of them began to distrust himself and each other for having somehow created Noah's condition. To make things not better, but worse, they had another son, two years older, who showed them every day what his younger brother might have been.

Mr. Greenfeld could hardly have been blamed if he had written a furious, screeching, or even maudlin book—but he has done none of these things. I found *A Child Called Noah* as poetic as it is harrowing. It is as much about love as it is about mental illness—or better yet, it is about the terrible intimacy between them. We see the imperfection that is inherent in most love, but we see it made huge. It shows how much strain love can survive. We see a man's fatherhood—one of the deepest roots of his capacity for commitment—being pulled out by the roots. And yet he and his wife survive.

They go on. They try to compartmentalize their lives, as they have been advised to do. They try to enjoy Noah while they can, until his illness overwhelms his beauty and their love. Before going to sleep at night, they debate the question of putting him in an institution as if they were saying their prayers. Noah probably wouldn't even notice the difference—but *they* would.

After a while, if you can hold onto your sanity in a situation like this, your sense of irony surfaces to help save you. It is the most painful kind of irony, not the kind that rises above or steps outside of a situation, but the sort that suffuses it with an excruciating, comic tenderness. You have to laugh at yourself, in surprise, so to speak, at having such an astonishing, unsupported ability to go on feeling.

Noah's father going to see the dog trainer: I dare you to try to imagine his emotions on that occasion. Or the time he took "a brood of children, including Noah, to the zoo, and bought them all Cracker Jack and balloons. It was fun to watch all the kids having fun. Except Noah—he couldn't care less. In his long camel hair coat he was like a little king wandering through his own captionless comic strip, one that lacked a last panel."

The Salutary Lesson of Smallness

"With regard to anything at all, not only has everything not been said, but almost everything remains to be said." "Fix your attention on the first object that catches your eye; you'll realize at once that no one has ever looked at it." "I suggest . . . a voyage into the depths of things, an invasion of qualities, a revolution or subversion comparable to the kind that the plough or shovel makes when, all at once and for the first time, millions of particles, flakes, roots, worms and little creatures previously buried are brought to light."

There is no hope of understanding things through science, because it would require several lifetimes. "The best thing to do then is to consider all things as unknown and to walk or stretch out under the woods or on the grass and to start all over again from the beginning."

Francis Ponge proposes to approach poetry through things. His best-known book is called *Taking the Side of Things*. We have been estranged from the stuff, the texture, the whatness of reality by the abstractions of science, and this estrangement colors—or rather discolors, bleaches the color from—our lives. It makes us rhetorical, sentimental. As Ponge expresses it, "Man generally embraces only his emanations, his phantoms . . . He can only waltz them around." Poetry's grand flights are often abdications, a retreat into an imaginary world that does nothing to keep us honest, accurate or alive. For himself, Ponge says, "The least suspicion of poetic purring warns me that I am merely back again on the merry-go-round and have to get off in a hurry."

Ponge is no newcomer to poetry. The earliest poem in this selection from his work is dated 1923. Jean-Paul Sartre devoted a considerable essay to him in his *Situations I* and he was admired by Paul Valéry and Albert Camus. In the nineteen sixties, Ponge was "discovered" by another generation and elevated to the rank of culture hero. But though he was a visiting professor at Columbia in 1966–67, he has been virtually unknown here, except for occasional translations in magazines such as *Poetry* and *transition*. (These translations—by Pierre Schneider, Richard Wilbur and Wylie Sypher—are infinitely better than those in the present volume.) The publication of *Things*—in an extremely handsome edition—is probably the result of our ecology craze rather than Ponge's growing reputation.

Ponge is in love with things; they replenish him. "Isn't it good," he asks, "after an airplane trip to go home and look at some peaches on a plate?" In his respect for the object, he reminds us of Wallace Stevens: "With my whole body I taste these peaches . . ." and of Marianne Moore and Theodore Roethke. The more insignificant the object, the better, for as Pierre Schneider put it in a brilliant essay on Ponge, we need "the salutary lesson of smallness" to restore us to a more natural scale, to reintegrate us in a landscape whose foreground we have been monopolizing for centuries.

Ponge will not be satisfied until the poem is "assassinated by its object." These objects are not "our decor, our frame," but "our spectators, our judges." They define us at least as much as we define them, and we must learn to give them their due. "The real secret of the contemplator's success is his refusal to consider as *an evil* the encroachment on his personality by things." What sort of things? Ponge begins in his own poems with the most ordinary, because "the wealth of propositions contained in the least object is so great that I still cannot conceive of how to do justice to any but the simplest things: a stone, a plant, fire, a piece of wood, a morsel of meat."

Things is about evenly divided between poems and speculations about poetry. The poems more than live up to their billing. The plant, for example, "is an analysis as act, an original dialectic in space . . . Its immobility shapes its perfection." Plants are "only a will toward expression . . . they pass their time complicating their form." The wasp "seems to live in a continual state of crisis . . . perhaps because of the narrowness of its diaphragm." "Contrary to popular opinion, stone, never reforming in nature, is actually the only thing in it that dies constantly."

The spider is "suspended without context by its own decisions . . . strumming unsuccessfully above the abyss." In breathing in the carnation, "you experience the pleasure whose reverse would be the sneeze." The insignificant is "all my exercise and my hygienic sigh." "Autumn at last is but a brew of cold tea . . . Nature tears up her manuscripts, destroys her library." The candle's light "decomposes furnished rooms to masses of shadow." Of stones, he writes: "Roses sit on their gray knees, and harangue them in their naive way." In pine woods, "Everything is done there, without excess, so as to leave man to himself. The vegetation, the animation, are relegated to the heights. Nothing to distract his attention . . . No anecdotes."

In a nervous age, Francis Ponge is capable of "prodigies of sustained attention." He helps us "increase *the quantity of our qualities,*" dreams of "a science whose material would be esthetic impressions . . . an elucidation of impressions." Almost single-handedly, he attempts to revise our speech, to correct "the comedy of its seriousness." For the adulterous romance of words, he would substitute the reality of what *is.*

Flowing from Form to Form

So many of us have lost our religion, our feeling of ethnic or national identity, our instinctive moral orientation, that the coordinates of our spirit are becoming increasingly rootless and vague—perhaps even precarious. One more—and perhaps final—root we seem in danger of losing is our sense of place, and we can ill afford it. For "the places we have roots in," as David Brower sees it, "and the flavor of their light and sound and feel when things are right in those places, are the wellsprings of our serenity."

A place, says the poet Richard Wilbur in his Introduction, "is a fusion of human and natural order." We need that fusion. We need it because it is as close as many of us can come to a religion. To be continuous with nature, intimate with it, is immensely reassuring in a world of abstractions and inconceivable distances. As Spengler said, religion is a tension between man and the universe that man can love. Our places are the bases of that tension, and we need to love them just as much as we need to love each other. Otherwise, we are "intellectual nomads" who walk the earth like ghosts, who have lost the landscape inside themselves and will never find it outside.

"Throughout the course of life on this planet, wildness has flowed from form to form . . . Then suddenly . . . man undertook to simplify that wildness, foreclose on diversity, dry up springs and praise himself." (This is Mr. Brower again, paraphrasing John Muir.) At this rate, we shall soon have nothing left but nostalgia, which is rapidly becoming the most American of emotions. It may not be true, as Robinson Jeffers wrote, that "the heart-breaking beauty/Will remain when there is no heart to break for it . . ." It may turn out just the other way around.

Still, the trend is not all negative. "People are groping toward a reconciliation with this planet," Mr. Wilbur says. Our love of the wild goes deep into the American grain. "It is a taste with political overtones, having to do with freedom and self-realization,

19

and it also entails an atavistic gesture toward the frontier." Though "panoramas are not what they used to be," according to another poet, "the quality of despair/cannot be the specialty of this ecstatic air."

Mr. Gussow's book has brought sixty American painters to the aid of ecology. Its tone is not that of a threat so much as a seduction. In sixty-seven extraordinarily well-chosen paintings—by artists ranging over four centuries—he is saying: Look at all you have and congratulate yourself. In William Sidney Mount's words, "nature beckons us one and all . . . to be great." Even the most ardent conservationist cannot match the eloquence of these paintings. And the painters themselves turn out to be spellbinders too, because Mr. Gussow has persuaded them to talk about their work as they experienced it in the act of creation. (He has skillfully dug out the words of the dead ones.) He has got them to define for us that "fusion of human and natural order" in their own words.

In the nineteenth century, Thomas Cole combined a Platonic sense of nature as morally, religiously and philosophically uplifting with a vivid grasp of the place itself in all its quiddity and color. Today, Sharon Yates says: "I need suspension for drifting . . . I need time to change me . . ." to prepare me for "that dialogue with nature, that struggle to yield instead of fight." Sidney Goodman is fascinated and repelled by the "way man-made structures often violate a place." In one of her paintings, Nell Blaine "was interested in the way the tops of the trees met the sky."

For Wolf Kahn, whose "Underside of the Barn" is one of the strongest contemporary paintings in the book, "Barns become as much nature as an orchard is." "The closer you get to the local quality," he says, "the closer you get to the universal." He believes that "nostalgia informs most of the best landscape painting," and that there are two kinds of nostalgia: antiquity and some sort of pastoral past. "We don't have any antiquity, so for us there is only eighteenth and nineteenth century rural nostalgia . . . a New England barn is to us as a Greek temple was to Poussin."

In these sixty artists' ways of looking at our places, we find a reassuring diversity, a security against the sameness, the monotony, that lurks like the rumor of a plague behind the facade of

American life. We have Albert Bierstadt's eagle vistas and Thomas Cole's leafy bowers that are like animal boudoirs. There is the leanness of Charles Sheeler, order "pruned to the formal bone." The work of Milton Avery, "the Matisse of Puritanism," gives us "the illusion of having been instantly abstracted from observation." Paul Resika says that "our temperate world has a long twilight . . . a light of sentiment."

Mr. Gussow is a good painter himself and his selections do him credit. John LaFarge, Georgia O'Keeffe, George Inness, George Catlin, Edwin Dickinson, Arthur Dove, Marsden Hartley are all shown to be more adventurous than we remembered—even in the perspective of today. Van Dearing Perrine, Karl Schrag, William Kienbusch, Thomas Moran, Elmer Bischof, Richard Bogart, Martin Johnson Heade, John Kensett and still others are all strikingly good enough to make us wonder why we haven't seen and heard more of them. Can it be that they've simply been crowded out of sight in the embarrassment of riches that is American art?

One can be forgiven a little flush of chauvinism on closing *A Sense of Place*. For all the fashionable rejection of everything "American," one discovers that there is far too much—too much that is truly great—for it to be denied. We are not yet condemned to "An existential landscape—without absolutes, without prototypes, devoted to change and mobility." As T. S. Eliot, who was not a notorious optimist, put it:

> *We shall not cease from exploration*
> *And the end of all our exploring*
> *Will be to arrive where we started*
> *And know the place for the first time.*

Seen the Enemy and They Is Us

Sooner or later, says Irving Kristol, the American people will decide that they would rather not die laughing at themselves. Though right now gallows or black humor at our own expense is a popular national pastime, Mr. Kristol thinks that the joke has gone far enough. This does not mean that he doesn't enjoy a witticism himself: in fact, he offers us a book full of better ones simply by turning the others inside out. Almost single-handedly, he outripostes an army of mockers. Irony, one might say, is one of the waste products of our age, like the omnipresent paper blowing in the streets. It is too easy; our intellectuals have been dining out on it so long that they've grown fat and complacent.

There could hardly be anyone better qualified than Mr. Kristol to startle them out of that complacency. To begin with, he is one of them, a man with impeccable credentials. Formerly managing editor of *Commentary* and co-editor of *Encounter*, he now shares the editing of *The Public Interest*—one of our best quarterlies—with Daniel Bell. And since, like most of our intellectuals, Mr. Kristol was born into the ideology of liberalism "as into a civil religion," he cannot be dismissed as one of the uninitiated.

The unifying theme of *The Democratic Idea in America* is the tendency of democratic republics to "progress" away from "their original, animating principles, and as a consequence to precipitate grave crises in the moral and political order." In substituting democratic faith for a democratic philosophy, we have assumed an optimism about human nature that would have astonished our founding fathers. This faith has placed our problems outside of the probing of our philosophy and encouraged a tendency to blame them not on ourselves, but on "vested interests," "outside agitators" or an arrogant Establishment.

We have chosen to worship the common man at a time when he is more confused and demoralized than ever before in his history. Conversely, we are disinclined to apply intellectual discipline and plain truth precisely when we need them most. With the whole world morally up in arms against us, we are busily incorporating an "adversary culture" into our school curriculum, injecting it into the very life stream of our national consciousness.

In a single far-reaching sentence, the author puts his finger on one of our greatest ills: the fact that "the unanticipated consequences of social action are always more important, and usually less agreeable, than the intended consequences." Every age, he reminds us, is Auden's *Age of Anxiety*; one can always say with Emerson that "things are in the saddle," or with Yeats that "the center cannot hold." Putting it even better himself, he says, "The premonition of apocalypse springs eternal in the human breast."

How do we usually deal with this premonition? By turning not to the spirit, but to the procedural and mechanical arrangements of democracy, by enacting more legislation, which likely as not is impossible to carry out. But we must, because in today's "revolution of rising expectations," the people demand "action." "To see something on television is to feel entitled to it; to be promised something by a politician is to feel immediately deprived of it."

Speaking of the plight or crisis of the cities, Mr. Kristol says that the problem goes further than that, because our whole civilization has become urbanized. There is no longer that healthy tension between urban and provincial, "progressive" and conservative, sophisticated and conventional, nihilistic and pietistic. The "republican morality" that the makers of the Constitution counted on to protect us from chaos has been robbed of one of the legs it stood, already unsteadily, on. In our current morality, the cynical " 'why not' is ceasing to be a question at all. It is becoming a kind of answer."

Some of Mr. Kristol's sentences open terrifying vistas: "Being frustrated is disagreeable, but the real disasters in life begin when you get what you want." "When we lack the will to see things as they are, there is nothing so mystifying as the obvious." For student radicals, "it is not the average American who is disgusting; it is the ideal American." In the last half-century or so, "high-minded hypocrisy has completely driven statesmanlike reasonableness out of the American public forum." "Once you surrender the liberty to speak plainly, you lose the capacity to think clearly."

In a brilliant mood of mischief, Mr. Kristol composes two

Presidential addresses, one full of the usual ritual platitudes and rhetoric and the other a small masterpiece of realistic plain speaking. Then he asks us: What would happen if the President gave the realistic speech? "Just imagine what our TV commentators and 'news analysts' would do with a man who sought elected office with the promise that, during his tenure, he hoped to effect some small improvements in our condition."

Shifting the blame, dodging the issue and turning a blind eye are time-honored American pastimes, but Mr. Kristol doesn't take kindly to them. Invoking "the immortal words of Pogo," he says, "I have seen the enemy and they is us."

A.C. or D.C. Death?

"Mr. Buxton will adjust all of the straps—there are eleven of them—as rapidly as possible. Since you will no doubt be perspiring, he will towel your head dry where it has been shaved and then adjust an electrode to the spot; he will adjust another to the base of your spine where your clothing will have been cut for the purpose . . . You sit at once; no delay, understand? If the new method is to serve, speed is of the first importance. I should say promptness, because I don't mean that you are to run as if it were a race. Simply step along smartly beside the warden, neither before nor behind him." This is the chief electrician rehearsing the death of the first man to be "scientifically" executed in the electric chair, in the year 1890. In just over a hundred words, it says more about the dehumanizing effect of technology than a shelf of sociology books. Here is the machine age in its infancy, like a little boy dispassionately pulling the wings off flies.

Though *A Peep into the Twentieth Century* is based on extensive research, it is not the richness of the documentation but Mr. Davis's talent that gives the novel its remarkable bite. He uses the distance and the detachment of science to approach an abstraction called a prisoner, a convict, a condemned man—and then smack! we are up against flesh and blood. A shaved head, perspiring, wiped dry by the warden with a towel, one man wiping another man's head before throwing a switch that will send 1,700 volts humming through his body.

Rupert Weber is a murderer, and murderers are notoriously hard to portray. In fiction, the act almost always seems rhetorical; it is too exotic for us, we can't empathize into it. When Raskolnikov brings the hatchet down on the old woman's head in *Crime and Punishment*, it is never more than a metaphor, even in the hands of Dostoyevsky. But when Weber uses the hatchet with which he has been fixing a door to kill his common-law wife Jenny, we believe it. We believe it because he has that capacity to surprise us that makes almost anything possible. And his motive is so unpretentious, so close to the bone: He killed Jenny because he was drunk and she had been complaining about the infrequency of his love-making.

Weber is so palpably alive that everyone wants him. The inventor of the electric chair wants him for his machine; Chaplain Snow wants him for God; Warden Buxton wants him off his conscience, if he can get his sentence commuted. Weber teases them all. He has an incorrigible animal quality that can't be cornered. He teases the scientist with insanity, which could cheat the chair; he teases the chaplain with his refusal to kneel and pray, the warden with a fatalistic determination to "take his medicine like a man." Around them, meanwhile, a great debate rages: Shall the condemned man be "taken off" by alternating or direct current? By Edison or Westinghouse?

Snow, the chaplain, is another fine portrait. Young, slim, blond, almost girlish, he woos Weber with Christian love, with caritas. When this fails, he falls back on a more secular appeal. Trying to link man's magic to God's, he reads No Darkness on the Deep: The Romance of Electricity to Weber. He himself is "electrified" with ecstasy. He sees this new invention, this uncanny chair, as another cross, a nineteenth-century novelty offered up to God. He has never felt so thrillingly intimate with death, our ultimate gift to our Maker. The sensation is so voluptuous that it quite carries him away.

Then smack! we are up against Weber once more—Weber the man, not the convert, the soul to be saved, but Weber the murderer who kills the chaplain's dream by groping him at the very moment they kneel to pray. Weber wants to see whether there is life in Snow's love; he wants to remind the chaplain that his immortal soul is housed in a mischievous animal.

Like the chaplain, Weber too is ecstatic with the nearness of death. In a constant state of erethism, he spends himself as if there were no tomorrow. In his dreams he ravishes the chaplain, the warden's wife, Jenny, everybody. His impending death—like an existentialist demonstration—makes him omnivorous for life. And his is the last laugh: When the machine falters, Weber puts on a show for the witnesses that they'll never forget. With every part, every product, of his body, he derides the notion that science or anything else can tidy up the dirty business of dying.

Mr. Davis's ironies are so deft that we are never obliged to feel the cosmos itself creaking with them. In costuming his virtuosity in mock-Victorian quaintness, he has made it more effective. His characters are real far beyond the strict necessities of their roles, and he has used them to build a brilliant fictional conundrum around the idea of death. When, with the prison doctor, we watch Weber's dissected body being dumped into the lime pit, we feel that we've learned quite a lot about how men are put together and how they come apart.

Of Human and Other Animals

It's so easy to forget what a satisfying thing ordinary life can be. Where it exists, people seem to take it for granted, instead of shouting it to the housetops. You would think it would find its way into fiction—surely, novelists must have noticed its joys, like a hungry man with his nose pressed to a bakery window—but ordinary life just about disappeared from fiction somewhere in the nineteenth century. Dickens could bring tears of gratification to your eyes with the placement of a bay window in a room or a pub; anyone who's ever read Trollope will feel a permanent nostalgia for small towns and plain people. Even as late as Hardy, it was possible. He too could make you feel that the life he described evolved logically, inevitably, *rightfully*, from his characters' immanent qualities. When all was right with the world these men knew, it was as cozy as a fourposter bed with a fire in the grate.

It is superfluous to dilate on the contrast with the contemporary novel. There's a splendid sentence in Saul Bellow's *Herzog* that definitively sums it up. Near the beginning of the book, he describes the modernized or retouched beauty of a sunset as seen through the smoke of garbage burning in New Jersey. Now and then in a memoir—a sort of halfway ground between fact and fiction, because the facts are *felt*—now and then, you'll come across the ordinary raised to an almost heroic splendor. *All Creatures Great and Small* is one of these, an ardent acknowledgement of the gift of life.

James Herriot, a British veterinary surgeon, is one of those rare men who know how to appreciate the ordinary. He reminds one of T. E. Lawrence's remark that he would never drink anything but water because he didn't want to spoil his taste for it. The ordinary bubbles like a cool and musical fountain in the Yorkshire hills where Mr. Herriot went as a young veterinarian's assistant just out of college in 1937. The way he describes it, it seems so blessedly long ago. The people—even the animals—in

his pages are . . . well, different. Not larger than life, but large *as*
life. They are not stunted by unimaginable perspectives. They
belong to a time when we had not yet come to see man as a
colossal anticlimax.

Mr. Herriot is a natural storyteller because he is tremendously
interested in everything and manages to invest his stories with
that interest. When he is in a drafty byre in the wee hours of a
freezing night, lying stripped from the waist up on a cold stone
floor with his bare arm reaching as far as it will go inside a cow
whose calf is stuck in a transverse position—we are there with
him. We share his satisfaction, too, as his numbed hand finally
gets a purchase on the calf and pulls it right. We taste the hot
tea, the eggs and bacon, the grateful farmer's wife gives him
when the calf is safely suckling.

In the Yorkshire hills in 1937, things as they were, as the poet
said, had not yet been destroyed. The tractor had not replaced
the horse and men still felt that they too were creatures of the
land. Custom continued to rear its hoary head, and the author
enjoyed it with all his heart, as he paused between removing a
wire from a cow's throat and a cyst from a dog's side to stand and
stare with pleasure at "the ragged miles of moorland rolling
away, dipping and rising over the flat fell-top."

There's comedy and fine old-fashioned tear-jerking too in his
tales. Filling in for an elderly, ill-favored veterinarian who was
sick, the author finds himself called out at night to remove a bone
from a dog's throat for a Mrs. Mallard. He is met at the door by
a voluptuous blonde of a certain age, heavily perfumed and wearing an evening gown. "Body and Soul" is playing softly on the
phonograph, the lights are low, the sofa is pulled close to the fire.
Mrs. Mallard is surprised to see the young assistant. Fiddling with
her earring, she comprehends the situation long before he does
and calls in her perfectly sound dog . . .

A dying old woman with several animals asks the author
whether she will ever see her dear four-footed friends again. She
has been assured that animals have no souls and cannot reconcile
herself to a separation in the hereafter. "Is it true?" she asks the
young veterinarian. "You've been to school, and you must know."
"Of course I know," he replies. "They teach us vets all about
animals' souls." "That is what you really believe?" the old

woman persists, looking at him with a steady gaze. At the crucial moment, he can't carry off the souls, but he retrieves the situation as well as any man could. "Wherever you are going," he says, "they are going too."

It's no secret that people often reveal themselves with their animals more readily than with one another. In fact, this peculiarity is enough to give pause to a philosopher. But Mr. Herriot has lain on too many cold stone floors, has reached into too many horses', cows' or pigs' innards to make a proper philosopher. He's a veterinarian, that's what he is, and when his right arm is free, he's a helluva writer as well.

Education as Tragicomedy

When a liberal educator behaves in a dogmatic manner, his action is ascribed to a "passionate concern." It is not that he is forcing his personality or his convictions on someone else: rather, he has taken "a selfless position" in the best interests of the community. But should a conservative insist on *his* principles, he is immediately anathematized as "coercive," "autocratic" or "imperious." His sincerity and his seriousness are questioned by committees.

This is what has happened to Donald Barr, headmaster of the Dalton School and author of *Who Pushed Humpty Dumpty?* Mr. Barr has complicated the picture by being witty, even ironical. Is irony appropriate to headmasters? Would you want your child to go to an ironical school? In this book, the author has laid his cards on the table, presented his collected writings for the outraged parents' inspection. At a time when most educational theorists are tragedians, he has dared to write a tragicomedy.

In reading a book for review, I generally jot down particularly quotable lines or points; in this case, I soon had to abandon this practice. I was writing down almost as much as I was reading. Mr. Barr's aphorisms and insights came at me so thick and fast —his texture is so rich—that I often had to put the book down after a few pages to give my intellectual appetite a chance to burp.

But lest I be suspected of hyperbole, let me give you a few samples: "To the modern liberal mind, the word discipline has an almost pornographic sound." "Though discipline and freedom seem antithetical, each without the other destroys itself." For the alienated young, "The meaning of every experience leaks away even at the instant of occurrence, so that life is like sitting and endlessly eating a sort of dry existential bran." "A few years ago, adolescence was a phase; then it became a profession; now it is a new nationality." "Parents who would never give their children an unbalanced physical diet proudly give them an unbalanced psychological diet." "We think unthinkingly (so to speak) that 'yes' is a loving word and 'no' is a hostile word." "It is by waiting [for the gratification of their desires] that children learn what time is."

Of the "sexual revolution," Mr. Barr says: "An adolescent in his joyless round of promiscuity is no more a revolutionary than a pickpocket is a socialist." "They go through the motions of emotion . . . like robots in heat." What is needed, he urges, is not education in sex, but in sexuality—and especially in passion, because passion is the most difficult thing adolescents must learn to cope with.

On the use of drugs as a means of extending awareness or intensifying perception, he writes: "There is no point in asking 'Perception of what? Awareness of what?' These perceptions need no object. It is masturbatory awareness. The children 'turned on' by marijuana, cocaine (now common), LSD, or methedrine are like radios tuned to nothing, they play the noise of their own tubes."

"When a bright child begins to do badly in his studies, the question to ask him (but not in so many words) is: 'Whom are you punishing?' " "The permissive fallacy is that children learn good things from bad experiences." "The trouble with many children is that their fathers are mothers and their mothers are sisters." "When should a parent turn over authority to a child? When the child stops reaching for authority and reaches for responsibility."

Speaking of student revolts, Mr. Barr says: "The more arbitrary their demands the more 'idealistic' it will seem to the sociology department and to the radicals' parents." Many of the disaffected young, the author feels, are suffering from "the enormous fatigue of trying to live without religion." About the feeling of superfluousness so many young people have, the sense that the world doesn't need them, he writes: "Many men begin to die when they retire from their jobs, and something like this is going on at the other end of life as well."

The college student has become the new proletariat for the revolutionary. The old proletariat is too prosperous to be proselytized, while the student is ideal material, because he sees himself as a serf at school. While student radicals are fond of espousing large causes—what Mr. Barr calls "macro-morality"—they are often indifferent to the personal or "micro-morality" of cheating on tests, stealing, being cruel to their parents, lying and destruction of property. In fact, he says, they may feel a negative connection between these two moralities. "Consistency is only a kind of chastity of the head; the times do not regard it much." And finally we must learn not to think always of the child as the victim: often it is the parent.

If I seem to have given over most of this review to quoting Mr. Barr rather than criticizing him—as a critic is supposed to do—it is because I found very little to dispute. I wish I could say that he took the words right out of my mouth, but I'm afraid it's just the other way around.

The Obstetrics of the Soul

"I don't understand what I'm supposed to do," Tolstoy said on his deathbed—and neither do most of us. The conspiracy of silence with which we surround the subject of dying led Geoffrey Gorer, the British anthropologist, to coin the phrase "the pornography of death." But a "good death" is an indispensable end to a good life—so crucial, in fact, that a German writer called it the "obstetrics of the soul." To die with dignity is important not only to the dying person, but also to his or her survivors, who will always be able to remember the one they loved in this light.

According to David Hendin in his *Death as a Fact of Life,* dying today is often rendered obscene by technology. Many patients are kept alive when they are no longer human beings, but simple circulatory systems, breathing but otherwise unresponsive tissue. Under these circumstances, life may sometimes be more terrifying than death. The dying person's relatives and friends are elbowed away from him by machines. And since these machines interfere with the natural course of decline, no one knows exactly when death will come and the patient often expires with only technology for company. In this connection, the author quotes Theodore Fox's famous remark: "We shall have to learn to refrain from doing things merely because we know how to do them."

Mr. Hendin quotes surveys to show that most dying people would prefer to talk about it, and are greatly relieved when the silence is broken. I know that as I read his book, I felt my own anxieties about death first articulated, then partially assuaged. It *is* therapeutic to bring that immemorial enemy of ours out into the light. As the author points out, for some of us the threat of death can have an integrative rather than a disruptive function. It can make us see our life as a coherent whole and give us an opportunity to sum it up emotionally and intellectually—to deny the fashionable charge of "meaninglessness or absurdity."

Accepting death is not necessarily a form of resignation, of

giving up: it may be a positive reorientation. We can look *back*
over our life as well as forward to its end. We can congratulate
ourselves on what we have done and reverse the old saw that
"you can't take it with you." By renouncing the terrible duty of
pretending, Mr. Hendin says, we can take the bandages off our
fears and our feelings and die with love instead of lies as the last
thing we hear.

The author has done a brilliant and highly sensitive job of
bringing together the literature of death—from the need for
revising our legal, medical and psychological criteria to the fact
that the dead are forcing the living into an ever-decreasing space.
He discusses the science of cryonics, or freezing the body in the
hope of future resuscitation (cost, $20,000); the case for and
against euthanasia; the need to train doctors to *face* death as well
as to fight it; the "hospices" being built for dying people, so that
they can spend their last days in as homelike an atmosphere as
their medical needs permit; the advantages of cremation and its
relative unpopularity in the United States, and much more.

I found the chapter "Children and Death" especially moving. Mr. Hendin knows how to evoke a feeling as well as most
novelists and he is never, as far as I can remember, guilty of mere
sentimentality in dealing with the most highly charged subject in
our emotional repertory. Warning us against feeding inane eu-
phemisms to children, he cites the case of a little boy who was
told that his dead mother "went up into the sky." Shortly afterwards, the boy was taken on a visit by airplane and was very sad
and disappointed because he had looked on every cloud but had
not seen his mother. Informed that his infant brother had been
picked up by God and taken to heaven, another child kept his
windows locked, refused to cross open spaces and played only in
the shade of trees for fear the same thing would happen to him.

Unacknowledged death haunts us far more effectively than the
ghosts of our childhood. The author feels that the more fully it
is faced, the sooner we are likely to recover from the shock of
someone's death. If we do not make peace with them and separate ourselves from the dead through appropriate periods of
mourning and grief, we may find it difficult to attach ourselves
to anyone who might help replace them afterwards.

Though there is not a superfluous page in *Death as a Fact of*

Life, I found myself—emotionally, not morbidly—drawn to those passages dealing with the dying person. When Mr. Hendin speaks of the indignity of deterioration, I remember the humiliation I saw in my own father's face when he was a Rube Goldberg tangle of tubes and life-coercing machines. His difficulties were increased by his "stiff upper lip" philosophy that locked both of us in the anguish of all that we wanted to, and could not say. A terrible loneliness lurked in his eyes, but it was too late for him to learn or to change.

What the author does not say because it may be beyond the scope of his intent is that our entire life is a preparation for our death, and we may expect to die well or badly depending on how we have lived. Freud told a story of visiting William James at a time when the American psychologist and philosopher had a brush with death in the form of a heart attack. He could not refrain from asking James afterward how he had felt about the prospect. James replied that he had lived his life and done his work. Death held no terrors for him. Edmund Bergler, the psychiatrist, remarks in one of his many books that, after a satisfying sexual experience with someone we love, it is natural to feel sleepy. I mention these two remarks because I feel that, somewhere between them, we may find the answer to one of life's most intimidating questions.

Wash Your Feet with Poetry

At a recent reception given by the New School for Yevgeny Yevtushenko, I learned that the Soviet poet's books are published in printings running to hundreds of thousands. Then a distinguished American poet said that, when he was visiting Russia, he was ashamed to confess the size of his books' printings. The novelist John Cheever got up and told a story about driving through a Russian city with Mr. Yevtushenko at the wheel. After dramatically breaking just about every traffic law, they were finally stopped by two policemen who asked the poet for his license. On seeing his name and recognizing him, they handed it back, crying, "Go! Go and write us more beautiful poems!"

Now, Mr. Yevtushenko is a good poet, but not *that* good. There are other factors influencing the size of those printings. For one thing, there aren't all that many readable new books published in Russia. And then people are not distracted from them to the degree that we are by television, movies, the theater or the other temptations of relative affluence. Nor does their technology abstract them from the texture of life as much as ours does. In fact, the average Soviet citizen lives very close to things. He couldn't afford to get away from them if he wanted to. And this texture makes up a large part of Mr. Yevtushenko's poetry.

I got the feeling, that night at the New School, that the distinctive texture of American life was not getting a fair shake: there were lots of people present who were aware of it only in terms of air pollution, ecological suicide, the war in Vietnam and so on. Others—a minority—are beginning to realize that this is an incomplete and damaging view and they're trying to do something about it. There is a spate of movies right now, for example, about earlier, more "American" eras in our history. And people are squinting all over the landscape, trying to *see* nature again. They are taking sensitivity courses or treatments in an attempt to learn how to feel the feel of things: one popular book advises lovers to wash one another's feet in rock salt.

What I propose instead is that we wash one another's feet in poetry. And we can start with Peter Klappert's *Lugging Vegetables to Nantucket*. His book has just been published as the winning volume from some 500 manuscripts submitted in the 1970 Yale Younger Poets competition. Unless you buy it, he will probably be read only by the 499 losers, not altogether objectively. And he deserves better, because he knows things that you and I don't. In fact, to take it a bit further, he knows things that your doctor, lawyer, psychiatrist, tax accountant and favorite news commentator don't know—and you listen to them, don't you?

"How the hell can you expect me to read poetry," you'll say. "I can't even understand the stuff." Well, try to tell me that you understand Beckett, or Pinter, or Godard, or Antonioni. But you don't have to understand them—or Peter Klappert either. You can *experience* them. It is the great triumph of our time that the American public has learned to enjoy—even to applaud—what it doesn't understand. The Museum of Modern Art is never empty, nor the Whitney. And *Lugging Vegetables to Nantucket* is a museum too—a little museum of modern feelings and perceptions, one that's a lot easier to come to terms with than op, pop or abstract expressionist painting. Especially when you have Stanley Kunitz playing the perfect host in the introduction, serving cocktails and hors d'oeuvres, helping you feel at home in this strange place.

If you can learn to play golf, tennis or bridge, you can learn to read poetry—because poetry has changed. It has "prepared a face to meet the faces that it will meet"—including yours. It is no longer academic, forbiddingly erudite, full of allusions to other books you haven't read. Poetry today is sexy—not so much in the sense of mere content, but in its texture, its directness, its emphasis on sensation and the "feel" of ideas. It lays its hand on parts of you that no one has ever touched before—and if you can accept it, it feels wonderful.

Poetry has always been under suspicion in American life. It has been thought precious, delicate—even sissified. And with some justice, for it *is* delicate. Just as a male dancer dares to move in ways that would make the average man feel uncomfortable, or at least self-conscious, so poetry dares you to feel tender, or awed, or all-out loving. But poetry is not only tender: it is tough too, especially about people. It points a rude, accusing finger at *our* cowardice, *our* timidity in matters of sensibility.

Listen to Mr. Klappert: "She arched her heart/up from the mattress/and took the room into her eyes." "She aches enthusiasm . . ." "She wants a prominence she cannot climb . . ." One of my favorite lines is "Why can't we go somewhere and talk about dichotomies?" As I read it, the line refers to lovers' fondness for fitting their ideas as well as their bodies together, for dividing up the world into what *they* like and dislike, into mutually exclusive realms of "us" and "them," all as a way of intensifying the cocoon-like quality of their imagined uniqueness.

Mr. Klappert can say, to all of us, "Do you plead filthy or not filthy?" He quotes the "Dean of Menopause": "If you see something ugly, run it over." He regrets that "one is so seldom struck by lightning." There are many other rich and unexpected things too, but since I have to choose, I'd like to leave you with this:

> *It may have been a waste of time*
> *from here, to go back through*
> *and hear myself confess that I*
> *am an ex-florist, to harangue*
> *myself in the greenhouse, to hear*
> *the echoes that would have been there,*
> *to prune and prune and pick*
> *the slivered glass, witness*
> *the execution of an act of love,*
> *sweep together one last confusion*
> *of orchids, and take them for myself.*

Seeding the Wasteland

What Theodore Roszak offers us in *Where the Wasteland Ends* is nothing less than a State of the Union Message on the condition of the human soul. He begins it by saying that most of us hardly have anything resembling a soul left, that we have "matured" under the influence of science to a point where the very word soul has a childish and sentimental connotation. Our religious feelings as we once knew them—what the author calls our "transcendent energies"—have been virtually exiled from the social order, except, he points out, where they have taken refuge in psychedelic experiences, sensory awareness groups and Oriental philosophies, all of which are looked upon as either crimes, fads or lunatic fringe activities.

As William Blake said, our "mind-forged manacles" have tried to "vegetate the divine vision." Mr. Roszak finds that we have "progressed" from physical to spiritual starvation. It is the paradox of our time that things get worse as they get better, that we need ever more expertise to extricate us from the predicament in which our experts have landed us. The odor of alienation still clings to liberal humanism, the finest flower of urban-industrial civilization. The best it can offer, in Bertrand Russell's words, is "the firm foundation of unyielding despair."

Science can only condescend to "conquered" nature, whose warm embrace once "precluded both arrogance and that dispiriting conviction of cosmic absurdity which haunts contemporary culture." Nature now is almost as prepackaged as a supermarket. "While urban-industrial society grows intellectually fat on a smorgasbord of cultural tidbits, the world as a whole becomes steadily poorer in real *lived* variety."

The problem is an old one. In claiming historical validity, and subjecting itself to the scrutiny of science, Christianity destroyed the power of myth, and "the rhapsodic reports of the past became the obituaries of religion." As Calvin said, "the mind of man . . . is a perpetual manufacturing of idols"—he is forever *imagining* what he needs. Fear of this idolatry led the church to "desacralize" nature, to separate it from God, who then "became that cosmic bouillon cube in which all holiness was now to be concentrated for safe keeping." In such a world, beauty is cut loose from its sacramental base and becomes an idle or decadent pleasure.

In our diminished mode of consciousness—stripped of its transcendent energies—we suffer from what Blake called "single vision." Mr. Roszak suggests that sleep—our only regular escape from chilling reason—may be a compensating "natural high," an alternative and replenishing kind of consciousness. But dreams —our repository of wonders—are censored for that very reason. The body's reality is suppressed by the head, which, under the influence of science, seeks to *imperialize* the senses. Sex is the least of our repressions, for it is still alive and fighting. Our horror of the organic—"anything alive, mindless and gooey . . . anything sloppy, slobbering, liquescent, smelly, slimy, gurgling, putrescent, mushy, grubby"—attests to the larger denial of the flesh.

Speaking of psychotherapy as a remedy for some of these repressions, Mr. Roszak calls it "mysticism with all the metaphysical commitments drained off." It deals with that part of ourselves —ignored by modern life—which is left "to wither in the coward heart." "Sacramental consciousness," a *participation* in nature, would be the ideal of therapy, for where this has atrophied, "there can be no confirming epiphanies," no awareness of the things we *feel* beyond knowing.

The scientific act of knowing "is an act of alienation," a forcing of experience out and away from the grip of the personal. But "it is as irresponsible to leave unintegrated knowledge lying about as to produce babies and abandon them on the nearest doorstep." Not many of us—our artists are notable exceptions— can be expected to join with Nietzsche in "the thrilling sensation of our own nothingness." As science gets further from the lay citizen's understanding, "the resulting spiritual strain will be much more than most people can live with gracefully." One can't go on indefinitely acknowledging that that which makes one's world go round is hopelessly beyond one's comprehension. At least when the church's higher theology passed its flock's understanding, they were given an active ritual life as a consolation. Science, though, is stingy with consolations.

Its goal, says B. F. Skinner, is "the destruction of mysteries."

We see this same tendency imposing "a politics in which nothing remains but the administrative adjustments of people to specifiable standards of conduct and interaction." This is a bleak picture, a moon landscape indeed, but Mr. Roszak does not propose to abandon us there. In the second half of his book, he shows us, with a tough-mindedness and erudition that these qualities can rarely command, what the irrational, the transcendent and the rhapsodic can do for us. He believes that though "humanism has not the necessary psychic leverage" to lift us out of the wasteland, contemporary man may still have a few other tricks up his raveled sleeve.

The fate of the soul, says Mr. Roszak, is the fate of the social order, and only a religious renewal—in his special sense—will generate our next politics and perhaps the final radicalism of our society. The sensibility that accompanies technological omnipotence lacks both the tragic dimension and the regenerative imagination that could save us from the feeling of nihilism and absurdity that has labeled ours the Age of Anxiety and the Age of Longing.

Without rapture or participation—what the author calls "sacramental consciousness"—knowledge can only be functional. Science, as he puts it, has become our religion simply because we cannot *see around it*. We have been fed the prestige of the infinite—to use Santayana's phrase—in place of the experience of nature. Romanticism—the archenemy of science—has progressively been dismissed as a form of "emotional indigestion." Sometimes the charge, the author admits, is justified: "So much genius flawed by so much banality." But romanticism's sense of life redeems its puerile histrionics. It struggles to save the reality of experience from evaporating into a starvation diet of theoretical abstraction or disintegrating into a chaos of bare, empirical fact.

Romanticism is a critical counterpoint to the empirical advance of science. Not only in the laboratories, but in the Christian church as well, its typical *enthusiasm* for things has always been regarded as a form of heresy. For however much Christianity had borrowed from Judaism, it had left behind "the lyric spirit of prophecy, preferring desiccated theological discourse." The lid is clamped on so tight that the dark side of the mind—the landscape of romanticism—exists only by way of negative definition, in the word *un*conscious.

Mr. Roszak heroically makes his way through the prophetic poems to show us how much William Blake knew, already, of our predicament. Turning to Wordsworth, he says that he felt the "speaking presence" of nature more keenly than most, that his poetry was "an archeology of consciousness." Of Goethe, the author remarks that he was so faithful to the idea of the natural that he even resisted spectacles when his eyes grew dim. In his Ur-Phänomen, or deep-down phenomenon, Goethe confirmed Mr. Roszak's presentiment that "mystery is truth's dancing partner." Poetry, in the author's definition, is "the therapeutic subversion of language by language; it is language doctoring its own worse disease of literalism with the medicine of symbolic play."

Unlike our anesthetized urbanites, pagan or primitive peoples see reality as polyphonic, full of overtones, counterpoints and resonances. Both Martha Graham and Ida Rolf, in her Structural Integration therapy, have made "extensive explorations of gravitational dynamics within the body," which scientific empiricism has ignored. Coming back to Goethe, Mr. Roszak says that, for him, a plant was not *merely* a plant but "a choreography of symbolic gestures."

In a healthy culture, invention would properly be indistinguishable from art and ritual, and technological progress would be simultaneously a deepening of religious consciousness. The invention of agriculture, for example, was a rich joining of technique and religion, of fertility rites, rain dances and crop rotation. A tool was originally an elaborately symbolized and highly decorated art object, used by those for whom work was not a bore or a burden, but a form of prayer. Today, the author sees this spirit being reborn in the handicrafts of the "tribes" and communes now blossoming all over the country.

We are prisoners of literal surfaces, educating our young largely through letters and numbers. But the basis of all learning is what Ivan Ilyich discovered in Tolstoy's great story: that every logical premise—in his case, that "all men are mortal"—has an experience attached to it. Death lurks beneath this particular piece of logic—his own death. Mr. Roszak feels that we can best resuscitate ourselves by setting our minds "rhapsodically afire." And we must go back to nature, flee the cities, which few are interested in saving because they are more cage than home, congenial only to intellectuals and merchants.

Of course, many of the current communal experiments in living will fail, but wisdom can grow out of failure and a failure can be a moral victory, too. Our new religion, supported by the same dissenters, must be a subversive force: in Buddha's words, "A turning about in the deepest seat of consciousness." Mr. Roszak suggests also that our artists relent at last from the Grand Guignol of their nihilism, where "the repressed collective unconscious of our culture is being turned inside out before our eyes."

There is enough inspiration and provocation in *Where the Wasteland Ends* to fuel a thousand seminars in Contemporary Civilization . . . enough eloquence to make each reader *feel* in his whole self, as well as in his regenerated "sacramental consciousness," the truth of its message. Few of us will find cause for anxiety, though, in the author's final, gentle suggestion: "There is nothing to do, nowhere to get. We need only stand still in the light."

An Unfriendly Ornithologist

"All I could talk about was babies and recipes!" This is the headline of a recent advertisement on the plight of the woman who is intellectually out of it. While no one would call Mary McCarthy intellectually out of it, the line comes to mind in connection with her new novel, *Birds of America*. Forsaking the group and the groves, Miss McCarthy has elected to take us into the kitchen and nursery of her imagination. In many ways, it's a fascinating experience. (Can you imagine Julia Child writing a political novel?) We find out how she feels about frozen foods, injected turkeys, bean pots, mixes—oh, all sorts of things.

And we meet Peter, the baby. He's nineteen years old, but a baby nevertheless, and only a mother could love him. As the book opens, Peter and his mother, Rosamund, are taking a refresher course in Americana. They're revisiting "Rocky Port," Maine, where they had spent a happy summer celebrating her second divorce four years ago. But alas, Rocky Port has been invaded and occupied by that arch villain of American imperialism, the tourist. The Great Horned Owl has died of a broken heart, the cormorants are gone, and Peter and Rosamund can't find their favorite waterfall, which has undoubtedly been bulldozed under for a superhighway.

There's nothing for it but Peter must go to Europe. And once there, he takes over the book. It's not a turn for the best. Miss McCarthy's sensibility is uncomfortable cooped up inside a nineteen-year-old boy who is not only a political virgin, but a physiological one as well. In *The Golden Bough*, Frazer describes a sacrifice to the corn god in which a young person is flayed and a priest squeezes into the skin. It's something like that in *Birds of America*—only it's not clear why Miss McCarthy made the sacrifice. She is at her best in her own skin.

One always felt that Miss McCarthy understood men—she understands so many things!—but perhaps she can't come all the way down to boys. Though she works very hard over him, the blood simply won't flow through Peter's veins. Like a mother trying to fatten up her child, she loads Peter down with idiosyncrasies. But you can't see the forest for the trees: he is all idiosyncrasy and no boy. For example, he can't stand dirty toilets, so in his cheap hotels in Paris and in Rome he is forever scrubbing down the johns, which the whole floor uses. Because it won't bud in his room, he takes a large potted plant for walks.

He goes to incredible lengths and suffers all sorts of anguish to avoid being caught in a white lie by a group of perfect strangers. He picks up a sleeping clochard's bottle and puts it into a trash basket because someone might step on it—then retrieves the bottle and returns it to the clochard because he might have put down a deposit on it. With the whole Left Bank to choose from, he falls for a vegetarian who's a better softball player than he is.

But Peter doesn't spoil *Birds of America* all by himself. There are some bludgeoning attacks on "American types" that are astonishing coming from a writer of Miss McCarthy's talent and sophistication. Where she was once ironical about her country and its people, she now seems merely exasperated—an exasperation with an edge of hysteria in it. A Thanksgiving dinner given by an American general in Paris lies very heavily on the reader's digestion. So does a scene in a train in which some middle-aged, Midwestern schoolmarms exhibit a denture one of them has just broken, holding it up to Peter as if it were a naughty French postcard.

The "serious" American novel has been dining out on moral indignation for quite a while now, but sometimes it sounds like "the insistent out-of-tune of a broken violin." In a last-ditch attempt to bring color into Peter's cheek, Miss McCarthy injects him with passionate political commitments. After meddling with the French police and muddling here and there, he sits down and writes his mother a twenty-eight-page letter. She is a harpsichordist—which may inspire unfair comparisons with the author—and he wants her to cancel her government-sponsored tour of Europe as a protest against the war in Vietnam.

Before she can answer yes or no, Peter goes to the Jardin des Plantes and gets himself bitten by a swan. The bite becomes infected and he is taken to the hospital, where he is given penicillin. But he's allergic to penicillin and goes into shock. Then, in his delirium, Immanuel Kant comes to his bedside and announces that Nature is dead. What does this mean? It means that they're not making boys the way they used to. And Miss McCarthy isn't writing books the way she used to, either.

No, But I Read the Review

I remember a friend of mine, an older writer, commenting on one of the first book reviews I ever wrote. "It's a nice piece," he said, "but you don't *have* to include the cosmos." He was telling me, in a kindly way, that I was young and inexperienced and straining too hard. I mention this here because, in reading Pauline Kael's *Deeper into Movies,* I realized that *she* includes the cosmos, but with no strain at all. I don't think she could keep it out, and I hope she never tries.

Her typical piece not only evaluates the movie itself: it also presents you with a theory of film-making, of acting, directing, shooting, scriptwriting, everything. It tells you how these and other aspects of film are influenced by, or cater to, the quality and condition of life in America today. Reading a Pauline Kael review gives you a pretty good idea of the current state of our morality, our esthetics, our politics—and, yes, I might as well say it: our souls.

There's a school of French literary criticism in which the critic tries to outstrip, in the brilliance of his own style and images, the artist he is discussing. In the case of Pauline Kael on the movies, it's simply no contest. Very few pictures are worth a thousand of her words. At first sight, it seems a terrible waste to ask a writer as gifted as Miss Kael to criticize films—but when you stop to think about it, you realize how badly they need her. Who else could find so many interesting things to say about their failures? The mere fact that she accepts the job is reassuring —even if only for a weekly column six months a year in *The New Yorker* magazine. She wouldn't do it, one feels, unless there was a real possibility that the medium might improve.

Speaking of improvement, I don't see how the people who have exasperated Miss Kael can make the same mistake again. Nobody can expose a mistake quite so nakedly as she can. Yet it is not rancor that makes her displeasure so voluptuously definitive— she simply calls the shots as she sees them. A few examples: "Nicol Williamson is a violently self-conscious actor whose effect on the camera is like that of the singers who used to shatter crystal . . . he stares so much he's in danger of wearing out his eyeballs." Of Omar Sharif, she says he "is a great sufferer . . . what a Camille he'd be!" In her *Duet for Cannibals*, Susan Sontag shows so little dramatic sense that the actors "seem to be stranded on the screen . . ."

Of the pseudo-Hemingway spareness of speech in *Downhill Racer*, Miss Kael remarks that it is "as if speech were what athletes are supposed to sublimate." Writing of *Zabriskie Point*, she suggests that "Death Valley is the perfect Antonioni location, because his infatuation with desolation has become his defining characteristic." His clumsy attack on the United States fails to convince us, because "we have such a lot to choose from that we've become connoisseurs of anti-Americanism." Fellini fares no better: "Like Cecil B. de Mille, who was also fond of pagan infernos, Fellini equates sexual 'vice' with apocalypse." The youth cult in films moves Miss Kael to observe that "any work that is enjoyable is said to be counterrevolutionary."

The author is a formidable literary critic when she defends books like *Women in Love* and *Tropic of Cancer* from oversimplification or flattening for cheap effects. Generally, she finds the "new" movies most sentimental about youth and most despairing about America. "Austere mortification of the audience" is so well established by now as a sign of "seriousness" that the most gratuitous attack will stretch a masochistic line around the block. Among her personal dislikes, Miss Kael lists "brain-damaged heroes; virgins driven mad (particularly when played by Sandy Dennis); aging virgins (particularly when played by Joanne Woodward); anything with Anthony Quinn as a peasant; and Christ figures."

Occasionally, Miss Kael strikes me as indulgent—but if these are in fact indulgences, what a case she makes for them! It's not surprising that she should sometimes be disproportionately grateful for small pleasures like *McCabe and Mrs. Miller* or *Z*. I know that I myself have a peculiar weakness for a particular detail in *The Bride of Frankenstein*: the long-awaited lightning storm has arrived, and as the doctor's hunchbacked assistant scuttles up the steps of the ruined castle to send the huge kites aloft, he pauses to pull up one of his stockings.

Sometimes the author's eye is so penetrating that she sees

through pictures that I find entertainingly opaque. I thought Paul Morrissey's *Trash* was both funnier and sadder than she did, and I didn't see *Patton* as a meretricious glorification of a military monster but as an attempt to examine a dream of glory that was at once pugnacious, pathetic and impressive in some darkly human way. And as for Jean-Luc Godard's *Weekend*, which Miss Kael reviewed in an earlier volume—well, I'm ready to concede, hands down, that she is the *only* person with a legitimate claim to appreciate it.

That's enough caviling. A regular reviewer—of any medium— is lucky if he or she can maintain a modicum of "grace under pressure." And Miss Kael does quite a bit better than that.

Recycling Junk into Art

Contemporary painters and sculptors often talk about closing the gap between art and life, but Kurt Schwitters did, almost fifty years ago. He literally inhabited his art. Gutting his house in Hanover, he turned it into a "Merzbau"—a multistoried constructivist sculpture. From the inside, the Merzbau resembled a rain forest of abstract forms, a warehouse of surplus imagination. It was like an immensely complicated lock into which Schwitters himself fitted as the key. Every night, he climbed up this gargantuan creation and slept on top of it, as though resting on his achievement. "Merz" was the root name of all Schwitter's art, derived from a scrap of the word "commerz" in one of his collages. The Merzbau began as a sort of stalagmite combining several Dada-like constructions with titles like "Cult Pump" and "Gallows of Desire" into a "Cathedral of Erotic Misery." Composed of pieces of junk that Schwitters incessantly collected and then plastered over, it eventually became the visual poem of a man who recycled the waste products of his environment and made them into art.

Like the corpse in Eugène Ionesco's play *Amédée*, the Merzbau continued to grow and occupy an increasing amount of living space. As it grew, its rather literary origins were synthesized in an overall architectonic scheme. When it filled the room, Schwitters evicted his upstairs tenant and broke through the ceiling. His son, too, was forced to move to another room. The work finally extended from the basement, even penetrating the cistern, to the roof. Inevitably, it pushed up through the roof and Schwitters added a windowless penthouse at the top, which served for years as his bedroom. Under the stress of its owner's enthusiasm, the side wall of the house developed a species of hernia, also, and this became a balcony. Besides working night and day himself on his Merzbau, he also employed a carpenter and a painter full time.

Only photographs have survived, for the Hanover Merzbau

was destroyed by a bomb in 1943. They reveal a structure of astonishing imaginativeness and considerable beauty, a "Cabinet of Dr. Caligari" carried to its ultimate conclusion, an architecture as intimately related to its occupant as the most intricately convoluted shell of any mollusk.

Schwitters also toyed with the idea of designing a system of weights that would automatically adjust the esthetic balance of a room to the movements of a person in it. To refine this idea, he projected a series of experiments using white mice. In another equally far-fetched but delightful scheme for "doing away with the uninhabitability of houses," he proposed to incorporate into the architecture of a room the typical trajectories of the tenant. His designs for an experimental theater would pack any of today's off-Broadway houses: "Take gigantic surfaces conceived as infinite, cloak them in color, shift them menacingly and vault their smooth pudency. Shatter and embroil finite parts . . . find a sewing machine that yawns . . . Take lights and deform them as brutally as you can . . . Take petticoats and other kindred articles, shoes and false hair, also ice skates and throw them into place where they belong, and always at the right time . . . Inner tubes are highly recommended." With his characteristic good-natured irony, Schwitters added, "Even people can be used . . . they can speak on two legs, even in sensible sentences."

The New Theater, Happenings, Environments, Combines—Schwitters anticipated them all. He did not so much practice art as live it. He rushed forward on all fronts, wrote "phonetic" poetry and recited it in cafés, helped revolutionize typography and advertising, made drawings with rubber stamps, created scores of collages that often surpassed those of Picasso and Braque in lyric as well as iconographic interest. Though he flirted with the Dadaists and surrealists, Schwitters disliked their politicalization of art. Politics came to his door nevertheless in the form of the Gestapo and he had to flee to Norway. There, in Lysaker, near Oslo, he began another Merzbau. (It was burned to the ground by children in 1951.) In 1940 he fled to England, where he died eight years later at the age of sixty. In spite of his failing health, he was working on a third Merzbau in a damp, unheated barn in the Lake District.

Schwitters' personality was inseparable from his work, and Dr.

Werner Schmalenbach, director of a Düsseldorf Museum, gives us a wealth of well-chosen selections from the artist's writings, as well as first-hand descriptions of the man and his work by friends, critics and other artists. One of the most interesting things about Schwitters was his complete conventionality in everything but his work. Though he was one of the most unusual artists of the century, "the way he looked, dressed and spoke and the establishment he maintained in the family home at Waldhausenstrasse 5 could hardly have been more bourgeois . . . His art, his writing, and his flamboyant public appearances were in utter contradiction to this style of life . . ."

Richard Huelsenbeck, spokesman for the Berlin Dada group, described Schwitters as "a genius in a frock coat." A publisher who was a close friend called him "a complicated fool." Schwitters was also a successful advertising man, acting as an account executive and art director for his own agency. Besides his Merz works, he also painted conventional, even sentimental landscapes and portraits. This "ordinariness" was probably one source of Schwitters's strength as an artist and innovator. It was a fixed point, a solid center, in the esthetic turbulence of his time. Like meter in poetry, it helped to keep his work coherent. It gave him perspective, objectivity, independence, saved him from the melodramatic silliness that characterized the lives and work of so many avant-gardists. As he himself said about his fellow Hanoverians, "They never get dog's diseases." This might have been a mischievous hint that it is not necessary to foam at the mouth, in the stereotypical image of the "mad-dog" genius, in order to be an artist.

Though they were abstract in design, Schwitters's Merz pictures were composed of the sloughed-off skin of his culture; they were warmed by a history of human contact. It was as if he were saying that even the by-products of bourgeois life could be made into art, that there is beauty to waste in this world of ours. One can sense a peculiar poetry in the picture of this frock-coated man gathering his materials. As Dr. Schmalenbach says, "He was manic, almost kleptomanic, in his obsession with the waste materials of everyday life . . . Wherever he went, he collected used streetcar and theater tickets, worn scraps of paper, bits of wire, old nails, rusty tin cans. To find them, he went through wastepaper baskets, ashcans, attics, junk piles; he was always stooping down in public places to pick up things people had thrown away."

Schwitters was like a man determined to retrieve life from the gutters, garbage cans and wastebaskets where the unimaginative had mistakenly discarded it. He cleaned up behind his culture; his art fed off its offal like fish in a balanced aquarium. He was a redeemer, someone who believed that human use gave a patina of pathos or *Gemütlichkeit* to objects. He liked things that were dog-eared with touch, rusted with time, wrinkled with relevance. He was an archeologist, reconstructing a civilization from the scraps and shards of its constantly changing mind.

A Talked-Out Case

I remember a scene from *The Power and the Glory* in which the fugitive "whiskey priest" stumbles onto a house that is abandoned except for a fierce, half-crippled dog. There is a bone on the floor and the famished priest notices a few scraps of meat still clinging to it. But when he moves toward it, the dog growls and prepares to attack. Feigning nonchalance, the priest hums a few lines from the litany. Then, begging the Lord's forgiveness, he snatches the bone and escapes.

In another scene in the same book, the priest revisits his tiny village, where the people are forbidden to harbor him under pain of death. The police arrive and search the village and while the priest hides, his common-law wife throws his satchel containing his sacred paraphernalia on the reeking garbage dump. When he goes there to retrieve it, a small girl watches him rummage in the filth. He meets her eyes and realizes that she is his illegitimate daughter.

In these two episodes, Mr. Greene achieves a perfect union of pathos and irony. The action could not be closer to, or more consonant with, the symbolism. Speech is unnecessary because everything else is eloquent. Nothing could improve on the economy or intensity of these passages, and I cannot think of a better lesson in how literature seizes life by the throat. But this is a talent that Mr. Greene seems to have shelved. He has become talky, and what's worse, his most recent characters are melodramatically out of step with things for reasons that are barely sufficient. They have declined from inevitability to plausibility.

Plarr, the central character of *The Honorary Consul*, is a doctor, with all the predictable, world-weary pragmatism we have come to expect of doctors in fiction. I should think that Mr. Greene, of all people, would have known how to transcend this cliché, just as his "whiskey priest" both personified and contradicted his calling. Like the protagonist of one of the author's other novels, Plarr is a "burnt-out case," but we see only the ashes, not the fire. He is mechanically absorbed in his work and an occasional mistress, whom he meets only on the operating table of his desire.

The one woman who stirs him is Clara, an enigmatic young prostitute at the brothel of Señora Sanchez. This establishment, with its reputation for order, its ritual procedures, its tiny clean cells, each with its crucifix and candle, is like a gangrenous arm of the Church. Not only prostitutes, but all of Mr. Greene's women are "fallen." They are deflated by fate and the men he offers them have not inspiration enough to blow them up again, to give them "the kiss of life." Love appears to be woman's original sin, a hubristic hope of happiness. But she is inevitably disappointed, because her partner lusts for a different kind of communion. He exhausts himself trying to love God.

The Honorary Consul revolves around the kidnapping of old Charlie Fortnum, an unofficial symbol of England in the small South American town where he and Plarr live. But the revolutionaries are amateurs—like all revolutionaries except Jesus, the author seems to imply. They meant to seize the American ambassador and got Fortnum by mistake. Doggedly, they decide to hold him anyway and demand the release of ten political prisoners in exchange for his life. Two of the revolutionaries are former school friends of Plarr's. Aquino is a poet, who with typical Latin bombast, writes only of death. León is an unfrocked priest who has come for the catechism lesson we now expect from Mr. Greene.

Small ironies buzz like mosquitoes through the plot. Saavedra, an old-fashioned novelist who is obsessed with *machismo*— Saavedra was Cervantes's family name—offers himself as a hostage in Fortnum's place. He still supposes that literature can play a direct part in politics. But of course nobody wants either of them. In their impotence, León and Aquino fall back on bravado and propose to kill the irrelevant Fortnum, to mask one mistake with another. They will show the world that they mean business, even though they are obviously in the wrong business. Plarr, who has come to treat a wound suffered by Fortnum in trying to escape, attempts to heal his own wounds in an interminable theological debate with León. In the course of this talkathon, God turns out to be the least interesting character in the novel.

If this is not Mr. Greene at his best, it is quite a good book as books go. Confused as he is by his comic-opera *machismo*, Saavedra still has the absurd, last-ditch dignity of a Don Quixote. Fortnum's drunken muddling through achieves a forlorn majesty in the best British tradition. Lost in the labyrinth of their revolutionary principles, the kidnappers resemble rats in a maze. And then there are always the fine Graham Greene sentences: In their dwelling places, ". . . the poor always cling close to the river . . . as though they plan one day to swim away . . ." Plarr's mother, who sees her widowhood as a penance not so much of prayers as of éclairs, has pouches under her eyes—not "the pouches of grief, but of constipation."

It is the preaching, I think, that damns the book. Though most good novelists are preachers to a degree, their pulpit is flesh and blood, the word incarnate. When Mr. Greene crucified his "whiskey priest" in *The Power and the Glory*, the reader underwent that religious experience we call art. But when, in *The Honorary Consul*, he turns religion into an importunity, when he offers us an apostrophe dressed up as a dramatic progression, he forfeits the element of magic that both his mythologies need.

A Lynching in Black Face

"What this town needs is a good old-fashioned lynching. The real thing. With all the trimmings. It would be like going to church. Puts things in their proper perspective. Reminding everybody of who they are, where they stand. Divides the world simple and pure. Good or bad. Oppressors and oppressed. Black or white. Things tend to get a little fuzzy here in the big city. We need a ritual. A spectacular . . . Now I'm not talking about grabbing just any old body and stringing him up to the nearest lamp post. That's not it at all. We must learn to do a thing correctly with style for immediate appeal and depth for the deep thinkers, the ones who concern themselves with history and tradition . . . What could be more dramatic? A great artist must have conceived the first lynching. As a failed poet myself, I envy his sweet touch, the sure hand that could extricate a satisfying, stable form from the raw fantasies of his peers."

The speaker is Willie Hall, better known as Littleman because of his stunted legs in their metal braces. He is black, and what he is proposing is "a lynching in black face." The victim is to be a white policeman. "If we lynch a cop," Littleman says, "we will be declaring ourselves a nation . . . since the total community gives its sanction in a lynching."

He is talking to his recruits, repeating himself hypnotically, elaborating theme and variations like a musician until what he says becomes familiar, no longer a witticism but a concrete proposal, complete with ways and means. He is wearing down the incredulity of Saunders, the street man who is capable of violence, Rice, the secretive fool who can provide the necessary hideout, and Wilkerson, the schoolteacher, whose only function may be to appreciate Littleman as the others cannot.

Along with Littleman's recruits, the reader too is finding his incredulity worn down, is seeing a bitter witticism harden into a troubling threat. Though we have heard the themes and variations of violence before in black writing, *The Lynchers* touches us in a more personal way, for John Edgar Wideman has a weapon more powerful than any knife or gun. His weapon is art. Eloquence is his arsenal, his arms cache. His prose, at its best, is a black panther, coiled to spring.

Not that *The Lynchers* is flawless; far from it. Mr. Wideman ripples too many muscles in his writing, often cannot seem to decide whether to show or snow us. His two intellectuals have swelled heads, heavy with introspection. They are too expensively dressed in their ideas, out of place against the soiled honesty of the other passages. The author even resorts to the same device to try their souls. Both Littleman and Wilkerson have a "dream girl," a woman who offers an alternate vision of self-realization, an island they can escape to where waves lap peacefully on a private shore.

Though he is a former Rhodes scholar who has become associate professor of English and director of Afro-American studies at the University of Pennsylvania, Mr. Wideman's best scenes are homely, set in a kitchen. Grandiloquence cannot compete with gut truths. The history taught in the lecture halls cannot touch the stories told around a table, between sink and stove. When Wilkerson visits his mother and father in order to introduce them to his girl, he arrives before her, trying to prepare the ground. He is not clear in his own mind why he is bringing her there, but we sense that he is trying to persuade her that he is real, that his Hamlet-like vacillation has been earned the hard way.

And his mother gives him a dose of reality, all right—like the sulfur-and-molasses purge that Southern children used to have to swallow every spring. She mocks his dashiki—worn for the first time—and his attempt at an Afro hairdo. Satirizing his separate arrival, she asks, "Is you all going to leave at the same time?" His father, who is a garbage man—no, it somehow doesn't seem too thick—arrives drunk, but gallantly cradling a second-hand box of flowers—they've hardly been smelled—that he found along the route. It would have made all the difference if we could have seen Wilkerson's cool dream girl reacting to this cozy domesticity, but in one of several missed opportunities, the author refuses to let her enter the room.

Littleman's girl is no better. She resembles the heroine in one

of those rainy, talky, pretentious movies—a girl all high-falutin'
phrases and forced circumstance. Then the author puts Littleman
himself *hors de combat* in a hospital, where he can do nothing
but lie and think—a fatal prescription for a character—and try to
proselytize the ward boy.

Like Antaeus and most authors, Mr. Wideman is strongest
when his feet are on the ground. He can make an ordinary scene
sing the blues like nobody's business. There is a beautiful passage
in which Wilkerson, wandering distraught through the sleeping
city, comes upon a man hunched over a conga drum beneath a
lamppost in a playground. The man has no talent for drum-
ming, but again and again, alone in the forsaken playground, he
tries to get a rhythm going. It is an image that says everything,
that could not be improved upon.

Mr. Wideman is wordy, and *The Lynchers* is as shaky in its
structure as some of the buildings his characters inhabit. But he
can *write*, and you come away from his book with the feeling that
he is, as they say, very close to getting it all together.

A Most Unpedestrian Walker

In the last few years, psychologists seem to have discovered, as if for the first time, the importance of people's touching one another, of establishing palpable contact in an increasingly isolating emotional atmosphere. Touching, they suggest, is one of the few certainties still open to us. In the beginning was, not the word, but the touch. In a similar spirit, sociologists and philosophers have now begun to warn or exhort us to get back in touch with nature, to reintegrate ourselves with our first history, to seek the softening and soothing touch of our original mother.

In walking, John Hillaby has found a way to join both these schools of thought. Walking, for him, is a form of touching, and being touched, through his whole body. As Henry James remarked somewhere, landscape is character, and for Mr. Hillaby, walking is like making love to the landscape and letting it love him back.

He is reviving a very old way of life, once shared by mendicant friars and beggars, pilgrims, bards and traveling artisans. His values are equally venerable, or anachronistic. Everywhere, we have seen the qualitative moving out to the quantitative; we have found ourselves more and more often in transit instead of simply *in*, more talented in getting somewhere than in *being* somewhere. We have developed the surface habits of the hurried as against the earned experiences and destinations of those who do their traveling on their own power.

People who live in the country are used to the sight of teenagers at the peak of their physical powers hitching a ride rather than walk a quarter of a mile. On Compo Beach in Westport, Connecticut, the girls have everything but calf muscles: in fact, those few who do have them tend to regard them as a deformity. Mr. Hillaby, though, talks about walking as a feeling of well-being, a pleasure with a strong sensual component. Those of us who have marched to drum music may have experienced something of this.

In their way of walking, many of our young men today are imitating their movie or ethnic heroes—cock of the walk, foot-dragging dropout or feline black cat—while their female counter-parts have evolved a method of locomotion you can't find anywhere else in the world. It can be described only as a panto-mimed resignation or resentment at being a biped. Their stride is too long for efficiency or grace and their movements seem dictated either by an embarrassment of breast, buttock and thigh or an unfamiliarity with these parts.

Mr. Hillaby has already written two very good books about walking. In *Journey to the Jade Sea,* he took a 1,100-mile stroll in Africa, through arid desert, to Lake Rudolph and back. *A Walk Through Britain* followed, and now the author has begun below Amsterdam and passed through the Netherlands, Belgium, Germany and France to end in Nice. The journey took him sixty-seven days, but it required more than six months' planning to avoid the ubiquitous highways in each country, and even then he was not entirely successful.

Mr. Hillaby is a naturalist and a bit of a historian and he studies up on the places he walks to, because, as he says, if you know something about what you're looking at, it is infinitely more interesting. His mind is as nimble as his legs, and he observes people and customs as well as wildlife and landscapes. Unlike some physical culture enthusiasts, he is not averse to talking and drinking all night if he finds good company in a tavern or inn.

When he meets a hippie couple from America carrying a "just married" sign and waiting for a hitch, he finds that nothing he asks interests them. All they are willing to divulge is that, after Europe, they are going to India. Why India? "Because it is logical." In searching for a Belgian priest he once met, the author is led to a brothel, whose madam, his informant tells him, knows everybody. She doesn't know his priest but in talking to one of the girls at the bar he learns a lovely word. The girl's customers are mostly older men, who patronize the place, she says, out of "Torchlusspanik," fear of the closing of the door.

Mr. Hillaby discourses on wine, on food, on the peculiarities of the people he meets, on the characteristics of Dutch as against Renaissance painting, on architecture and on ecology. He turns a very neat phrase: When someone tries to bargain with the madam who knew everybody, she looks at him as if he were advocating "a foreshortened form of the mass." A prostitute in another place resembles "an old doll in a bankrupt toy shop." The first tulips the author sees in the Netherlands are "waxy-looking blooms for the sick room and the cemetery, entirely scentless and too stiff for grace."

In dull stretches of country, Mr. Hillaby ponders the reasons for the misogyny of a lusty man like Rabelais. He ruminates on the ecological indifference of most of Europe and aptly quotes the remark that "Greed shows up more clearly on a landscape than on a man's face." He finds that the tidelike drift of people from rural areas to towns and cities is eroding their individuality.

In this book, more than in the previous two, Mr. Hillaby allows us to see quite a bit of himself along with everything else and this gives *A Walk Through Europe* a depth and intimacy the other two books have never tried for. Reading it, one is tempted to agree with Nietzsche, who said something to the effect that our best thoughts come to us while we are walking.

Genius, Buffoon—or Both?

What makes a man "a great lover"? In these days of sexual revolution, instruction manuals, sensitivity therapy and "raised consciousness," the case of the Italian writer Gabriele D'Annunzio should be instructive—for, if any man was, he was certainly one of the greatest lovers in history. Compared to him, Casanova, for example, seems a mere sensualist, a man for whom seduction was something like a hobby or a sport. Casanova's sense of irony inevitably inhibited him and reduced him to a sexual Machiavellian, while for D'Annunzio each encounter was, while it lasted, the Absolute, the Ultimate. He was a true believer who made a religion of love, a man who proved something our age seems to have forgotten: that the mind is the first and foremost of the erogenous zones. Who else could have said to a duchess he hardly knew: "Come, we shall have a profound evening."

We know that it was not his looks that fascinated so many famous and talented women, for Philippe Jullian tells us in his brilliant and copiously furnished biography that D'Annunzio was very short and thickset, with hips that were wider than his shoulders. Born in 1863 in Pescara in the Abruzzi region, he had inherited the build of the southern peasant. His face was rescued by his personality, which printed power, intelligence and something like exaltation on his rather ordinary features. For most of his adult life, he was bald as well, for when his scalp was laid open during a duel, the surgeon panicked and poured so much antiseptic into the wound that the hair roots were destroyed.

D'Annunzio's books are difficult to assess. As Mr. Jullian puts it, "His writing is most dated when the language of the soul is employed"—but this language made up a considerable part of his work. The English writer Ouida said that D'Annunzio totally failed to perceive those times "when the ridiculous mars the pathetic." Furthermore, he plagiarized, borrowed and imitated, using Flaubert, Daudet, Goncourt, Bourget, Boccaccio and Nietzsche as models. His work was so much a part of himself and his time—the final flowering of the Decadent movement—that one might almost regard it as organic material that aged and died with its author.

Though some of his poems are good and his plays no worse than most of his contemporaries', D'Annunzio's novels often seemed like blast furnaces of euphemized erotica. Almost indistinguishable from parody, they are saved only by the utter conviction one feels in them. The skeptical reader's laughter is restrained by the uneasy feeling that the author has experienced these exalted or hyperbolical sentiments, that he has enjoyed something that we are too "reasonable" to try. Like a great actor salvaging an absurd part, D'Annunzio used the force of his personality, the impenetrability of his humorlessness, to carry the moment.

Italians, however, had no difficulty in adoring D'Annunzio. During his lifetime, they were passing through their most "operatic" period, and though he often shocked them, they thrilled like secret sinners to his pages. And his rise from a lowly bourgeois with the body of a peasant to the "conqueror" of international society's darlings was the daydream of the man in the street, who probably believed the rumors that D'Annunzio drank champagne from the skull of a virgin and that his pillow was stuffed with the locks of a hundred mistresses.

The most famous of these mistresses was Eleonora Duse, Italy's finest actress and a considerable personality in her own right. Although Mr. Jullian does not mention it in his *D'Annunzio*, there is a story that someone asked her what made her lover irresistible. Her reply was significant: He makes you feel that you are so beautiful. A remark that D'Annunzio made to Isadora Duncan shows how carefully he custom-tailored his compliments. During a walk in a forest, he said to her: "All other women destroy the landscape; you alone become part of it." His loves were so numerous and his reputation so formidable that an unusually level-headed observer of the time commented: "The woman who had not slept with him became a laughingstock."

At the outbreak of World War I, disillusioned perhaps by the fact that he had contracted his first case of syphilis at the age of fifty, D'Annunzio turned his attention to politics. Living in

France at the time and loving the French, he tried—and to a certain extent succeeded—in talking Italy into coming in on the Allied side. As a public speaker he was superb, for he found here the immediate emotional involvement that literature could not offer—and he was able to make love to not one but 40,000 people each time he mounted a balcony.

His entry into politics brought him into a long flirtation with the idea of power, and with Mussolini as well. They used each other liberally, but the younger Mussolini was too much for D'Annunzio's failing energies. The poet retired to his villa, the Vittoriale, which he typically "gave" to the Government as a museum, so that it could be enlarged and maintained at the expense of the state. Surrounded by trinkets and mementos that included the airplane he had flown during the war—"so many precautions against oblivion"—D'Annunzio, even into his seventies, sent out for prostitutes. He would serve them tea in semi-darkness, bewilder them with elevated conversation until dawn, then reenact his old rituals. He lived until 1938 and, like the pilot he was so proud of being, he tried to soar until the very end.

Art and the Anxious Object

"The artist has become, as it were, too big for art. His proper medium is working on the world: Ecology—Transforming the Landscape—Changing the Conditions of Life." This is Harold Rosenberg's view of some of the newest movements, from Action Art to Pop to Earthworks. In *The De-definition of Art*, he quotes a contemporary artist who says: "I choose not to make objects. Instead, I have set out to create a quality of experience that locates itself in the world." Because so many artists feel this way today, the very nature of art has become uncertain or ambiguous. Mr. Rosenberg describes a work of art in this context as an "anxious object," one that does not know whether it is a masterpiece or junk—or both, as in the case of the collages of Kurt Schwitters, composed of the detritus of modern life.

In some instances, the author says, "nothing is left of art but the fiction of the artist." The art object is often eliminated in favor of an idea for a work "or a rumor that it has been consummated." We have only Claes Oldenburg's word for it that he created a work of art and then buried it where no one can see it. More and more, art is being reduced to a conception, rather than a visual or sensual experience. Esthetics has been rejected in favor of "a solitary dialogue between man and the universe." This dialogue has taken such artists so far beyond direct perceptual experience that "awareness of the work depends upon a system of documentation." We must have what amounts to an explanation before we can "see" the work.

"The eye's outrageous philistinism" must be conceptually corrected: "Paintings today are apprehended by the ears." Instead of deriving principles from what it sees, art criticism now teaches the eye to "see" principles. In abstract art, subject matter was banished to clear the way for direct response of the eye to optical data. Abstract art was speechless; it had "eliminated the verbal correlative from the canvas." But, continues Mr. Rosenberg, the place of literature in painting has been taken by the "rhetoric of abstract concepts." "Looking has become a professional matter."

Earthworks and Action Art are uncollectable art objects that serve as advertisements for the showman-artist "who markets his signature appended to commonplace relics." We recognize an art object today only because it is segregated from nature by the language used to describe it. Increasingly existing as an excrescence of theory, the art object is to be considered only as a record of the artist's creative processes.

Overpowering the eye by words, of greater intellectual than visual interest, the work of the new movement is being pushed in the direction of speculative philosophy. As a result, "It is a hardship of the times that before an artist can fashion an icon, he must compose the theology that his icon will reinforce."

These remarks do not mean that Mr. Rosenberg is hostile per se to all the more extreme forms of contemporary art. As long as painting remains painting or can be recognized as such, he is willing and able to appreciate it according to its merits. While criteria for evaluating or responding to Earthworks or Action Art are difficult to arrive at, are entangled in an "opaque rhetoric of half-thoughts" passing for analysis, the author can and does bring a rich and complex appreciation to the work of painters such as Barnett Newman and Mark Rothko.

Of Newman, he says that he "worked with emptiness as if it were a substance. His program was to induce emptiness to exclaim its secrets." He defines a Newman work by saying that it is there, "an entity that keeps nature at bay." Newman is one of those artists who conceive of painting as "a marathon of deletions," seeking to arrive at an ultimate sign. This, says Mr. Rosenberg, "is the century of 'the last painter,' whose formulas of negation have promised to defy further reduction."

The negationists of painting feel that the artist should vanish and take art with him in order to "restore to everyone full responsibility for his relationship with the world." In the negationist view—or the World Game of Buckminster Fuller, in which each person living on it approaches Space Ship Earth as a work of art—everyone may become an artist, composing "geosocial scenarios." In embracing negationist views of art, in eagerly welcoming them as "views" or as "relevant," institutions such as our own Museum of Modern Art may be radically changing their roles. It is possible, Mr. Rosenberg says, that "any object or spectacle that falls into no other category will be accepted as belonging to a new art form." But "when everything has found its way into the museum, the place of art will have to be outside it."

Mr. Rosenberg's sentences have elegance, precision and a satisfying sense of things uncannily clicking into place. He consistently goes beyond the clever scoffing that must be a temptation to modern art critics. When he discredits an absurdity, he usually hangs something better on the wall. And while wits tend to be cagey about their own convictions, he is perfectly willing to commit his to print. He says, for example, that "the basic substance of art has become the protracted discourse in words and materials echoed back and forth from artist to artist, work to work, art movement to art movement, on all aspects of contemporary civilization and of the place of creation and of the individual in it. The student-artist needs, while learning to see and execute, above all to be brought into this discourse, without which the history of modern painting appears a gratuitious parade of fashion." Amen. And hooray.

On Crossing the Frontier

There are some writers who seem to have a private path into people's souls. They lead you there through unfamiliar streets; you don't recognize any landmarks. The journey is uncanny. And yet, when you have arrived, there is no question that you are there. The characters *exist*, all the more so because you don't quite know how they've been created. There is only the peculiar fact, the unanalyzable presence, of these people. Without knowing anything about them, you know *all* about them. And you wait for them to do what they must. Like them, you are in the grip of an originality that bemuses you.

James Hanley is one of these writers. It is not surprising to find that he is admired by Henry Green, who is another. An Irishman, Mr. Hanley is even less recognized in the United States than is Mr. Green, who is English. Perhaps each has captured too much of the national character of his country, has dipped too deeply into its essence, to be readily accessible to our average reader. They are both, in the best sense, writers' writers, the sort of authors who work in such mysterious ways that most readers feel uneasy with them, are bored or fatigued by their strangeness.

Reading them can never be a casual act; the commitment is as total as if you were dreaming. You must let go, let yourself plunge into the author's singularity, muttering helplessly, "Where are you taking me?" In a sense, the talent of such writers lies in an ability to make you feel a kind of madness—like a potential for glory, or ecstatic individuality—beneath the clothes, behind the eyes, in the startling speech, of "ordinary" people.

Like Henry Green, James Hanley works with minimal materials—everyday people in everyday situations—and like Mr. Green again, his style is at once spare, understated and poetic. Though you are aware of his eccentricity, it is so convincing that there is rarely a feeling of artiness or affectation. One is tempted to make an invidious comparison with someone like Samuel Beckett, whose characters, at least in his later work, are stripped not to blood, bone and obsession, but to pretentious and oversimplified symbols.

In *Another World*, love is Mr. Hanley's theme, and he illustrates its infinite range in two antipodal couples. Jones, the little jack-of-all-trades in the Decent Hotel, loves Mrs. Gandell, its towering proprietor, and she loves him with all the accumulated ardor of her fifty-five years. "I am sure," he says as they prepare for bed, "that you are looking forward to crossing the frontier, Mrs. Gandell." "I always look forward," she replies, "to you doing your duty, Jones." "I'll set you on fire," he says matter-of-factly. "Soon, I'll send color flying into your Yorkshire mug . . ." "The explosion, Mrs. Gandell," he continues, "much better than a mere collision." He is small, Jones is, and he muses erotically on Mrs. Gandell's great size: "D'you know, the first time I saw you, I wondered where your leg ended."

Miss Vaughan, the single tenant of the Decent Hotel during the cruel Welsh winter, is loved too, by Mr. Thomas, the minister, but she doesn't return his feeling. "Mr. Thomas depends on smiles," she says to herself, refusing to return his or to pity his vulnerability. Where once, in her youth, "life had seemed to rise up, vaunting," now, in her middle age, it was different. It "crouched." But she is content, "she rises and falls upon the turbulent waves of the world, and is unharmed."

The minister has persuaded himself, in the teeth of her denial, that Miss Vaughan is lonely. He insists on this because he feels he has nothing to offer—no thrill or thrall—but the symmetry of twoness. Talking to her through her locked door in the hotel, he says, "What great big eyes daylight has, Miss Vaughan." "In your face I see an ocean of loss," he urges. "Your bed is cold, Miss Vaughan . . . Po---lar."

But Miss Vaughan is satisfied to lie in her bed and dream. She dreams of a captain and a ship that will not sail, an anchor, dragging deep, that will never break dead water. "You are not quite real, Miss Vaughan," the minister pleads through the door. "Yet I know I could make you happy." In his desperation, he even listens to Jones, but can't rise to his advice: "Hug her, Mr. Thomas, *hug* her . . . and remember to take your collar off."

In his tiny study, full of damp, of spiders, of "books big and little," the minister thinks, "I am walking out of my life." Held together for fifty years by faith, he is being torn to shreds by his first passion. His experience has not prepared him for it. When at last he comes face to face with Miss Vaughan, on a beach where "the air rings like a bell," he can only cry, "What shall I do with the moment?" He asks not because he is a man of the collar: Mr. Hanley goes deeper than that. He implies that this is a collar we all wear—unless, of course, we are, like Jones, willing and able to cross the frontier.

Those Who Shut Up and Put Up

No one looks at the world with pristine eyes, Ruth Benedict said in *Patterns of Culture*—but right now there are tens of thousands of young people in this country who are trying to do just that. In some two to three thousand communes and communities, they are trying to put aside their habits and prejudices, their very histories, to start from scratch. Or, as some of them would say it, from consciousness. They have succeeded, to a degree, in stopping the world and getting off. No longer content to criticize or satirize the Establishment, they've elected to shut up and put up. Some of them have put up shacks and some geodesic domes. All of them have patched together their own images of man—and if these Frankensteins are not conventionally handsome, they're not quite so bad either when you get used to them. In *Getting Back Together*, Robert Houriet has captured quite a few of them in a wonderfully freaky family album that may make some of us want to revise our own.

Mr. Houriet was a young night editor of a Jersey paper and quit his job when the publisher ordered conformity in dress and haircuts. He was not exactly a rebel—the idea just rubbed him the wrong way. Once he was out of a job, he felt that need for stepping back and taking stock that has become a common syndrome in American life—so he decided to do a book on the new life styles being born all over the country. By looking into these behavioral laboratories, by sampling their socio-sexual stews, he hoped to learn something not only about America, but about himself. He did, but not in the way he had expected. His trip turned into a "trip" and he became a part of the experiment he had set out merely to report on.

Mr. Houriet was the ideal man for the job. He was just conventional enough to bring some kind of recognizable perspective to what he experienced, but not enough to prejudice his reactions. He seems to have been accepted wherever he went, so that he was more a witness or a participant than an outsider. In the course of his odyssey, he went through experiences many "straight" people secretly yearn to have. For example, he describes his first acid trip without the customary bombast. In a delightful passage—which could have been merely funny, but goes much further—he tells about his "baptism" into a primitive pentecostal group. There was the usual laying on of hands and then he was told to "speak in tongues." Embarrassed and inhibited, he hesitated, then "blathered" for two or three seconds and stopped. Urged to go on, he began again and found himself effortlessly speaking in what "sounded like Greek and was very rich in vowel sounds and inflections."

Peace, New Leftism, natural diet, rural living, sexual freedom, group marriages, mysticism, nudity, psychedelics, psychotherapy, art, crafts, historical romanticism—these were some of the dominant motifs of the communes. Some were perpetual encounter sessions; others were disciplined even to drawing up graphs of their behavior. Some were founded on drugs and others prohibited even alcohol. In one commune, ideal anarchism proved to be impotent in the face of such questions as who shall wash the dishes or whether the dogs should sleep in or outside. Some groups were rich in tarot occultists and poor in automobile mechanics. When it was time to draw off the maple sugar, the members of one settlement chose instead to hold a "love heap" and lost most of the harvest.

Hardly a single commune managed to be economically independent, many of them relying on family handouts, donations, part-time jobs in the other world and welfare. Some were swamped by noncontributing visitors who, on principle, could not be excluded. Bombings, shootings, beatings, arson and "legal" persecution were just some of the forms of harassment the groups suffered. Even worse than these, though, they suffered one another—the inevitable abrasion of living together with a minimum of privacy, of being condemned to sharing almost everything.

Mr. Houriet finds pockets of eccentric poetry. Almost every commune he visited, he says, "had gone to special lengths to make its outhouses unique and artful," with junk sculptures, driftwood, candelabra, splendid views and fragrant herbs. He shows us the incessant coming and going of the members, the endless, unconscious quest for the missing ingredient. We learn that, in group marriages, there is a competition to see who can be the *least* jealous. In one group, Claudia is pregnant and Bill, the baby's father, leaves her because "he has to climb a mountain —alone." At a commune called Lewd, nudity is mandatory at breakfast.

For the reader as well as the author, *Getting Back Together* is a trip you can't take without being touched. In forcefully reminding you of the infinite choice you once thought you had, it makes you not only wistful but a little high as well. Of course, a lot of the things described in the book are absurd, but as a Chinese proverb says: "To be sincere in love is to be grotesque." Mr. Houriet is not afraid to be grotesque, and he makes you want to try it too.

That's No Lady, That's My Wife

Though she knows all about men, Diana Balooka can't seem to pick a good one. She is such a sophisticated machine for satisfaction, a veritable computer bank of polymorphous pleasures—yet her partners keep walking out on her. In fact, this is the only thing her third husband, Jason, enjoys—for he will neither talk to her nor touch her. When Jason fails to return from one of his walkouts, Diana decides upon a divorce. While her lawyer tackles the legal problems, she addresses herself to the literary ones: How many similes, metaphors and conceits, how many flights of rhetoric, of fantasy, can she find in her predicament? For a woman who had such a notoriously unsuccessful marriage, who was so vociferously unhappy in it, she certainly takes its dissolution to heart.

Diana's first husband hated women. Her second husband had a different failing: like a premature ejaculator, he died before she was finished with him. With a fine disdain for our curiosity, she disposes of him in what may or may not be a metaphor: We are told that he "slipped in a pagoda and died in the lotus position."

While her divorce is pending, Diana has an affair with Haig, who spends all his time looking at TV and telling Diana to get off the phone because he's tired of her pressing him for an audible, visible or palpable response. Diana has other troubles too: at thirty-three she seems to have worn out her genitourinary tract. There are trips to the doctor and to the hospital, as well as detailed descriptions of symptoms and psychosomatics. And, oh yes, Diana has four children coaxed out of Jason with fertility charts and a thermometer. They are the most self-sufficient toddlers in the world, intruding on her for only a line or two now and then.

In her memory book, Diana has one happy page: her affair with Philipe. He was "fantastic . . . the world's greatest lover." His secret? He was gentle, "sensually available," and he "never said anything but beautiful things." "Not once," she tells him, "have we never pleased each other." But then, paradoxically, she goes on to add: "I say goodbye to you easily, because never once have I suffered anxiety with you." One gets the impression that, for all her protestations, satisfactory sex is something of a redundancy. Judging by her history, our heroine seems to prefer problems to orgasms.

With her heart on her sleeve and her soul in a sling, Diana still manages to give a good account of herself. She is a tap dancer and sometime poet when she is not busy breathing life into her current paramour, and her prose style has the staccato impact of one and the febrile invention of the other. As Jules Laforgue said about Baudelaire, she has captured the true miaow of city life. Her imagination stalks the back fences and overturns the garbage cans of our emotions. Improving on the act of one of her lovers, who was a stand-up comic in the borscht belt, Diana becomes a lie-down comic of the sexual revolution. "I am holding on to this little death for dear life," she says of her Morty Gross. Another lover inspires this line: "When you have an affair with a married man, you hear a lot more about his wife than you do about yourself."

Like Joan Didion and Lois Gould, Sandra Hochman writes of a new kind of woman, one who can't be satisfied with the old familiar formulas. In a way, these novels of theirs resemble those portraits of the artist as a young man that we used to read. Like artists, their heroines are in the process of emancipating themselves from the ordinary to discover who they are and what will make them complete. As Wallace Stevens put it, they have "wiped away moonlight like mud." They have said no to everything in order to get at themselves.

Have they succeeded? After reading them—first preparing ourselves with Kate Millett and Germaine Greer—we still know very little about them. Like their philosophers, they tell us mainly what they don't want. They seem to be groping toward a new choreography, or revised equation, that is just beyond the reach of their books. Everything so far is prelude. The male reader's admiration for them is tinged with misgivings. After such knowledge, he wonders, what forgiveness? And who will be doing the forgiving? Is Diana Balooka the pinup of the future? He looks at the naked photographs she has sent him and thinks that though she's a nice girl to visit, he wouldn't want to live there.

As Green as a File Cabinet

I was trying to plow right through *Home Life* in order to get my review in on time, but it was impossible. Every few pages, I had to stop and admire the book—or simply sit back and feel it. My God, but my fellow creatures are fascinating! I found myself thinking. How touching, how absurd, how real they are! All at once I was delighted to be sharing their destiny. Not that *Home Life* is a happy book—far from it. But it doesn't matter, because its people are so dimensional. It's so reassuring—positively exhilarating—to find that we haven't yet been flattened out by life, our features abraded away by the sheer rush of phenomena.

Dorothy Rabinowitz can make you feel the very sweat in people's palms, the jitters in their limbs as they struggle with their anxieties, the restless flickering of their eyes, seeking or avoiding recognitions, the confusions of tongue and teeth as they try to say two contradictory things at once. At the home for the aged, a son is describing the idyllic life he offered his unappreciative parent, when suddenly he stands up and points: "See that, the color of the file cabinet, see that color? That was the color of the *grass* out there." And yet his father complained. A daughter is explaining how much she loves her mother, how she'd like to keep her at home. Only her son, her son is seventeen now and he needs a room to put a desk in. He needs a desk to study at. It's not a question of her mother's age, the daughter says over and over, not her defective hearing or her funny little habits—it's a question of a place for a desk for her son. A desk to study at.

Another son has a mother who lives contentedly alone—but he worries about her. What if she were to fall and break a hip, both hips? She would be unable to reach the telephone. True, he calls her daily, but she might fall after he calls. Though she had no difficulty whatever in walking, he felt that his mother had to fall sooner or later and he couldn't bear the waiting. Like so many other sons and daughters, he felt that it was unreasonable, illogical, for such an elderly person to go on standing upright.

She stubbornly refused to progress in life, to advance to meet her inevitable fate.

When these mothers and fathers finally do enter the Home, they sign away everything. Of the fourteen paragraphs in the contract, there are thirteen detailing the things the resident surrenders and only one stating what the home offers in return. It is unconditional surrender: besides all property, real and personal, the resident even relinquishes the right to choose the manner of his own funeral. What they cannot sign away, though, are their egos, their value systems, their judgment. Many die soon after arriving—the largest number in the first thirteen weeks. Most of them die alone; there is rarely time to summon relatives. One old man was universally admired at having beaten the rap. While visiting his daughter for a weekend outside the home, he had the good fortune to die there. In his old bedroom.

There are some fierce spirits who stand out, like Mr. Blazer. In the central hall of his home, there was an enormous Matisse candelabrum—a $25,000 donation from a philanthropist. Approaching the work in the spirit of one who has received a gift, Mr. Blazer habitually hung his hat on the uppermost branch, tucked his books and papers in the recesses of the sculpture and sat down to write on the base. Not everyone, however, knew how to use what was given to him. Mr. Stone, for example, had not wished to enter the Home. He was only persuaded by singing. The staff discovered that he liked to sing and sang him into signing up. For a while, he was happy, in a sing-along sort of way —until he found that no one ever talked to him. When he tried to formulate the questions his new life raised in his mind, the people just sang at him until he stopped trying.

There are two Homes described in the book. Mr. Trommler's is run on scientific lines. He explains to his staff that there must always be a physical object, preferably a table, between a staff member and a "client" (resident). In the absence of a table, a brief case, a notebook, or a wastepaper basket may be used to symbolize the interdynamic relationship between them. Unless people are separated into distinct sides, symbolized by an object-barrier, there can, naturally, be no interdynamics.

Mr. Byron, director of the other Home, likes to be surrounded by creative people. His staff is heavy with writers, film-makers, tap dancers. One young man is hired mainly because he spent a year in South Africa and was going to bring "a certain exotic background" into the Home. Mr. Byron would have liked to hire someone with a prison record too—not a murderer—to share some of his experiences with the residents.

Home Life is presented as "a documentary, which employs some of the techniques of fiction." Its people and institutions are described as "composite portraits." We know better. Yedida Nielsen has devoted many years to professional work among the aged—but with all due respect to her, it is Dorothy Rabinowitz, the writer of the book, who enables Miss Nielsen's knowledge to lay living hands on us. Where another author might have raged, accused, exhorted, she has made us experience her subject as only an artist can. She has captured scenes and conversations that upstage the Theater of the Absurd and churn our guts at the same time. At the end of the book, she quotes an old woman's answer to the question: What would you do if you had your life to live over again? What would I do with my life? the old woman muses. "I'd grasp it." This is what Dorothy Rabinowitz has done: she's *grasped* it.

The Music of Time: Adagio

Anthony Powell may be the last major novelist to deal at first hand with the English aristocracy, which is disappearing much as the lions, elephants and rhinos are disappearing from Africa, leaving each country the poorer for it. The manners of the English upper classes were a cornucopia of incongruities that furnished at least two centuries of novelists with material even the best of them could not have invented. It took hundreds of years to develop these lordly eccentrics, who were not casual cranks but a crystallization of the best and the worst in English history and culture.

Though their personalities were often integrated around absurdities, they *were* integrated and they *were* personalities, which is a great deal these days. The gentry, the choice vaudeville of the lower classes, were blessed in having novelists, not sociologists, for biographers. Ford Madox Ford, Evelyn Waugh—who could ask for anything more? Authors like these have seen to it that the last of the aristocracy have not fallen "as apples fall, without astronomy." There is grandeur in these ruins, and even the most grudging egalitarian ought to grieve for their antic dignity.

The American personality evolves so quickly that it often seems merely provisional, like so many of our buildings. The English character goes down fighting, laying about with cane, umbrella and riding crop. There are a few, though, who sip their tea and take notes, like the novelists already mentioned. These cool but rueful observers are the antique dealers of personality, the ambivalent elegists of an England they'll never see again.

Though Waugh can rise to grandeur—as in the case of his Englishman who is forever condemned to read Dickens to an African tyrant—I believe Ford is the greater artist. Nothing could express the decline of the upper classes more definitively than the closing scenes of *The Good Soldier*. Captain Ashburnham is suicidally in love with his ward Nancy, yet he is so suffocated by his manners, his gentleman's code, that all he can say to her as she leaves for India is "So long." As the narrator observes, "The signal for the train's departure was a very bright red; that is about as passionate a statement as I can get into that scene." When the Captain cuts his throat shortly afterwards, you feel that it is because he no longer has anything to say to his era. He is only ventilating himself.

Somewhere in *Parade's End*, Ford's hero Tietjens gazes out over his family's countryseat, which he has inherited, and reflects that he might well be the last Englishman ever to look at his land in precisely that way, with such a complex and historically rooted resonance of feeling. This is the way Ford looks at his people. He is like someone seeing old acquaintances off—not on a boat or train—but on the tide of history.

In England, according to ancient custom, the younger son never inherited the family property unless his older brothers died without leaving an heir. This is the position of Anthony Powell, author of *The Music of Time*. He is a younger son writing about younger sons. He and his characters have inherited only the ruins of the old estate. The blood has thinned, the line is about to end. Powell walks through the empty rooms and muses on the memory of what was.

Writing the obituary of an age can be a splendid opportunity or a bore. In Powell's work, it is a bit of both. I find him a very good writer, but I'm getting tired of seeing him praised for what he is not. I don't understand why his admirers can't be satisfied to appreciate him without comparing him to Proust or claiming that he is the most important British novelist of his time, which extends all the way back to 1931, when he published *Afternoon Men*. The comparison with Proust is simply silly: Mr. Powell is good, and Proust is great. The alleged likeness is based on nothing more than the fact that Mr. Powell has published eleven volumes of a twelve-volume work, and that occasionally these volumes contain moderately long, finicky sentences. The applause for this series has elements in it that remind me of the response a vaudeville tap dancer used to get when he persisted in one step for a longer time than usual.

Proust's lengthy sentences arise out of a passion or obsession to preserve, with the utmost precision, a perception or feeling he has experienced. In some ways, he is like those Americans who must take hundreds of photographs of places they have visited or of stages in the development of their children. They seem to suffer from an anxiety that they cannot trust themselves to remember a particularly precious occasion. Proust's sentences keep pinching their subject, as if to make sure that they have captured it alive. They do this with so much fervor that they very nearly describe a sexual as well as an esthetic curve. Proust always drives toward absolute definition, the experience both in itself and under the aspect of eternity.

Mr. Powell, now, is self-consciously low-keyed. When he adds clause to clause, he is only dressing a character in his gestures, opening an umbrella of idiosyncrasy over him. You don't feel, as you do in reading Proust, a thrilling intuition that literature itself is advancing with the sentence, that the experience described is sharing a consummation with the medium.

Because there are so many of them, most of Mr. Powell's people have little more than minor parts. They are bric-a-brac in an ambiance, not much in themselves. Like John Aubrey, whose *Brief Lives* inspired the author to write a book about him, Mr. Powell is gossipy, given to short strokes. Unfortunately, he lacks Aubrey's seventeenth-century gusto. His style is so circumspect, so deliberately innocent of éclat that it often slips into a rather prissy niggling. His narrator, Nick Jenkins, is so self-effacing that he lives, in effect, on our charity. His habit of understatement— that fetish of the subtle—sometimes amounts to a vice. His ego is repressed beyond discretion almost to anonymity, and this is a disadvantage in a storyteller, for it is the ego—naked or disguised—that gives ourselves and our perceptions their primary colors. It is no accident that some of fiction's greatest characters are egocentric.

You would expect to find in an eleven-volume novel some large emotions—yet I can't remember any. *The Music of Time* is a centipede of a book: many-legged, long-bodied, close to the ground. In his avoidance of the extravagant emotions, Mr. Powell puts me uneasily in mind of all the old chestnuts about the coldness and detachment of Englishmen. And it would have to be a very cold, detached taste indeed that would rank his work above a book like *Loving* by Henry Green or *Another World* by James Hanley. These two British novels appeared in Mr. Powell's time, and I would not exchange either of them for his entire oeuvre. Though they are both structured and controlled to the highest degree, there is also a beautiful banshee howl of stark humanity in them.

Temporary Kings is a porcelain teacup of classy conversation and who's sleeping with whom. Once again, the author goes up into the attic and brings down all sorts of relics from previous volumes—who prospered, who failed, who lived or died, who are gasping in the embrace of old age. The only really bloody character in the book is Pamela Widmerpool, bitchy, castrating, as fiercely egocentric as a Charles Addams infant. Her measured insults, her whims released like falcons after their prey, offer the only real flights in this slowest of the eleven volumes.

The author attempts to breathe life into a dead character—the novelist X. Trapnel of his last book—by introducing an American who is intent on writing a biography and a producer who wants to film Trapnel's final work. Aside from his affair with Pamela, Trapnel was always a doubtful figure, and he has not grown more vivid in his grave. Kenneth Widmerpool, who is as far as Mr. Powell will go in the direction of unpleasantness, suffers some reverses, but they are too murky and involuted to be interesting. A literary congress in Venice provides occasions for brilliant talk, but I wonder how many people still want to read that kind of thing, which today seems terribly old-fashioned and artificial.

I suppose you could say that *Temporary Kings* does give us some sort of picture of how literature used to kick up its heels in London society and how sex can cuckold art. Apart from that, as it nears its conclusion, *The Music of Time* begins more and more to resemble a very high-toned BBC documentary on the last quaint flutters of the English upper classes as they go to meet their unmakers.

On the Existential Rack

If anybody has the right to say "These are the times that try men's souls," it is not the book reviewer, but the drama critic. To be sure, I sometimes think I'm getting more than my share of the casualties of our exacerbated age. After a run of particularly bad books, I feel like an interne on the night shift of an emergency ward. Who can sew them all up, give mouth-to-mouth resuscitation to each one who is failing? Who can cure the human condition?

But these, after all, are only books. One can put a book down for a moment, slam it shut on the author's threats or importuning, even throw it across the room. And then, of course, there are the good books. Just one—one knockout—is enough to sustain you through a dozen catastrophes. You're so lit up by the possibilities, the goose-pimpling power, of literature that you're ready for anything—for a while.

The drama critic is in a far more exposed position. Playwrights are no longer satisfied to work out their problems at home, in rehearsal or in New Haven. The critic today is forced to sit through the excruciating spectacle of the creative act in the making—or breaking. He has to watch the actors running the gamut of emotions like people running for their lives. He has to see them sweat, groan, scream, scrabble on the floor, stare like zombies—without turning away in embarrassment for his species or his occupation.

If there is a social, sexual, psychological or political problem that is endemic to our age, he is compelled to experience it, in the flesh, night after night. He has to watch his fellow man writhing on the existential rack. He must have the patience of a saint in the faint hope that it will all somehow come out better in the end than one might have expected.

I'm talking, of course, of the new movements in the theater—and of Walter Kerr's *God on the Gymnasium Floor*. Mr. Kerr is so magnificently reasonable that one wants to say, "What is a nice guy like you doing in a place like this?" His reasonableness is something like normality raised to genius. He never says anything you can't *experience*, never *retreats* into wit, though almost everything he writes is witty.

He can spend two or three hours watching the most preposterous performance ever devised by the human mind and then come out and tell you—without condescension—what the playwright, the director and the actors were trying to do, where they got the idea from and why it didn't work. If the play is below the level of fruitful discussion as drama, he can summon up an elegant sociology to keep the evening from being a total loss. When the experiment succeeds—as it sometimes does—he is as moved by it as any student from the Yale School of Drama.

Mr. Kerr talks of the theater as both anachronism and discovery—as the "natural savior, outlet, regenerator, master matrix and all-purpose adapter in almost every conceivable phase of twentieth century life . . ." Yet, he goes on, "It is conceivable that, in the course of becoming everything else . . . it will never save itself. It will simply disappear into all the other things it is serving."

The theater has become the laboratory for our lives, a place where we dare what we never even daydreamed. In Joseph Chaikin's Open Theater, "We are shocked into realizing how close we are—how close we always are—to the edge of things . . . We are made aware, simply sensually aware, of the preparations we make daily for dying without acknowledging to ourselves what we are doing."

In the Living Theater, with the actors climbing all over you, "there was no togetherness, no secret sharing, no impulsive return of the performer's intimate gesture, no yes. Though you were not alone, these players were." In Jerzy Grotowski's Polish Laboratory Theater, Mr. Kerr finds the stripped-down "theater of poverty" slowly being impelled toward the luxury of language, which it had renounced as an ornament that obscured the truth.

Speaking of the mythic or religious character of so much current experimentation, he points out that the earlier religions that gave birth to theater—Greek and Christian—believed in themselves, but "Drama at the present time has no such functioning consensus," and so we must reverse the old process. "Drama once

grew out of religion. We are trying to grow religion out of drama
. . . so that we can grow drama out of religion once we have got
it."

Like Elizabeth Hardwick in her much-discussed article a couple of years ago, I had always felt that drama was still literature,
no matter what else it may have engorged these last few years.
And it seemed to me, from what I heard, that most of the new
theater was either the enemy of literature or a stranger to it. Mr.
Kerr has made me recognize my prejudice, enabled me to see
that it is not so much hostile as simply different. The next time I
go to the theater, I'll try to close my mind and open my senses.
Like the next man, I'm in the market for a new religion too.

The Poet and
the Anthropologist

The black man's rhetoric is one of the things that make it difficult for well-meaning whites to talk to him today. It goes without saying that he has earned the right to this rhetoric: like jazz, it is a natural expression of his feelings. Maybe even more than that. But not everybody understands jazz. Not every white knows that words like burn, pig, fascist and enemy—when applied to him—may simply be blue notes. This is why *A Rap on Race* is so important at this moment. It gives one white a chance to speak for all those who may be baffled, a chance to get inside black rhetoric with James Baldwin, one of the most publicized black writers of our time. The choice of a partner for him could not be better. Nobody can accuse Margaret Mead of being a racist or a "bleeding heart." Because she is an anthropologist, perspective is her profession. And in living on the closest terms among black people in other parts of the world—and writing brilliantly about them—she has surely demonstrated a high degree of empathy.

She and Mr. Baldwin talked for seven and one-half hours. They had three sessions, with no moderator, no audience but a tape recorder, to distract them. They came together not to debate, or for one to interview the other, but to "rap"—to talk as freely and as informally as they pleased. The result is the only published "confrontation" of its kind. Miss Mead takes her assignment seriously: she is determined to understand Mr. Baldwin, even when he doesn't himself. Unlike most whites who are concerned about blacks, she does not adopt an apologetic posture. She respects herself as a professional and rarely hesitates to probe Mr. Baldwin's sore spots. Like a doctor looking for the source of the injury, she prods and pokes wherever she feels it is necessary. Every time he tries to pull away, to generalize his complaint, she pins him down to particulars. What exactly do you mean? She doesn't mind pulling apart a fine metaphor to see what it's made of. Again and again, she returns Baldwin's rhetoric to him, translated into plain English: Is this what you're saying? Is this what you actually believe?

Understandably, Mr. Baldwin sometimes finds this inhibiting. At one point he protests, "But I'm a poet," and Miss Mead comes right back with "Yes, but I'm not." And she adds, with unconcealed ambivalence, that most of their conversation has been "poetic." Wallace Stevens has a poem called "Thirteen Ways of Looking at a Blackbird," and their talk is something like this. Baldwin specializes in descriptions—highly emotional descriptions—of what it feels like, to him, to be black in a white world. Miss Mead keeps replying, Yes, but I'm moved by your poetry and I would like to respond to it. Where do you suggest I begin?

As a social scientist, Miss Mead wants to do something. Mr. Baldwin, if one can judge by what he says, does not. Sometimes it almost sounds as if he is afraid of losing his subject matter. We have to "atone" for our history, he says. Atone? Miss Mead answers, Why atone? Because we are all guilty, Mr. Baldwin says. I am *not* guilty, Miss Mead says. I am responsible only for what I myself do. To Baldwin's insistent dwelling on the past—the oppression of blacks in the past—she says, Should we carry the past on forever as a feud? There is a difference between acknowledging and perpetuating. We can't undo the past, and the steps that got us here have to be incorporated into where we are going next.

When Baldwin accuses Americans of apathy, she disagrees. It's not apathy we suffer from, she says, but lack of knowledge. We are frustrated because we know something is wrong and don't know how to fix it. We are irritated because we can't fix our society any more than we can fix our vacuum cleaners. When Baldwin says, You and I are both exiles, Margaret—implying that all intellectuals are outcasts in our society—she says, No, I am not an exile. When he says that man's principal achievement so far has been the ability to destroy himself, she replies, "I think we have a few other little achievements around."

Dr. Mead says that she thinks whites and blacks have to learn, literally, to touch each other, as they once did in the South when black women took care of white children. Touching will help to dissolve the sense of strangeness. Baldwin agrees, yet it is clear that he himself is still too touchy to allow it. He often sounds like a cross between Beckett and Albee—the dramatic negation of one and the nervous shrillness of the other. When he says things like "My countrymen are my murderers . . . They murdered nearly all my friends and menace everybody left," Miss Mead is tactfully silent, or perhaps just resigned. From the way he talks, one would think that Baldwin went in daily fear for his life.

He constantly uses words like danger, terrifying, frightening, sinister, destroyed. He seems to revel in them. At times he is almost operatic, as when he says, "I will never, never, never, as long as I live, be at home anywhere in the world." This sounds like nothing so much as a grandiose promise he is making to himself. Sometimes too he will pile clause upon clause in what seems to be merely rhythms, without cognitive content. At one point, however, he really arouses Miss Mead. When he says, "I have been, in America, the Arab at the hands of the Jews," this is too much for her and she simply answers, "Oh, fiddlesticks!"

A Rap on Race may not be rich in tangibles, but it is in perspectives. Among other things, it shows that whites and blacks will never be able to act together—to really integrate the two races—until we stop segregating black writing and black rhetoric from analysis and criticism. While the black experience belongs only to blacks, the truth belongs to everybody.

Updike Rampant

When I began this book and found Rabbit Angstrom ten years older, fatter, softer, settled and no longer even running as he was in the earlier version, I wondered why Updike had locked himself in with this loser, why he had given himself so little elbowroom. He has this habit, I thought, of keeping his people small —old, precious or ordinary—so he can write all around them, pin them with his exquisite entomology. But then it seemed to me that he had broken out of that bind in *Bech*. Bech, being an intellectual, an artist and a Jew, allowed Updike to flesh out his fanciness, to get away from those queasy, pastoral towns that time forgot and move on into the world outside.

There were many of us who felt that *Rabbit, Run* was Updike's most solid book—or at least until *Bech*—and now it looked as if he was going to fall back on it and try to milk it for whatever was left. A tour de force about a creep—that's about what I expected. And I was never so wrong. *Rabbit Redux* is the complete Updike at last, an awesomely accomplished writer who is better, tougher, wiser and more radically human than anyone could have expected him to be.

He went back to Rabbit because he knew that it was too easy to have an intellectual or an artist as a hero. There is always a temptation to talk or think things out—but with a guy like Rabbit, you have to *act* them out all the way, *show* what's happening to him, nakedly, without offstage intellection or interpretation. The thought must be made flesh; the flesh, as in sex, made metaphor; the man in the street tormented into irony. Where Rabbit once ran away, he's now standing his ground, letting the world flow over and around him while he tries to keep his head above water.

Life grows stale, it loses interest, Freud says somewhere, when we stop risking our lives—risking in the sense of staking them on something and holding nothing back, no hedge or insurance. This is what Rabbit is doing now—climbing out on every limb he can find and swinging there. Feeling he has nothing further to lose, he lets himself go wherever the currents of contemporary life carry him. Philosophers and estheticians have talked about the role of chance in life and art, but Rabbit *takes* chances. He is like a man who is determined to reach the *reductio ad absurdum*—or sublime—in his life once and for all.

It begins with his wife's telling him that she is sleeping with Stavros, a car salesman in her father's agency. She loves Stavros, she says, for the way he searches out every nook and cranny in her body and soul and "sells" them to her as Rabbit never did. But though she is being literally reborn with Stavros, some vestige of conventionality makes her want Rabbit to resist, to say, "Cut it out or I'll kill you." He cares, he cares more than he cares to admit, but he's too deep in trouble himself, inside himself, to try to compete for her.

When she leaves, he vegetates in the house with his thirteen-year-old son Nelson, until Buchanan, a black co-worker in the printing plant, takes pity on him. Buchanan's "old lady," it seems, has been harboring a white eighteen-year-old girl named Jill who has run away from her rich parents, and, worried about the heat she might bring down on them, he deftly unloads her on Rabbit. Used to paying her way with sex—her only capital—Jill finds Rabbit resistant material at first. He feels, for example, that her habitual offering of oral love is an unconscious attempt to keep him at a distance, to deny him the real intimacy of her body. He doesn't like landlord sex or unripe anatomy, but since there's nobody else in the bed, they gradually bridge the generation gap.

She begins to kiss away Rabbit's hard-hat attitudes—toward Vietnam, blacks, sex, everything—until Skeeter arrives. Skeeter is a black friend of hers, a kid who has just jumped bail on a drug charge and wants a few days' asylum. Afraid that Jill will leave if he doesn't take him in, Rabbit does, but biting the hand that feeds him is Skeeter's philosophy of life and he sets about insulting, educating and shocking Rabbit not only out of his prejudices, but very nearly out of his personality. High on marijuana every night, Rabbit reads black history—courtesy of Skeeter—aloud to his son, his girl and himself.

Skeeter is something new in black characters, including those in books by blacks. He goes beyond the familiar anger and rhetoric into the wild humor that black writers are only now beginning to capitalize on. He is an inspired preacher of the inchoate religiosity that seems to be gaining ground with some militant blacks—a religion that seems to be midway between Black Mass and storefront revivalism. Skeeter is a compound of drug-induced delusions of grandeur, real indignation, homicidal rage and quirky genius. He has a talent for provoking, for getting to the absolute bottom, for traveling through disillusion and coming out on the other side, where *everything* is exposed.

He is a more potent bomb than any the black revolution has yet thrown. Neither good nor evil exactly, he is the ultimate catalyst or kibitzer, a blue-note howl of pain and laughter such as Charlie Parker might have blown. What Updike conjures out of the combination of Skeeter, Jill, Nelson and Rabbit makes most writing about blacks, sex and families seem like something out of a children's book. It will leave Americans shuddering for a long, long time.

Janice, Rabbit's wife, is a wiser, tougher, fuller character now— a wife to end all wives, funny, terrifying, tender, sexy and yet very ordinary too. Rabbit's acerbic old mother—"having the adventure now we're all going to have," as his father puts it—is full of feisty last words from the rim of the grave. Through Jill, Updike explores the incompleteness—in them and in ourselves— that draws us toward very young girls.

In *Rabbit Redux*, Updike's ear is perfect and he has finally put together in his prose all the things that were there only separately. He has sacrificed none of his sensibility—simply translated it into gutsier, more natural but no less eloquent rhythms. He moves now with the sureness, grace and precision of the born athlete. Let me give you just one random example: Jill's mother —rich, ripe, spoiled—feels, when she finds out what happened to her daughter, "a grieved anger seeking its ceiling, a flamingo in her voice seeking the space to flaunt its vivid wings . . ." But enough—for God's sake, read the book. It may even—will probably—change your life.

Some Unexpected Packages

However you define art, a man who will wrap a mile of rocky Australian coastline in opaque plastic and then drape and tie it into place and shape, demands a certain respect. At half price, the fabric alone cost something like $16,000. Sewing the bolts together and delivering them to the site cost $5,000. Thirty-five miles of rope at half price came to $2,200. A site engineer, four foremen, a dozen professional rock climbers, about a hundred student volunteers, four night watchmen and a four-man maintenance team were also required for the project. It all cost $56,000, less than half what it would have been if a thirty-six-year-old Bulgarian artist named Christo had not inspired so many people to work for nothing or to sell him materials at reduced prices.

The Minister for Lands, the people in charge of parks and wildlife, refused to grant permission for the project. It was the Prince Henry Hospital—a most unlikely sponsor—that lent part of its land, nine miles south of Sydney, for the wrapping. The result, eloquently photographed from all angles in *Christo*, was far more impressive than anyone who has not seen these pictures —or the thing itself—can possibly imagine. Though it might have seemed, in its conception, to be merely a publicity stunt, a happening, a "gratuitous act" intended as a catch-all metaphor for the relation between art and life, Christo's "packaged" coast achieved a genuinely eerie beauty and worked in uncanny ways on the spectator.

It had a powerful quality of surprise and an undeniable element of grandeur. The metaphor itself—if it was a metaphorical statement Christo was making, beyond the visual impact of his project—was highly ambiguous. Perhaps it would be best to call it ineffable, to say simply that Christo's wrapping of the landscape altered it in the mysterious way that art works. In the spectator's consciousness, that rocky coast became highly charged; it provoked thought and feeling without directing them into any familiar channels.

David Bourdon, the author of *Christo*, refers to this kind of packaging as "revelation through concealment." Christo has packaged everything from bottles and tin cans to bodies, machines and buildings. "In all of his packages," says Mr. Bourdon, "he transforms familiar objects into ambivalent presences, sometimes rendering them unrecognizable and often raising doubts about their past, present and future identity and function. In his more epic endeavors, he questions the relationship of art to both the urban and natural environments. In a materialistic age, his art is a profound comment on the chronic expectations and frustrations aroused by the increasing number of consumer products and services that are 'enhanced' through packaging."

Mr. Bourdon writes so well about his subject that one cannot resist quoting another passage: "Packaging can connote gifts, death, preservation, and eros, but it almost always implies value —that the object is *worthy* of such attention . . . a gift-wrapped object is guaranteed to elicit curiosity, the promise of a surprise withheld. Concealment also implies preservation and, in some cases, suppression and censorship . . . the erotic aspect of packaging has been with us as long as the strip tease. Clothing-as-packaging touches most of us every day." And here's one more remark worth mulling over: "The success of Christo's work is dependent upon the fine line he maintains between literalism and metamorphosis, two of the predominant themes threaded through twentieth-century art."

Not all of Christo's packaging is esthetically successful. Judging from the photograph, his wrapping of the Museum of Contemporary Art in Chicago simply looked like a bad job of doing up an awkward bundle. But though it may have been too close to literalism, it was good publicity for the museum. The Museum of Modern Art in New York must have felt that it too would cut a poor figure, for it refused to be packaged. Christo's sausage-shaped 280-foot-high air package, made for an international art show in West Germany, seemed to deserve the bad jokes it inspired.

Not confining himself to packaging, Christo has erected "temporary monuments" of multicolored oil drums—and here too the effect is greater than one would have expected. In designing storefronts, whose empty windows are simply draped, and corridors that lead nowhere, Christo has created still another form of art, halfway between literary metaphor and the compositions of Piet Mondrian and other geometric abstractionists. In these he achieves, in a totally different manner, the effect of eerieness or uncanniness that is so strongly felt in the packaged coast of Australia.

If he had succeeded in nothing else, Christo would at least have earned the title of the most *contemporary* of all living artists. To many this will be a title of doubtful value, an ambivalent tribute. But any artist who can offer us surprises on such a large, and often intense, scale . . . who can wrap the all-too-familiar elements of our everyday world in some kind of mystery or ambiguity . . . who can pursue his ideas with such a fine disdain for cost, permanence or practical rewards . . . is worth looking at and thinking on.

Of Art, Ecstasy and Water

After he and Mary McCarthy had separated, Edmund Wilson invited Anaïs Nin to see his house. It was in an "impasse" in the East 90's, narrow and bleak. He had forgotten his key, so they entered through the basement. Mary had taken away all the furniture, leaving only two rocking chairs in the empty living room with the long windows. They sat in the chairs and began to rock and talk: "He wanted me to help him reconstruct his life, to help him choose a couch . . . but I wanted to leave."

The scene is typical of the best moments in the fourth volume of *The Diary of Anaïs Nin*. People were always confessing to her and it is fascinating to see Wilson's tenderer feelings struggling with his critical taste. His review of her then current novel is a masterpiece of ambivalence: "There is not much expert craftsmanship in *This Hunger* by Anaïs Nin, but it is a more important book than either Marquand or Isherwood because it explores a new realm of material." The realm referred to was characterized by "the conflicts created for women by living half in a man-controlled world against which they cannot help rebelling, half in a world which they have made for themselves but which they cannot find completely satisfactory." He tells her: "I would love to be married to you and I would teach you to write." But she finds him a coldly intellectual father figure who would "destroy her spontaneity."

Miss Nin's *Diary* is quite a curious affair: though she herself is often naive, playing house with the idea of art like a child, she has a gift for attracting people and attaching them to herself. In some ways, she is like a woman who takes in stray cats. Lost or confused young men and women sit at her feet and find in her highly abstract utterances whatever it is they think they need. She has so much faith in herself and in art—they might as well be synonymous—that she makes an excellent muse. The young Gore Vidal is one of her neophytes, but he, alas, soon becomes "hard and cynical."

Miss Nin is a voice crying in the wilderness of modernity. Her vocabulary is out of some Victorian antique shop of literature: like feather boas, faded satins, ambiguous furs, words such as illusion, dream, beauty, soul, spontaneity, infinite, inspire and create are her stock in trade. Some of her passages are gnomic to the point of camp: "Think of the ballet exercises. The hand reproduces resistance to water. And what is painting but absolute transparency? It is art which is ecstasy, which is Paradise, and water." Or she will say: "It is possible I never learned the names of birds in order to discover the bird of peace, the bird of paradise, the bird of the soul, the bird of desire."

Miss Nin philosophizes as some women preen or comb their hair before a mirror. It is almost as much a part of her as breathing. She never doubts herself in the least: she has the assurance of insanity or genius. And it seems to warm everyone around her. She is like the only person with a fireplace during an extremely severe winter. It is not too much to call her a heroine, as we watch her printing her own books in editions of three hundred on her own press and then waiting for the world to beat a path to her door.

She and Henry Miller are now in the twilight of their long romance. He writes her undistinguished letters full of encouragement and encloses money when he has any—but then, when he is in town, sends a note to say that for some "strange" reason he doesn't dare see her. And when she visits him in California, she feels bad vibrations and leaves.

All through this volume of the diary, Miss Nin carries on a running battle with the critics. They want her books to be less abstract, more novelistic. "Lillian never goes to the icebox," one complains. But Miss Nin and her characters are interested only in essences and will not compromise with iceboxes.

The author quotes freely from the many flattering letters she receives about her books and about her influence on the writers. Whether it is the force of her personality, or the uniformity of the people she attracts, these letters are remarkably alike: I read your book over and over, you are so pure, you have helped me so much, etc. Humor is not often a part of Miss Nin's spontaneity, and those who value it must supply it themselves by adopting a perspective somewhat different from the author's.

For example, she tells us that the poet Charles Duits telephoned her to say that she must come and rescue him from the film-maker Maya Deren, who "is doing her courtship dance." Later, Mr. Duits "confessed that what frightened him was that she had hair on her chest." When a young soldier tells Miss Nin that during his training he was warned never to look into a dying man's eyes lest he go mad, she receives the information with that same impartial appreciation so highly valued by her friends.

It seems that the diaries are enjoying a tremendous vogue among young people today. It is a good sign, for Miss Nin is certainly an improvement over *The Prophet, Love Story* and *The Greening of America*. Also, turning her into a vogue may be the best solution to the ungallant task of evaluating her critically.

A World Well Lost for Love

Iris Murdoch used to teach philosophy, and it seems to have left her with a taste for toying with people's fates. In her novels, she is like a metaphysical practical joker, connecting her characters in such wanton and improbable ways that their lives seem no more than a series of freakish and passionate accidents. She takes a special pleasure in frustrating any attempt at rational proceedings, as if these were only the delusions of grandeur of a conceited animal. As a result, her people are often reduced to puppets in a philosophical Punch and Judy show, and while we may be amused, we are not convinced. Those of us who can still feel stubborn purpose, persistent as a toothache, throbbing in us, may even take offense at Miss Murdoch's eschatological flippancy.

She herself may have recognized this, for in *The Black Prince* she has reformed. Her characters still behave oddly, but for better reasons. Miss Murdoch concedes that it is only in extreme situations that people can be pricked into extreme actions, so that's where she puts them. She thrusts them into the arms of love and observes their convulsions as they struggle between pain and pleasure.

To Miss Murdoch's way of thinking, we are all sleeping beauties waiting for the kiss of love to open our eyes. But her fairy tales are not for children; we may as easily wake up screaming. Love does not mean living happily forever after—but it does mean *living*. It is the agent that releases our demon, that impels us into an antic pursuit of our slumbering potential. Goethe remarked that the only way to come to terms with the true superiority of another person was through love. Miss Murdoch agrees. She sees love as a necessary madness, a flow of adrenaline that gives us the strength to throw off habits, doubts, dead allegiances, inertia—anything in our way. Her characters run amok in what comes to seem a most natural manner.

When we meet Bradley Pearson, he is a writer who is so repressed, so puritanical, that he can neither write nor love. He fears imperfection in his work as some men fear premature ejaculation, and to protect himself he adopts a stultifyingly arty posture. "Every book," he pontificates, "is the wreck of a perfect idea." He *talks* about writing as some timid men brag about women. He is fifty-eight, divorced, author of two little-known books. And he pretends, as most of us do, to have chosen his fate.

In his friend, Arnold Baffin, he sees a horrible example of the alternative. Arnold is prolific, successful, a "gabbler." "Arnold was always trying, as it were, to take over the world by emptying himself over it like scented bath water. This wide catholic imperialism was quite alien to my own much more exacting idea of art as the condensing and refining of a conception almost to nothing." Arnold "saw significance everywhere, everything was vaguely part of his myth . . . life was simply one big gorgeous metaphor." As you can see, Miss Murdoch uses her two writers as clubs to beat each other in her own mischievous brand of literary criticism.

This is typical of her books. Whatever her characters do, or don't do, the landscape of the author's mind is always panoramic. Until her last two novels, she tended to suffocate her people in her own cleverness, just as the emperor Nero was said to have a trick ceiling in his palace which turned over to bury his guests in tons of roses. *The Black Prince* continues her steady improvement in this respect. Though the book is gaudy with asides on writing, relationships, manners, morals, love, hate, friendship, *Hamlet*, hypocrisy and sex, among other things, Miss Murdoch manages to pin most of her ruminations on one character or another. Sometimes, in fact, she drives them like a dagger into their hearts.

When Bradley falls in love with Julian, his friend Baffin's twenty-year-old daughter, the author shows us how sentimental, how unworldly and irrelevant, a writer's responses can be. Walking hand in hand with Julian, rendered fatuous by infatuation, Bradley says "the sun is shining." In love with everything, he asks her to admire a familiar tower, while she looks askance at his "senile" enthusiasm.

Bradley's love for Julian is so resuscitating, so full of surprises, that it makes you yearn for the invasion of a disordering passion —if you don't already have one. Though their happiness lasts only a few days, he feels that he has known "some great aeon of the experience of love . . . a sort of incarnate history of human love." He feels, together with his exaltation, torn to pieces by love, as if he is being "eaten by a large animal." As a frustrated writer and critic, Bradley is a performing anthology of erotic poetry.

I mustn't tell you—or even hint at—how it all ends, for Miss Murdoch's novels are, among other things, metaphysical suspense stories. Who will survive the human condition? Who will succumb to "the slings and arrows of outrageous fortune"? Is irony a fatal disease, like arteriosclerosis? I'm afraid you will have to run the gauntlet of Miss Murdoch's imagination to find out.

Lumps for the Leisure Class

First published in 1899, Thorstein Veblen's *The Theory of the Leisure Class* is probably the most original, ironical and revealing analysis ever to be made of American society. Essentially a study of snobbery and social pretentiousness, the book has something irreverent and unexpected to say about most of the widespread beliefs and behavior of its time. No one since has equaled Veblen's sense of our everyday absurdities and their origins, or his unerring instinct for the phrases that would simultaneously describe and deride them. Veblen's irony was both his nature and his protective coloration. Although his meaning is unmistakable to any reasonably careful reader, he escaped the wrath of the "ruling class" by assuring them that the pejorative terms he applied to them had been shorn of all evaluative content and used solely for descriptive purposes. His prose had a deadpan humor that was the intellectual equivalent of Buster Keaton and W. C. Fields.

When Veblen described as "honorific" any form of predatory, snobbish or ostentatious behavior, the word "honorific" removed the sting, although he had already defined it as "little if anything else than a recognized and successful form of aggression." "Conspicuous consumption"—buying solely as a form of display—and "conspicuous waste"—discarding as a sign of an unlimited capacity to replace—were not offensive to the thick-skinned pomposity of wealthy Victorians. Contrasting the honorific with the industrially useful, Veblen pointed out that the leisure classes had a "trained incapacity" for utilitarian action. In describing exploitation of their fellow men as the rich's only legitimate sphere of endeavor, he managed to give the word an ambiguous hint of "exploit" in the sense of a daring feat. "Reputable futility"—a synonym for socially approved idleness—is another of his mischievous coinages.

The leisure class could even be called "barbarous," since the word suggested bravery, force, blood sports and being a law unto themselves. In his description of their barbarous traits, Veblen closely paralleled the modern biologists who point out that our physical equipment is still that of the caveman. In the working classes, these "archaic survivals of prowess" were drained off by hard labor or drudgery. "Pecuniary canons of taste" referred to the leisure class's preference for the nonutilitarian. A bronze cow on the front lawn of a wealthy man's home was a perversion of a useful animal into a dubious esthetic object. In their search for the novelties demanded by the canon of conspicuous waste, the rich developed a taste for a "congeries of idiosyncracies"— a succinct definition of Victorian design. A cane and a silk hat disqualified their owner from practical activity, just as the "hazardously slender" waist of his wife proclaimed her a fragile China doll of adornment.

A teacher himself who, despite the number and reputation of his books, never rose above the rank of a poorly paid associate professor, Veblen naturally turned a sardonic eye on our institutions of higher learning. Distinguishing between esoteric and exoteric knowledge, he pointed out that the former was more respected, as being useless for material purposes. The chief appeal of the classics, as taught in the universities, he also saw in this light. The academic world was a stickler for form, its rituals of cap and gown, degrees, dignities and prerogatives all suggesting "some sort of scholarly apostolic succession." Innovation, as the author knew from bitter experience, found only "reluctant tolerance" in the higher learning.

As John Kenneth Galbraith points out in his useful introduction, Veblen's sociology wore a bit better than his economics. He was overly optimistic about the ordered rationality of the machine process. Socialist economies, says Mr. Galbraith, have not succeeded in translating either rationality or the machine process into effective economic performance. Also, organization, management and the problem of accommodating production to demand are more complicated than Veblen foresaw.

In his social criticism, Veblen is almost as pertinent now as he was at the turn of the century—in some ways, even more so. Our conspicuous consumption, for example, has been extended from the compulsory swimming pool and the impractical sports car to our very selves. The heavy drinker and the drug addict are both, in a sense, conspicuously consuming themselves, demonstrating an allegedly inexhaustible richness of regenerative power. The conspicuous consumption of women by "great lovers" is an advertisement of another form of personal wealth.

Veblen's "physiognomy of astuteness," which he detected on the faces of the sporting or "lower delinquent classes," is still worn by the baseball pitcher as he stares in for the sign, the boxer as he poses for the photographer, or the pimp as he makes his rounds in Harlem. Even politicians have adopted it. The author's analysis of the belief in luck still holds, too, even after seventy years of "enlightenment." Veblen describes this belief as an "instinctive sense of an inscrutable teleological propensity in objects or situations." When he cries, "Come on, baby!" the crapshooter or the spectator at a sporting event animistically believes that the propensity inherent in events "has been propitiated and fortified by so much conative and kinetic urging."

One element of Veblen's social analysis that has not survived is the instinct of workmanship. In an age of built-in obsolescence, this so-called instinct is now a matter of wistful memory. The spirit of the age, encouraged by sentimental liberals, has persuaded the working man that his talents are a source of social humiliation. Nothing is now done by hand that cannot more inefficiently be done by a machine. Just as the worker was once the servant of the consumer, so the machine is now the servant of the worker. And that servant is threatening to rebel, too, in the form of automation. When this last revolution is accomplished, we may no longer have any use for men like Thorstein Veblen. Our dehumanization may finally be beyond the reach of irony.

Elegy with a Southern Accent

It seems to me that American life has rushed forward so rapidly that it has created a vacuum behind it, and that it has become the special mission of certain Southern writers to fill that vacuum, to bridge the enormous gap between, say, life in Manhattan and in Mount Salus, Mississippi, where Eudora Welty has placed *The Optimist's Daughter*. Perhaps because it lost the Civil War—don't we always cling more passionately to what we've lost?—the South has always been history-haunted, tradition-obsessed, hungry for continuity and connection. Where else do people speak of "kin" so insistently? Some Southern novelists claim all the cardinal virtues exclusively for their towns, their life, their people, as if the country had been stood on end and all its vital juices had flowed downward.

For anyone who has not lived in the South, this may seem like so much sentimental nonsense, but there's more to it than that. The so-called "backwardness" of the South has had as much influence in our history as the overestimated frontier spirit. Perhaps their roles might even be called polar. In any case, what is not sufficiently understood by Northern readers is the terms in which Southern writers expressed their relationships to one another and to their environment.

The frequent bombast of Faulkner, the occasional quasi-mystical images of Miss Welty or Carson McCullers, are undeniably histrionic, but that is because they feel, consciously or unconsciously, that they are playing out the drama of American history. After them, our history ceases, in a sense, to be American: it becomes something without a recognizably national identity in any deep emotional sense, simply a chaos of contradictory, even foreign voices.

In writing about the death of the central character, Judge McKelva, as seen through the eyes of his daughter Laurel, Miss Welty is showing us the end of a peculiarly American way of life and hinting at what will follow it. She is trying to express, in a more elegiac way, what Mary McCarthy said with typically Northern exasperation in her recent *Birds of America*.

At seventy-one, Judge McKelva has a slipped retina and an advancing cataract in his other eye. Since his first wife died blind, we have to assume that the author is trying to tell us something. We can no longer see our way clearly? This may explain the judge's second marriage—to Fay, cheap, tough and traditionless. She's from Texas, the brashest, most progress-oriented of the Southern states, and as he lies dying after his operation, willing himself to leave a world he can no longer love or understand, she shakes him, trying to wake him from his long historical sleep, crying, "Enough is enough! This is my birthday!" She wants to celebrate the present. The hospital is in New Orleans and it is carnival time. It is always carnival time for those others, Miss Welty suggests.

Laurel, the judge's daughter, is forty-five, a war widow who never remarried. After her father's death, her main concern is to preserve his memory as accurately as possible, in obsessive, loving detail. She is offended by the affectionate hyperbole of his old friends as they praise him for things he didn't do, qualities he didn't have. The vulgarity of Fay and her family intrudes on Laurel's ritual farewell to her own family and her past. She wants to weep with dignity "for what had happened to life."

Dignity is the Custer's last stand of the South, something almost antediluvian to those Northerners who want to "let it all hang out." Sometimes, even for the sympathetic reader, this dignity is ritualized to a point where its original significance is lost. When Miss Welty talks of "betrayal on betrayal" between Laurel's supposedly harmonious mother and father, she is piling ambiguity on ambiguity. As far as I can make out, the judge's first wife carried her notions of consideration and moral obligation to the point where they came very close to being mystical. That, it seems to me, is one of the dangers of the Southern sensibility: its tendency to turn mystical just when the reader stands most in need of clarity.

Though I would say—without attempting to estimate how high this is—that Miss Welty is writing at the top of her form, she does let her scrupulousness slip now and again. Fay and her family are much too broadly drawn, like something out of Li'l Abner.

One of them, a small boy named Wendell, is unmercifully used to underscore, "with a child's innocent questions," far too many scenes. When we last see him, in the back of a pickup truck on his way home to Texas, he is shooting at Laurel and her friends with a toy gun: "Pow! Pow! Pow!"

There are a number of sentences I couldn't get comfortable with, such as this one, for example: "His whole pillowless head went dusky, as if he laid it under the surface of dark, pouring water and held it there." While Laurel is reminiscing around the house alone, reading old letters and recipes, she is pursued by a chimney swift, a "dirty" bird that beats its wings against her door and terrifies her with a bit of symbolism that should have been relinquished to the taxidermists of literary theory.

Most readers will be glad to forgive these little flaws, if they notice them at all. And Fay's parting words to Laurel are almost enough to redeem her cartoon quality: "The past," she says, "isn't a thing to me. I belong to the future . . ." I wonder, and you may too if you read the book, whether one couldn't find some middle ground.

Naked in His Raincoat

I come like someone naked in my raincoat,
but only a girl is naked in a raincoat . . .

He's right: Robert Lowell is not naked, but undressed, incongruous, in a raincoat. He's too old for striptease. His nakedness needs rationalization. He's too famous for us to be comfortable with him in this costume, with his "examining and examining what I have against myself." We expect him to manage things a bit better than that. "Everything is real until it's published," he complains, but that's the definition of the unsuccessful poet.

What choice have I but the one he has already given me?

the reviewer sent by God to humble me
ransacking my bags of dust for silver spoons—

Have I the right to contradict him? Doesn't he know best? Isn't he talking to himself all this while, instead of to us or me? "I have stood too long on a chair or ladder . . . I cannot hang my heavy picture straight . . ." And so he has come down to earth, to stand on the bare floor, unelevated,

writing out a line
as if listening to conscience were telling the truth . . .

The Dolphin, a completely new book, is a disappointment. These poems have moved, as the author puts it, "from the dismay of my old world to the blank/new—water-torture of vacillation!" Mr. Lowell, who was, or is, one of our best poets, has chosen to democratize himself. "Genius," he says, "hums the auditorium dead." Now, untidy life sprawls, scrawls, across the page.

The author is determined to hang loose, as they say. He slides from free association to incoherence: the leap is in his mind, not on the page. He tells us his troubles, his failings—but they sound

109

like anybody's, undramatic. Shamelessly, he rehashes his dreams
—would he listen to ours, unadorned like that? So much blabbed
biography, a hamburger of a life served up with little garnishes
of poetry like parsley. "The tedium and déjà-vu of home" indeed.

For Lizzie and Harriet, another book, is a series of revisions
taken from poems that first appeared in Mr. Lowell's previous
volume, Notebook. It is difficult to imagine his motives in re-
working them to this effect. The poems are full of lines like ". . .
your room was once the laundry"—lines in which we sense the
poet unconsciously checking the buttons of his memory and his
sanity. And so many leaves, trees, flowers, fish, birds, buildings,
stars, nights and mornings—simply jotted down, a debris of
ambiance, a dear diary in verse, a man maundering over a family
album. The structure of the poems is still beautiful, but the
content is so ordinary. They are like a woman with a wonderful
figure and no personality. Even when the rhythms are irresistible
no one dances to them.

Here and there, I found a line—

> The hours
> of shivering, ache and burning
> when we charged so far beyond our courage . . .

At times like this, you can glimpse the grand Robert Lowell of
old, but only as if he were someone at the back of a group photograph, half-heartedly standing on tiptoe, unwillingly twisting his
neck, to be visible. It's too easy to say what the poems are about:
the vicissitudes of family life and love laconically reported, random experiences, opened and shut like dusty books in a twenty-
five-cent stall, places like any others, uneventful events.

History contains almost four hundred poems, eighty of them
new, the rest "all changed, some heavily" from versions that also
appeared in Notebook. The author felt that, in their earlier
form, the "composition was jumbled," and adds, "I hope the
jumble or jungle is cleared." Well, perhaps it is, but it only
serves to show us more clearly their nervous barrenness. There
are few unexpected gifts of language, though it is never lame. I
rarely found an image that lit up a line, or a run of rhetoric that
pulled my pulse along with it. Among the exceptions are

"Leopardi, the Infinite," "Hugo at Théophile Gautier's Grave,"
"Baudelaire 2. Recollecting."

The eighty new poems are about history and historical figures.
They strike me as mere scavenging. Mr. Lowell rummages for an
aphorism rather like a man looking for a pair of matching
socks in an overflowing drawer. It is hard to understand how
someone who knew them so well could not find something more
particular, more defining, more excruciatingly human to say
about Delmore Schwartz and Randall Jarrell, two men who *suffered* poetry even more than the author. Surely, they deserve
better—or worse. For John Berryman, Mr. Lowell can offer no
better last line than "Suicide, the inalienable right of man."
While I knew Randall Jarrell and John Berryman only through
their works—I did know Delmore Schwartz—I can imagine all
three of them displeased with those poems, surprised at their old
friend's odd detachment.

Mr. Lowell's technique, though, is so splendidly intact that it
mocks his material. His new forms are fluent without surrender-
ing their staccato. Though they are less ejaculatory than his
earlier poems, they are far from flabby. If you heard these poems,
instead of reading them, they might work, might seduce you with
their changes. Because I admire his earlier poems, I feel a tragic
sense of loss here in these three books. I don't believe, though,
that a talent like Lowell's can lose its voice for very long. If I
were to hazard a guess at why these books are not the experience
I expected, I think I would say that the author is a very private
person who is awkwardly posing here for the public monument
he knows we owe him.

Unsentimental Education

Poor thing—she gasps for love as a carp gasps for air on the kitchen table. The man who described Emma Bovary in these terms could hardly be classified as a Romantic, yet Gustave Flaubert's earliest prose was as purple as anyone's. "Oh, how willingly I would give up all the women of the world to possess the mummy of Cleopatra!" This ejaculation is a fair sample. In *November*, a short novel completed before he was twenty-one, Flaubert wrote: "Oh, to be bending forward on a camel's back . . . unknown stars, four times the size of ours, throb in the skies . . . but on! Still further! I long to see furious Malabar and its dances of death: the wines are as deadly as poison, the poisons as sweet as wine . . ." The first version of *The Temptation of St. Anthony* must have been just as bad—or worse—for his two closest friends begged the author not to expose it to the world.

According to Francis Steegmuller, the editor of *Flaubert in Egypt*, young Gustave had been infected with a longing for the exotic by the Romantic writers who preceded his generation, especially the poems of Byron, *Les Orientales* by Victor Hugo and the *Arabian Nights*. When, in 1849, the journalist and photographer Maxime Du Camp asked Flaubert to accompany him on a trip to Egypt, he accepted. He was twenty-seven years old: it was high time he revised his fantasies and began to taste the reality he was to render so remorselessly in *Madame Bovary*.

After a series of epileptic attacks, Flaubert had given up law school and settled down contentedly in his parents' house to write. His friend Du Camp persuaded the recently widowed Mme. Flaubert that the trip would benefit her son's constitution—and she agreed to finance it. There was no truth whatever in Du Camp's argument, for Flaubert's epilepsy had ceased with his law studies and this muscular six-footer exposed his health to far greater hazards in the arms of various Egyptian women. Taking his mother by surprise, Flaubert left a day early to avoid a tearful scene, but sobbed nevertheless all the way to Paris. There, for two days, he ate and drank lavishly and frequented brothels to fortify himself against the absence of *Mère* Flaubert.

In Egypt, where "splendid things gleam in the dust," Flaubert straightaway plunged into his unsentimental education. Unable to speak to the women he habitually sought out, he stared into their eyes and at their shaven bodies, absorbing them through his unconscious, which is a relentless editor of youthful effusions. Although he had left an intelligent mistress in France, he soon began to feel that romance is a mere surface adornment, that Egyptian women had shaved it off with their body hair. In his travel diary, recording only what he actually experienced, Flaubert began to reshape his style into the gleaming surgical instrument it later became.

For our edification and amusement, Mr. Steegmuller prints parallel passages from Flaubert's earlier Egyptian fantasies and his factual record of the trip. In the original version of the *Education Sentimentale*, we find the young traveler climbing the Great Pyramid with torn hands and bleeding knees. At the top, he "sinks down half dead . . . amidst the carcasses of birds come there to die." In the event itself, Flaubert experienced little difficulty and found only graffiti at the top, including the name and address of a Parisian wallpaper manufacturer. He descended through a corridor like a sewer, slipping on bat's dung. His first view of the Sphinx reminded him of a dog lifting itself up out of the sand. As he and Du Camp wrote up their impressions that evening, fleas jumped on the pages of their notebooks.

In a visit to the local hospital, Flaubert observed that the syphilitic patients rose like soldiers at a signal from the doctor and exposed their sores. A psychotic woman turned handsprings at the sight of the young traveler. Rapidly becoming acclimated, our former Romantic found that he enjoyed not only these stark experiences, but the smell of crushed bedbugs mingling with the barbaric perfumes of his favorite prostitute. He likes, he says, a touch of bitterness in everything. At another time, after allowing himself to be coaxed and caressed by a group of girls whose "metallic eyes rolled like wheels," he decided to abstain in order "to preserve the sweet sadness of the scene."

From day to day, we can see the diary's style grow leaner, more precise—yet without losing its suppleness, its effect of graceful and effortless movement. One has only to compare his passages with some of Du Camp's—included for that mischievous purpose —to see the difference between a journalist and an artist. While Du Camp gives us a competent travelogue, Flaubert describes two women weeping as their husbands shear and sell their hair. He shows us a sheik accepting a box of cantharides pills ("Spanish fly") "on behalf of his father." His eye is caught by a camel that has been dying for three months of a broken back: it is watered and fed by passers-by.

Toward the end of the trip, in a letter to a friend, Flaubert says that he "feels the need to be settled." He is eager to get down to work—a different kind of work, for as he puts it: "What I have seen has made me hard to please." In time, his imagination will revisit Egypt for the third and final version of *The Temptation of St. Anthony,* and for Salomé's dance in *Hérodias*—but first he wants to turn his hungry eyes on a woman of his own country. For he senses in Emma Bovary a bitterness that goes beyond crushed bedbugs, a burning that not even the desert sun of Egypt can equal.

A Feudal Lord of Fiction

It is surprising, when you consider his fame, how few of Vladimir Nabokov's books are read in this country. In talking about him to a number of better-than-average readers, I found that most of them knew only *Lolita*. Some had tried *Ada* on the assumption that it was an equally accessible tragicomedy of sex, but had given up after fewer than a hundred pages. And though I feel that some of his early novels—like *Bend Sinister* and *Laughter in the Dark*—are among his best, I believe most readers have not looked into them, mistakenly fearing that they were as forbidding as, say, *Pale Fire* and *Transparent Things*.

There is a paradox implicit in Nabokov's work: though he is a most demanding writer, likely to be enjoyed only by a few select—I would almost say "professional"—readers, he has been catapulted into popularity by a book that is atypical for him. Though I have no ready explanation for this phenomenon, I find the characters in *Lolita* to be almost the only people in Nabokov's entire oeuvre who allow the average reader to feel that empathy which is so indispensable to full satisfaction.

It is no accident that chess and lepidoptery are two of the author's other interests, for in much of his work he treats his characters with the detachment of a Grand Master, and one feels he is less interested in them than in the transient and butterflylike beauty of his prose. It's interesting, for example, to compare his style with that of two equally language-conscious writers like Saul Bellow and John Updike. First, a sentence from Bellow's *Herzog*: "And Herzog, a solid figure of a man, if pale and suffering, lying on his sofa in the lengthening evening of a New York spring, in the background the trembling energy of the city, a sense and flavor of river water, a stripe of beautifying and dramatic filth contributed by New Jersey to the sunset . . ."

This is from Updike's *Rabbit Redux*, describing the wealthy mother of a girl who has just died in sordid circumstances: "The police had broken the news to her and her tone fluctuated between a polite curiosity about how Jill came to be living in this house and a grieved anger seeking its ceiling, a flamingo in her voice seeking the space to flaunt its vivid wings but cramped in a closet of partial comprehension."

Here is Nabokov, from "Ultima Thule," part of an unfinished novel that appears in *A Russian Beauty and Other Stories.* The narrator is addressing his deeply loved deceased wife: "Let us imagine—just an 'apropositional' thought—some totally new handbook of epistolary samples. To a lady who has lost her right hand: I kiss your ellipsis. To a deceased: Respecterfully yours. But enough of these sheepish vignettes. If you don't remember, then I remember for you: the memory of you can pass, grammatically speaking at least, for your memory, and I am perfectly willing to grant for the sake of an ornate phrase that if, after your death, I and the world still endure, it is only because you recollect the world and me."

Now I ask you: Isn't all of this last passage written "for the sake of an ornate phrase?" In the examples from Bellow and Updike, the beauty of the sentence is urgently *attached* to someone. Their characters *suffer* in a kind of bel canto. In Nabokov's passage, the sentence toys with and very nearly mocks the narrator's wife. And there's the rub: the reader is uncomfortably aware of the author's indifference. He feels like saying to him, "If you expect me to care, you'll have to go first. You show me yours, and I'll show you mine."

Nabokov's relation to his characters is so very different from Bellow's or Updike's. Where they are on the most intimate terms with their people, Nabokov's attitude to his is that of a benevolent despot or feudal lord. It would not be altogether unfair to call him a snob. Of course, he is brilliant, but brilliance is no substitute for sympathy. Literature is not a game, nor life a conundrum.

A Russian Beauty and Other Stories strikes me as a plate of confections. Though they were written between 1924 and 1940—closer in time to *Laughter in the Dark* and *Bend Sinister* than to *Pale Fire* or *Ada*—these pieces show the same detachment that keeps us at a distance in the later books. And some of them cannot even fall back on an art-for-art's-sake defense, because they are too unsubstantial even on these terms. "A Russian

Beauty" is almost anecdotal in its unadorned simplicity. An émigré Russian girl finally marries at the age of thirty, only to die during her first labor a year later. In "The Leonardo," a counterfeiter posing as a scholar is senselessly murdered by two brothers who resent his standoffishness.

"Torpid Smoke" is a rather torpid vignette, no more. So is "Terra Incognita." "Solus Rex" and "The Circle" I found impenetrable. Though "Lips to Lips," "An Affair of Honor," "A Dashing Fellow" and "Potato Elf" have redeeming virtues, they are made to seem conventional, circumstantial or "occasional" by the characters' lack of consequence. "Ultima Thule" is better and reminds me of Borges. It is a grudging dramatization of a cosmic riddle, but like Borges, it is provocative in a—dare I say? —"mind-expanding" way. Even here, though, I sometimes felt that the author was merely exercising his linguistic gifts, pursuing his beloved butterflies.

I think it would be useful to clear the air concerning Nabokov. If he doesn't want to reach out and touch us—if this offends his fastidiousness—fine! That's his affair. But I feel it's time we stopped pretending we like it.

The Shiksa's Revenge

To Isaiah Greene, his Jewishness has become a burden, a kind of elephantiasis of the self. He is as weary of his Jewishness as a prostitute is of her body, because he has been living off it, as a writer and lecturer on the Jew and the "Crisis of Identity." Like a man who has drunk too much at the well of the self, he has a hangover, a morning-after accidie. At forty, he can no longer even hear the promise of his youth. When we meet him, he is contemplating the awful daring, "the factitious excitement" of crossing Central Park, from east to west, at dusk. Anything, he thinks, to interrupt the dying fall of his days.

But on Park Avenue he runs into a Jewish demonstration at the Soviet Embassy. An innocent bystander, he suddenly finds himself being interviewed for television. One of the demonstrators is a beautiful blond girl: moved by her, he hastily exhumes his lectures and heats them up. The blond girl turns out to be a maverick shiksa, who has renamed herself Shoshana MacDonald. The Jew, it seems, is her favorite charity. As a result of the TV exposure, she and Greene become talk-show stars, cross-country lecturers at high fees.

When the brief candle of their newsworthiness begins to gutter, Shoshana retires from lecturing to finish her Ph.D., but Greene makes one more tour. He has been offered an astronomical sum to appear in a symposium at Donner Pass College for Women, located on the top of the Rockies, or "some other mountain range." Here the real drama for Greene and *Heartland* begins, for Donner Pass College is shiksapolis, a frontier our hero has never before reached. The students in this college, which has an Olympic-size swimming pool in the library, are descendants of those pioneers who, caught in a blizzard, had fallen to eating one another.

These are such shiksas as Alexander Portnoy and his literary confrères never met. Like their ancestors, they are carnivorous under their superb manners. "Swimming, scuba-diving, mountain climbing, skiing and slaloming," they are not human as Greene defines it, but somewhere else in the space between animal and angel. They inhabit the ineffable; their language is an onomatopoeia of cheerleader cries.

For Portnoy, the shiksa was an anthropologist's delight, a forbidden fruit, bought at the cost of a surrender of intelligence and identity. Assimilation was a sexual swoon that subverted one's sense of integrity. The shiksa lured the Jew out of the Talmud into "The Child's Garden of Verses," invited him to escape the catechizing eye of the Jewess and run barefoot in the grass. She pulled him from the shadows of history into the sun of the futureless present, where he bathes in the reflected glow of her golden mimicry.

In *Portnoy's Complaint*, the shiksa was like a lobotomy; in her snug harbor, the Jew was safe from the existential nagging of his tragic sense of life. The frog, with his all-seeing, unwinking eyes, was transformed into a prince who lived happily ever after because happiness was the only thing on the menu.

In Saul Maloff's *Heartland*, for perhaps the first time in the history of modern fiction, the shiksa is unmasked. She is not innocent, a flower or fruit ripe for plucking, but predatory. She works in mysterious ways, stalemating the Jew's classical appeal to reason. To her, he is like a talking, dancing bear. She has listened to him as *guest*—notice the word—lecturer, not one who belongs, and she has the answers before he even speaks.

It is not Greene, but a fellow symposiast, Fox, who is to become the shiksa's victim. Greene has dissipated his sexual aggressions in self-doubt; in recognition of his surrender, she will accept the bed sheets as a white flag, on her own terms. But not so Fox, who boasts that he is the Eastern visitor come as conqueror, "the new Vandal, Goth, and Visigoth . . . bearing sad tidings." "While the East wept, the West smiled," Fox snarls. The girls have too many teddy bears and a paucity of books. They must come down off their magic mountain and move toward a synthesis between "fantasy and work, illusion and reality, childhood and maturity, dream and fact."

Mr. Maloff offers us a superb scene in which Fox tries to teach one of the girls to make guttural "Hebrew sounds," using her diaphragm, her spittle, her body's quiver. In another brilliant passage, the girls' "courtesy" is turned on Greene, and it is difficult to tell whether this is a seduction or an inquisition. While his self-appointed hostess gives him artificial respiration, as a preliminary to their love-making, her breath whistles out in something that sounds suspiciously like "Jew."

The shiksa is no longer a park or pastoral landscape for the Jew's picnic on the grass. Answering Greene's wish to "immerse myself in your native element," his hostess says that it would "do you more harm than good," succinctly summing up a generation of novels on that theme. In a climax that it would be unfair to *Heartland* to reveal, Fox learns the hard way that, in the rough and tumble of American sociology, the shiksa has finally learned to defend herself.

The Wilder Shores of Imagination

Every culture could use a good dose of revulsion from time to time. In this century especially, we seem to grow by continually becoming disgusted with ourselves. We fatten so fast that it takes something like an attack of dysentery to keep us in shape. And this is what Dada amounted to: a crisis in the bowels of the *Zeitgeist*. Coming of age during World War I, the Dadaists were cosmic kibitzers, paranoid poets, elegant fairy godfathers of today's lumpen protesters. Though they pretended to be nihilists, most of them had the histrionic bitterness of disillusioned lovers. Several—like Jacques Vaché and René Crével—died of broken hearts, so to speak, in committing suicide.

Dada was not so much a school of art as a parodying of all schools. But, since brevity is the soul of wit, the Dadaists soon exhausted their material, and in the early twenties Surrealism was born. Surrealism set itself the task of cleaning out the attic and the closets of the modern imagination. André Breton, the housemother of the movement, "discovered" the unconscious while serving as a medical orderly in the war, and under his leadership the Surrealists stormed it as their ancestors had stormed the Bastille. Breton was himself the most Surrealist feature of the entire movement: totally humorless and pedantic, he had a compulsion for issuing manifestoes. He was constantly defining and redefining their position—while the Surrealists as constantly ignored or transcended these definitions.

Much of Surrealism, especially in literature, is spontaneity by formula, an anticipation of the speed or acid trips of today, resulting in what Mario Praz called "the reductio ad absurdum of the romantic inspiration." It is both sentimental and naive to suppose that a rampant unconscious or perception run amok is going to refresh art. This is another of those "profound banalities" to which the French are so prone. Even at its best, Surrealism is never far from parody, but that may be a strength as well as a weakness. We may have reached a point where we can discover new images only by distorting the old ones.

The Surrealists indulged in the theatrical gestures and Happenings of today's art, but their antics were more amusing. They were not as pompous, in practice at least, as the current champions of the Absurd, who take themselves as seriously as a suicide on Golden Gate Bridge. Though literary Surrealism soon proved to be a bore, a persistence in a bad habit, like fingernail biting, the painters had better luck. In their medium, which was more exposed than language, mediocrity had fewer places to hide.

In spite of its posturing and politicking, Surrealism was important. It helped to break the ice in European painting of the twenties. Cubism was beginning to ossify, and the Fauves were pretty well domesticated by that time, too. Art had become increasingly autonomous, addressing itself to its own possibilities, the artist and his art living like a balanced aquarium. Surrealism offered "poetic" imagery as an alternative to "pure" painting or "painting painting." In reintroducing subject matter, it represented a left-handed sort of humanism, a going home again to personal history.

By focusing on the unconscious, the Surrealists tried to turn art inside out, to disembowel it—and, in fact, this is what many of their pictures look like. *Dada and Surrealist Art* often reads like case histories in "the crisis of consciousness"—a favorite slogan of the movement. But pathology has never been so pertinent: we are all patients in the clinic of the twentieth century.

As Mr. Rubin points out, the biomorphism of Hans Arp, André Masson, Max Ernst and Joan Miró introduced a much needed note of lyricism into the austerity of experimental painting. It softened the shape of things to come, prepared the way for Arshile Gorky, William de Kooning and Matta Echaurren. In Giorgio de Chirico's ambiguous perpectives, we have the inevitable metaphor for the dilemma of contemporary man. In joining the antic and the erotic, Miró has given us a lovely object lesson in happy sex; Gorky and Matta have carried the romantic agony to its melodramatic conclusion.

Surrealism had its share of bad painters also: Victor Brauner, Oscar Dominguez, Wolfgang Paalen, Kurt Seligman, to name just a few, and there were times when René Magritte, Ernst and Masson floundered too. Dali's *brio* only partially camouflaged his charlatanism and the poverty of his pictorial vocabulary. With the exception of some trenchant remarks about Dali, Mr. Rubin usually contents himself with a little compassionate headshaking when confronted with the clumsy composite monsters or Krafft-Ebing cartoons that some Surrealists doggedly ground out.

Because it is so literary, Surrealist painting lends itself particularly to iconographic ingenuity, and Mr. Rubin is such a virtuoso here that even comparatively poor works provide him with rich occasions. He is not henpecked by his erudition, however. He gives as good as he gets in responding to the direct emotional appeal of the less doctrinaire pieces. His book is not only important as art history: it is also a voluptuous picnic on the wilder shores of imagination.

Shoppers with Nothing to Buy

I used to think that I was open-minded about women, that I was ready to meet them on their own grounds, but Joy Williams makes me feel that this is like saying I'll meet you on such-and-such a corner when that corner has disappeared in one of the abrupt and brutal changes of modern life. Her heroine Kate has "answers to questions no one would ever ask." She takes Freud's famous "What do women want?" and makes it obsolete with "What *is* a woman?" Kate proves that men and women are in pretty much the same predicament, except that men are more accustomed to it. So much so that they may have grown complacent; they unthinkingly take it in their stride.

But women have only now collided with themselves, like someone turning a corner of history and slamming up against a stranger. Suddenly they are like shoppers with nothing to buy. Their shopping list is a blank page, Mallarmé's "purest poem." Like Kate, they are finding that "it's difficult to tell at the end of the day whether it was theory or need that got you through it."

Kate has Grady, whom she loves—but he is not an answer, only a comfort. He is one of "those people with things to do, moving through their landscapes, victimized by their sceneries." She finds that "she has taken away his energy and replaced it with premonition." Now "he is not satisfied." He wonders "what can be beyond love?" And "he wants to get there." Like her reverend father's flock, she and Grady predicate their lives "upon the interpretation of the absence around them."

State of Grace suffers from a certain amount of repetition and first-novel floundering, but after a while you don't mind because you've discovered that you're never very far away from a beautiful scene or sentence that will gather the book up in its embrace. The unevenness derives in part too from the fact that this is unmapped territory the author is entering. To my knowledge, Miss Williams is the first to set foot there, and in that sense she may be the most "relevant" woman writing at this time. I can't tell which moves me more: her historical inevitability or her talent. When they are joined together as they are here, they should put any man in his place, if he can find it.

As I said, Kate has a man, a good man, but we can see that this is not the answer to the basic question she was born into, like a congenital disease. There is no magic symmetry, no paired equilibrium, no two-seater hammock or porch swing that can soothe or lull her ferocious appetite for identity. Kate sounds as if she never expected to hope for anything special—but life is *there*, blindly pushing in her blood. If anatomy is *not* destiny, then she and her "sisters" may have to find cold comfort between the icy sheets of books like this one until something else turns up.

Kate has a child by Grady, but it too is not an answer. It is an appendage, or dependage, a biological accident that uses her body as a boardinghouse. Perhaps she will love it anyway, will dance with it, as she and her reverend father danced to Bach when she was a little girl. Perhaps, as her mother did, she will take it to the amusement park and, like her mother again, lose her mind there, as it "enmeshes itself in the workings of the merry-go-round, entwines itself in its cheerless and monotonous music." In any case, she will know, even as she places and straps the child on a horse or ostrich, that this is not a solution. Following her father, she may read it the Golden Book about the Ten Commandments in which "Thou shalt not commit adultery" is accompanied by a drawing of two little children running away from a broken window. But even as her lips form the words and her finger traces the illustration, she will understand that this is only a game parents play.

Kate cannot strike on a significant action, so she stops and tries to think. She is not optimistic. As she puts it, "I'm taking time off and I may never take it on again." Her father pursues her, pleads with her to come back home, tells her that "truth removes the need for freedom," but she cannot locate a truth. Like some men, her father thinks he has the truth in his pocket, in his head, his heart, his pants—but she knows better than to believe his boast that he'll "absorb the harm she'd bring to others."

State of Grace folds back on itself like a fugue, phrasing and rephrasing Kate's problem like a tongue seeking out a painful cavity. Miss Williams's book is not pretty, but neither is a new-born baby, especially if you include the afterbirth. Her scenes, like her heroine, are drastic. When Kate's sister is killed in an automobile accident, their father gravely removes the chewing gum from his dead daughter's mouth. When Kate is seven and her mother dies, her cousin tries to console her. " 'I'm sorry about your mother,' he says quickly. "It's very sad and I'm sorry.' " But Kate is not taken in by this transparent show of feeling. " 'Well,' she says, 'you certainly didn't have anything to do with it. You don't even live around here.' "

There have been other despairing books by women, but since existentialism, despair comes cheap. It is like a new style in costume jewelry or men's trench coats. Miss Williams has nothing in common with this chichi angst. You might say that she puts the dignity back into despair. She is like someone who has run amok with Occam's razor. With him, she holds that, all other things being equal, the simplest solution is most likely to be the true one. She has cut away the fat, and now, the razor dripping in her hand, she says: "I am left with almost nothing, but I enter it. I enter it."

A Welsh Guinea Pig in Africa

Most of us think of Africa in either political or esthetic terms: as the newest of the "liberated" countries, hellbent on progress and self-determination, or as a great park-cum-museum, the last frontier of nature and natural man. It was C. W. Nicol's bad luck to get caught in the no man's land between these two conceptions when he served for a couple of years as a game warden in Ethiopia.

Nicol is a young Welshman who had already worked in the Arctic with Eskimos and with Japanese whalers off the coast of Canada. He had lived in Japan and was married to a Japanese; he could not be accused of cultural narrow-mindedness. Hired by the Imperial Ethiopian Government, he was sent into the remote, beautiful and primitively feudal Simien highlands of Ethiopia to found a national park and to save from extinction the rapidly disappearing Walia ibex, which had retreated there.

From his arrival to his resignation, his experiences were closer to the theater of the absurd than to ecology. He came to know Africa as only someone who has worked there can. He found that language, for most uneducated Ethiopians, was a kind of waste product, having little or no correspondence with reality. Every statement he heard had to be examined, like a bad poem, to get at the meaning behind it. He discovered that Ethiopian peasants could not take in, for example, the relation between cause and effect. They were more ready to accept the supernatural than an empirical proof demonstrated before their eyes.

Erosion, they said, was inevitable: it had nothing to do with destruction of trees that provided protection from the sun or held soil together on the rocky slopes. Burning of forests might lead, in a few years, to unusable land, but this meant nothing to people who thought only in terms of today.

Though they liked and respected him, Nicol discovered that his guards could not be honest with him because it conflicted with older loyalties—or, more importantly, because they could not grasp the principle, the importance, of honesty. Like rationality, it seemed to be a strange and inconvenient habit of foreigners. Faced with an unpleasant admission, they dissembled as instinctively as a man pulling his hand away from a flame or coming in out of a cold rain.

Nicol lectured them again and again in Biblical baby talk, explaining what the park meant to them, what ecology was, how, in the long run, it would all be for their benefit. They listened to him as if to a concert; they were moved, but unchanged. Their lives had not prepared them for the idea of a future, which was a prerequisite to the idea of planning. When Nicol tried to inspire them with pride in the beauty of their country, he found that they had not the slightest feeling for it. They knew almost nothing about the habits of the animals in the area. In fact, Nicol could not even find a word for nature in their language.

Some of his immediate superiors regarded him as a usurper of their power and sabotaged everything he tried to do. Some of them were in the business of selling leopard skins, which was against the law, but Nicol could not get them punished because bribery was the customary answer to everything. Promises were repeated like litanies, and ignored.

When it got to be too much for him, Nicol would take it out on his punching bag or go off with his binoculars to forget everything and just look at his park. The punching bag and the karate he had learned in Japan came in handy when he was attacked in the dark by assailants with heavy iron-tipped sticks.

He built a home of three circular huts for his wife and two children and was briefly happy with them until she became pregnant and had to be sent back to Japan. He loved his handsome German shepherd dog, but had to kill him when he became dangerous through being left alone too much and being stoned by children.

His guards left his wife's horse outside and hyenas killed and ate it. One guard carried an important letter in his pocket for a year and could offer no explanation. When Nicol brought another guard back from the brink of death with antibiotics, the first thing the man did was demand his back pay. At one time, three of his guards had advanced cases of gonorrhea and another was in jail for stealing a horse.

The American game warden who had preceded Nicol had resigned after a few months, but whenever he tried to resign, even the man who had opposed him tried to talk him into staying on. When he pointed out that his Ethiopian assistant was a competent and well-trained man, they answered that no one would listen to an Ethiopian. Apparently, a white man's very eccentricity—in their eyes—was a guarantee of good faith.

With the road to his park not even begun, with the peasants burning more forests than ever, with no funds and no official interest in his project, Nicol finally resigned. What precipitated it was an act on the part of his guards that showed him how little he had accomplished in almost two years. After all his lectures, they cut down for firewood two beautiful old trees right in front of their own huts.

After Nicol's resignation, the Emperor declared the Simien a national park, but there was still no road and the peasants were still burning away the forest. There was a new administration and some improvements, but not enough to be able to say that the park's existence was assured. Nicol had been tough, tireless, imaginative and fired by love of his project—and he had lost. He had lost because what he was trying to promote—a national park —seemed beyond the imaginative reach of most of the people concerned. His experience gives us a much-needed, down-to-earth idea of how much the Africans' image of the country differs from ours and how that difference inevitably affects our relations with them.

Apocalypses and Other Ills

Just keep it up and see where it gets you: this is the message of the futuristic novel. It takes our present behavior and carries it to its logical conclusion, which almost invariably turns out to be a *reductio ad absurdum*. The futuristic novelist is more interested in ideas than in people. His characters are merely manikins for a moral; they wear it like an ill-fitting suit or dress. In *Love in the Ruins*, Walker Percy has worked hard to avoid this dehumanization. His hero, Thomas More, is almost redundantly human. To demonstrate that he exists, the author has given him satyriasis, psychosis, lapsed Catholicism, large bowel complaints, alcoholism and hives. He fairly itches with humanity. All the same, he is a charming fellow, an appealing tragicomedian who is closely related to Percy's hero in his first novel, *The Moviegoer*, which won the National Book Award ten years ago.

We meet More in the 1980's, as he is preparing to save the people of the United States from the consequences of our contemporary foolishness. The whole country is violently polarized: black and white, liberal and conservative, dropout and Establishment. We have been involved in the war in "Ecuador" for fifteen years and there is no sign of a resolution. The country is crumbling into ruins because no one wants to be a repairman any more. Under such circumstances, conservatives have begun to fall victim to "unseasonable rages and large bowel complaints." Liberals are more apt to contract "sexual impotence, morning terror, and a feeling of abstraction of the self from the self."

A ne'er-do-well physician and psychiatrist, More is tinkering toward a machine to treat these symptoms. His "lapsometer" enables him to locate and measure areas of psychic imbalance—lapses—in the brain, but it can only diagnose, not cure. For treatment, More is forced to rely on homely, rule-of-thumb remedies. When Ted Tennis, for example, becomes so abstracted from himself that he cannot make love to his wife, the doctor prescribes "recovery of the self through ordeal." He orders Ted to walk home from work through Honey Island Swamp, which is infested with mosquitoes, leeches, vampire bats, tsetse flies, alligators, moccasins, copperheads, Bantu guerrillas and Michigan State dropouts. Reinducted into reality by these agencies, Ted falls happily into his Tanya's arms.

The stage is set for Dr. Faustus, and he arrives on cue, in the form of Art Immelman. Representing the CIA or something "a bit more exalted," as well as the combined Rockefeller, Ford and Carnegie foundations, Art wants to go into partnership with More, who in a weak moment agrees. Then all hell—or all human nature—breaks loose. Following More's lead, Art has developed an attachment for the lapsometer that enables it not only to diagnose symptoms, but also to intensify them as well. He uses it to disinhibit the whole population, until everyone erupts and a cloud of psychic fallout drifts over the country. Only blacks are immune to the fallout, because the gas cannot penetrate their pigmentation. Everyone else carries his prejudices, hatreds and desires to—as we predicted—their logical conclusion.

It all ends in open warfare between black and white, murderous rampages by members of the love community in the swamp, wholesale burning and general disorder. The blacks win and become the dominant race; the spoils of war are golf, birdwatching, ulcers and hypertension. More gets his first case of abstraction from the self in a black. It's not the cleverest plot in the world, but then it's not the worst, either. Far less preachy than *1984* or *Brave New World*, it's much funnier too. There's a passage in which Immelman stimulates the "musical-erotic" area of More's brain and turns his psyche into a kind of Kierkegaardian practical joke. And Percy uses an interesting trick of having the doctor refer to his mistresses' parts—never the obvious parts —by their abstruse medical names. (It's true that Thomas Mann did this infinitely better in *The Magic Mountain*, where Hans Castorp propositions Frau Chauchat in the same sort of language and for better reasons, but nevertheless . . .)

Percy's writing has improved considerably since his second novel, *The Last Gentleman*. His sentences are no longer *faux naïf* or unadventurous, and his eye and ear are sharper. There are many fine capsule characterizations like this: "She's not my type, being a certain kind of Smith girl, a thin moody Smithie who props cheek on knee, doesn't speak to freshmen, doesn't focus her eyes, and is prone to quick sullen decisions, leaping onto her little basketed bike and riding off without explanation." Or this one: "Maybe he's the best American type, the sergeant-yeoman out of the hills, the good cop. When the hurricane comes, he's the fellow with the truck: come on, we got to get those folks out of there."

What Percy is saying underneath his satire is going to put some Northern intellectual noses out of joint. Immelman, who presumably speaks for the Government, says of his shenanigans with the lapsometer: "We never 'do' anything to anybody. We only help people do what they want to do. We facilitate social interaction in order to isolate factors. If people show a tendency to interact in a certain way, we facilitate the interaction in order to accumulate reliable data." Translated, this argues that a liberal—or "scientific-objective"—government gives every social group its head until they break one another's.

It turns democracy into a laboratory experiment with white and black rats—a wholly idle experiment without a goal or even a guiding hypothesis. It all stems, Percy suggests, from a knuckling under to soulless pragmatism, a belief that everything is measurable—and manipulable. We've lost our feeling for the essential mystery of life and of ourselves. At the end of the book, Percy gets off a good "bad Catholic" crack: The trouble started, he has one character say, "when we abandoned the Latin mass."

School: Most Addictive Drug

Not acid, speed or junk but school is the most destructive drug in America today. This is the theme of Ivan Illich, a man with a truly Dostoyevskian flair for revolutionary thinking. We're so stoned on schooling, he says, that we can't think for ourselves any more. Education has put the dunce cap on the whole country by confusing "teaching with learning, grade advancement with education, a diploma with competence, and fluency with the ability to say something new." Nor is modernizing our schools the answer. We can gentle them with permissiveness, stuff them with gadgets or varnish them with liberalism—they will still be schools, and it is the very *idea* of the school as an institution that Mr. Illich dislikes.

Institutions are destroying our independence, putting us in a passive "client" relationship with life, in which we are eternally waiting for an answer to our applications for professional services. Mr. Illich would like to see us educating one another, substituting personal encounter and personal surprise for bureaucratized boredom. He feels that we should learn from things themselves, from people who are doing what we would like to be able to do, from our peers and from our elders. Life itself should be our teacher.

School, he believes, has become a stifling religion, a ritual for disguising dissonances, a promise of salvation won through the penance of attendance and the submission to dogma. Born in original sin, we are baptized into first grade. The myth of unending consumption of education and other consumer goods has replaced the myth of life everlasting. The curriculum of the "free" school is simply a dogma of a different kind, like the liturgies of folk and rock masses.

A life of action instead of a life of consumption: this is his prescription, and it deserves a round of applause. *Deschooling Society* proposes "opportunity webs" in place of schools. These would consist of access to educational objects, skill exchanges,

peer-matching and educators-at-large. Libraries, museums, laboratories, factories, airports and farms might all offer students
opportunities for various forms of learning. Storefront depots on
every city block might provide similar materials on a lesser scale
and help to humanize city life by revitalizing the neighborhood
concept. People who could "model" various kinds of competence
might be available to interested groups in skill exchanges. Peer-
matching would bring together those interested in the same
learning activity. Educators-at-large could be engaged as the need
arose. In effect, Mr. Illich proposes a total learning experience
embracing every aspect of life and beginning with the question:
"What kinds of things and people might learners want to be in
contact with in order to learn?"

In its projections, *Deschooling Society* is an affirmative *1984*.
Though it is flamboyantly visionary and inconceivably remote
from acceptance, this does not mean that the book is impractical.
On the contrary, it merely shows that we have reached a point
where the practical seems utopian, where common sense is more
far-fetched than fantasy. Mr. Illich does nothing to soften the
impact of his originality: he has a fondness for wild generalizations and sourceless statistics that is positively cavalier. Much of
his work has been done in Latin America and his style owes a
good deal to the old anarchist *dinamitero*. But though he throws
a rhetorical bomb on almost every page, very few of them are
duds.

While he has confined himself mainly to a discussion of schools,
Mr. Illich feels that his argument applies to all institutions. He
is especially eloquent on the subject of poverty. In constantly
creating new needs, institutions are continually expanding the
definition of poverty. Anyone who falls behind the latest advertised ideal of consumption is "poor." And the "modernization" of
poverty has added psychological impotence to its other disadvan-
tages. Self-reliance, pride and ingenuity are all subverted by the
passivity and conformity imposed on the poor. From an idiosyn-
cratic, rough-and-ready type, the poor man has degenerated into
a "client" of the welfare state, a squatter in the outer offices of
bureaucracy. Drawing his first and last breath in a hospital ward,
he goes through his whole life being "treated" by one agency or
another. Like a character in a Kafka story, he is trapped in the

"logic of irrational consistency," a nightmare dreamed up by social planners.

It is not difficult to pick holes in some of Mr. Illich's propositions, because in leaping from peak to peak he sometimes stumbles. Schools aren't as bad as he maintains; most learning isn't acquired casually, as he says; the "street education" that he advocates entered schools a long time ago; schools are not entirely self-perpetuating, because even the scholarship students are clamoring for change. Instruction does not invariably "smother the horizons of the imagination": sometimes it enlarges them. But this is like criticizing the grammar of someone who has just delivered a speech that gave us goose pimples. Flaws and all, *Deschooling Society* ought to be read by everybody.

Statutory Immortality

For a French bourgeois, says Frederick Brown, heaven is eternal status. In death, he wraps it around him like a shroud. Père Lachaise, Paris's most select cemetery, enshrines an "ossified social hierarchy." To be buried there is to achieve a "statutory immortality." In life, "like Beckett's anti-heroes, we inhabit nowhere; only the dead . . . enjoy place." A harried, crowded span is crowned with hallowed space. In the grave, "absolute selfhood" is forever guaranteed to those most "fearful of self-loss." This promise of beatitude is a permanent "reprieve from the anguish of personality." Père Lachaise is Paris's wish-fulfilling dream, fossilizing its clients' unconscious in "the maternal anonymity of earth, the virile self-proclamation of an obelisk, or the eternal real estate of a family mausoleum . . ." For the Frenchman, "fashion extends beyond the grave, where, for many, to be damned is to be eternally *démodé* . . ." We are not surprised to learn that the cemetery and the stock exchange were the works of the same architect.

Though Père Lachaise was founded in 1780, it reflected then, and still does, "the modern nostalgia for consecrated identity." A Frenchman's grave is his last word on himself. *J'ai dit.* The ugliness of so many of the cemetery's monuments can be blamed on their self-conscious gravity, in which symbolism squeezes out beauty, as the dead, each eternally "reciting his stone tirade," attempt to outface one another through time. Here, in a country "which sought to legislate being and nothingness," is a contest of dignity, solemn as stone, a *société* where everyone is mortally *sérieux*. "This cemetery," wrote an eighteenth-century commentator, "the first to be a true cemetery, will gather into itself the memories of all the generations death deposits there to avenge humanity for the insults of time, destruction and oblivion."

In *Père Lachaise: Elysium as Real Estate*, Frederick Brown has exposed the pomposity, has "tickled the catastrophe," of an otherwise sophisticated and ironical people. Corrupted by pragmatism, French Catholicism produced a grotesquely secular greed for immortality. While Americans deny death, the French declaim it. Who else but a Frenchman like Gide could say, as he lay dying, "Before you quote me, make sure I'm conscious"? For the Parisian bourgeois, "seeming equalled being"—form was everything. In the privacy of the tomb, each man strove, like Napoleon, to "seduce the absolute."

Though the French bourgeois has always been anxious to advance himself, this ambition had to struggle with his love of stasis. It "collided with an aversion to any moving object." In a nice example of *noblesse oblige*, the princess in Stendhal's *Charterhouse of Parma* carries this aversion to a proportionate extreme: she considers any form of haste a mark of vulgarity. Death is the antithesis of the haste that lays waste to austerity. It must be solemnized in the weightiest manner imaginable. The ingrained conservatism of the French finds infinite comfort in the notion of a perpetually dignified posture.

Mr. Brown's book is ripe with inspired mischief as he carries on his ambivalent love affair with the French. (He teaches, translates and writes about French culture.) The very idea of characterizing the French in terms of their corporeal last will and testament, of posing them against their gravestones, is a triumph of affection and insolence. But the author has been punished for his irreverence: some of the pomp and circumstance of death have seeped into his style. Now and then his sentences are as weighty and over-adorned as the mausoleums he mocks; others are the epitaphs of a buried idea. Intoxicated with his subject, he makes extravagant use of the dying fall. His book has such a high design that it would be damning it with faint praise to call it grandiose. The movement of his mind is at once so subtle and so bold that we are reminded of Mallarmé's remark: "If a person of ordinary intelligence and insufficient literary preparation opens one of my books and pretends to enjoy it, there has been a mistake. Things must be returned to their places."

In publicizing Père Lachaise, its director Frochot "needed classics" to give an "instant patina" to his creation. His first client—a police commissioner's errand boy—"was unlikely to draw the crowd whose eternal beatitude he had in mind." In search of embellishments, he shamelessly raided a museum con-

sisting mainly of sculptural spoils of war and these were strategi-
cally scattered throughout the grounds. The alleged bones of
Molière and La Fontaine were dug up and transferred to Père
Lachaise. When the casket of Louise de Lorraine, Henri III's
Queen, was accidentally unearthed, Frochot traded for her the
corpses of two poets and what remained of Hélöise and Abelard,
who had six times been torn asunder and reunited. The price
of the cemetery's "eternal ground" was raised to keep out the hoi
polloi. When Baron Desfontaines, the former owner of the property, repurchased three yards of Père Lachaise for his own repose,
he found Frochot's rate two hundred seventy-two times higher
than the original cost. However, discounts were sometimes made
to dignity when an illustrious applicant proved to be impecu-
nious.

Death had not always been treated so ceremoniously in Paris.
Before the establishment of Père Lachaise, the Cemetery of the
Innocents had served the city for some eight centuries. Two
million citizens lay thirty feet deep in what Mr. Brown describes
as a "historical mulch" or "human geology." Until Napoleon III
decreed that they be laid end to end, the poor were piled seven
deep in pell-mell intimacy. During the Middle Ages, this bulging
burial ground lay cheek-by-jowl with the town's central market,
as if the earthier spirits of those days saw death as something
akin to the decease of digestion.

Père Lachaise's name derived from the circumstance of its once
having been the estate of Louis XIV's confessor. Because of this
association, every owner of a plot in Paris's palace of the dead
saw himself as a king. This ennoblement was not, at least in
earlier times, extended to his wife. Male chauvinism persisted
into the hereafter. While she was allowed to reproduce his image,
the bourgeois's wife was never permitted to invade his soul or
share equally in its honors. She might be buried in Père
Lachaise, but only as the completion of her husband's persona,
just as other peoples inter certain of their possessions with them.
While he was "real and austere," he regarded her as merely
inchoate, an apprentice human being who, until recently, was
denied legal status, along with children and the insane. And he
saw nothing strange in this. To a Frenchman habituated by history to the "divine conundrums" of the Sun King's behavior,

nothing he did himself seemed unreasonable. In his theatrical conception of society, his wife was only a supporting character.

Père Lachaise is almost as rich in photographs—also by the author—as it is in ideas. Mr. Brown has not provided these with captions, as if he wished to encourage us to speculate freely on them. One of the oddest is of a tomb surmounted by an effigy of its occupant lying down in his street clothes, but with his hat fallen at his feet, as if death had unceremoniously knocked it off. The list of names of those buried in this purchasable heaven ranges from Oscar Wilde to Samuel Hahnemann, the founder of homeopathic medicine. It would be interesting to hear what these two have to say to one another.

The Contagion of Crime

Like people who hate drinking alone, readers of mystery or suspense novels tend to urge them on you. They seem to feel a need, also, to defend the taste. Suspense novels are often better written than "serious" ones, they tell you, which is like saying crossword puzzles are good for your vocabulary, or you follow *Playboy* for its fiction. Some years ago, Edmund Wilson expressed his irritation at this kind of proselytizing. In a crotchety article on the subject, he asked, "Who cares who killed Roger Ackroyd?" To him, the effort of reading mysteries was like unpacking a crate of straw only to discover a bent and rusty nail at the bottom.

Like Wilson, I too have been urged by addicted friends to try suspense novels, and my first reaction was much the same as his. If I succeeded in suspending my disbelief, I was dogged by my taste. I remember a sentence in one of Len Deighton's books that was pure, if inadvertent, Perelman: Across the major surgery of the sunset, the trees stood like sutures. (That may not be the exact wording, but it's close.) There was another one, in the old Humphrey Bogart canon, that particularly struck me, too. I think it was from Erle Stanley Gardner, and it went something like this: She used her smile carefully, the way an old chorus girl hoards her last pair of silk stockings. (I'm afraid I've improved that one—it doesn't seem so bad now.)

Why can't you just admit that you want to relax or escape? I said to my friends. It's all right. Masturbation is no longer frowned upon by enlightened people. Besides, you're in good company. Even W. H. Auden is a mystery fan, though he says he can read them only if they are set in an eighteenth-century vicarage. But in spite of my patronizing tone, I must have caught the contagion. After pointing out that mere curiosity is the most primitive of impulses; that a fascination with the minutiae of police procedure is anal-compulsive; that Le Carré's angst is too glib, etc. . . . after all this, I found myself reading the damned things and enjoying them.

Some of them, anyway. Like the books of Edmund Crispin,
James Fraser, David Ely, Kenneth Giles and Peter Dickinson.
Michael Innes ought to belong in there, too, but for all his
erudition, urbanity and wit, he is somehow too slow. "Fast-
moving" is one of the requisites of the form, though why one
should want to move fast while relaxing is in itself a mystery. I
suppose Georges Simenon is as good as anyone writing suspense
today. He is the Zola or Balzac of the genre, but for that very
reason his people and situations offer less opportunity for imaginative capering.

This may seem a long way around to writing about Peter
Dickinson, but a reviewer can only talk in a general way about a
suspense novel. Like the scene of a crime, the springs of its action
must not be touched. What I can disclose, though, is that Peter
Dickinson's books are just as carefully written as "serious" novels
—with one difference. He doesn't ask you to carry the same
moral burden; in reading him, you don't have to bring into play
the whole unwieldy apparatus of responsibility. We go to suspense novels when the world is too much with us: Dickinson
discreetly eliminates our world. He does this by simply having
one of his characters commit a murder. None of us knows any
murderers: this is outside our experience, unreal. We don't have
to take sides or get involved. We can follow the action playfully,
even esthetically, if we like. We can slump in our armchair or bed
without slumming.

Dickinson has published four books in the last three years.
Though the first two won consecutive awards in England, I think
The Glass-Sided Ants' Nest was overpraised. (Overpraise is endemic in this field.) All the critics were taken by the very premise
of a mystery involving a transplanted tribe of aborigines living
in a commune in London. *The Old English Peep Show* was less
labored and more fun. Its upper-class eccentricities and architectural follies are fairly familiar stuff, but brilliantly done—and
there is a man-eating lion in the book that you can actually
smell. *The Sinful Stones* has a character who could be Bertrand
Russell's stunt man, and a sinister religious cult that is building
the Eternal City out of damp cement.

Sleep and His Brother revolves around a hospital for
"cathypnics"—children who are mentally deficient, literally cold-

blooded and possessed of telepathic powers. It contains the following sentences:

" 'Despite what you have done to it, this remains a gloriously typical example of High Domestic Grandiose.' "

". . . Pibble felt as though he had only just withstood the blandishments of a door-to-door salesman on the threshold of his soul."

" '. . . if he's growing freesias he always sends us a bunch for the funerals. Bad taste is more touching than good taste, sometimes.' "

" 'Come,' said one of the children, and the three of them turned away from him as starving villagers might turn away from a lorry which they thought brought rice but in fact carried a cargo of birth control leaflets."

Each One of Us a Christ

The ugliness of life in America today seems to provoke beautiful books. Our best writers are at their best in describing the sense of loss, the loneliness, the absurdity, the anxiety, the yearning many of us feel. The pathology of our society fills their pens with paradoxes, ironies, pathos, even poetry. Our failures are great enough to lend grandeur to their diagnoses.

Our illness is so grave that the most high-minded doctors have had to be called back from their laboratories of pure research. Here, for example, is Professor Lionel Trilling, who writes of our raucous and discordant culture in the prose rhythms of a Proust. And though his eyes are cool with irony and distaste, we are grateful that he has come. If we can engage *his* attention, we cannot be wholly low.

In *Sincerity and Authenticity*, Professor Trilling has attempted to "observe the moral life in process of revising itself." The revision in question concerns the substitution of the idea of authenticity for the feeling of sincerity in our preferred description of ourselves. It is no mere semantic quibble, but a case of our very quiddity, our essential whatness, the weight, in a sense, of our being. As Nietzsche said, according to the author, the realization of the death of God had the effect of making all things, and especially man, seem "weightless." The concept of authenticity is our latest attempt to fatten our Giacometti-like figures to respectable proportions, to regain in our psyches what we've lost in our souls.

Before authenticity, says Professor Trilling, came sincerity, and before that, man was so consonant or congruent with his self that he had no mirror, so to speak, in which to look and see what he was. It would never have occurred to Moses, for example (or to President Eisenhower), to ask himself whether he was sincere. But then, following his fatal curiosity, or perhaps to show off for his new "society," man began to take himself apart, much like a child who takes apart his favorite toy to see what makes it tick. And he broke it to pieces in the process.

He looked at what used to be called the "noble life"—led by what Hegel termed the "honest soul"—and saw an idyllic picture in which man was at one with himself and with nature. But in the act of looking, he lingered too long and discovered that he had inadvertently stepped out of the picture. This sudden distancing, this first stirring of self-consciousness, was his undoing. The idyllic picture eventually became Karl Marx's "idiocy of village life," and the human spirit split into a wound impossible to heal.

Sincerity was man's first attempt to stanch the flow, to keep his self from bleeding away into ambiguity. But it was ultimately unsatisfying, this notion of "genuine" feeling, for as Oscar Wilde pointed out: "All bad poetry springs from genuine feelings." Sincerity simply wasn't flattering enough to float man's sinking self-esteem. He needed something more radical, more securely rooted in his shaken identity—and in this way he arrived at the idea of authenticity.

To be authentically himself gave man something of that "sentiment of being" Rousseau saw as the meaning of life. He wallowed in it, made a pig of himself in the slough of despond. As a result, says Professor Trilling, authenticity today is seized upon "as an affirmation of the unconditioned nature of the self, of its claim to an autonomy so complete that all systematic predications about it are either offensively reductive, or gratuitously prescriptive, or irrelevant." Here at last we have the ultimate human vanity, in its most modern, most masochistic expression: the conviction that, as far as the self is concerned, "whatever is, is right."

Never was a religion so perfectly custom-tailored to its time. I'm authentic: therefore I am. This was just what the doctor ordered: "to extricate ourselves from the generality of the commonplace and stand forth in the authenticity of particular being." Anything and everything could be justified—even exalted—in these terms. Our confession includes our absolution: if we are not better, our mediocrity is, at least, our very own. Our essence shines through its sad truths in a heroism of humility. And should we show signs of backsliding into self-esteem, "serious" literature is always ready to supply us with fresh images of abasement.

For Freud, the author remarks, the unmitigability of the human condition was the proof of its authenticity. In newer schools of psychoanalytic thought, even insanity may be glorified as a form of "being true to thine own self." "Madness," says Dr. David Cooper, "has in our age become some sort of lost truth." His collaborator, Dr. R. D. Laing, contends that schizophrenia may be merely an insecurity of being, a result of the parental imposition of inauthenticity. In a crazy world, he suggests, it may be the only sane strategy.

"The doctrine that madness is health," Professor Trilling comments, "that madness is liberation and authenticity, receives a happy welcome from a consequential part of the educated public." Not from him, however. As he views it, "The falsities of an alienated social reality are rejected in favor of an upward psychopathic mobility to the point of divinity, each one of us a Christ . . ." Or what Nietzsche called a "culture philistine" who, because he sees himself as damned, believes that he is saved.

The hydra-headed distortions of the idea of authenticity have led to an alarming vulgarization in American art and life. As a "parfit, gentil knight" in the lists of literature, Lionel Trilling has done what he can to rescue us from it. Now it is a question of the thickness of the monster's hide.

In the Cradle of the Deep

Precise ambiguity ought to be an oxymoron, a contradiction in terms, but in Stanley G. Crawford's *Log of the S.S. The Mrs. Unguentine*, it is not. It is a quality that enables his book to go on ricocheting through my imagination long after I've laid it down. Though I am not certain how much of the action his characters have actually experienced and how much they have only projected, this uncertainty does not make them vague or unsatisfying: rather, it lends them a terrible pathos. It is as if the author were asking: "Can romance *ever* live up to our expectations?" Or "Do you *dare* to believe this?"

Mr. Crawford has calculated his ambiguities so nicely that they balance, and his story hangs in that balance. This is not the catch-all, do-it-yourself symbolism of the lazy or incompetent writer: the author seems to be suggesting that these near-incredible things *could* have occurred, and if they did not, more's the pity. We are haunted, not frustrated, by the possibilities he refuses to pin down.

I'm not fond of what is usually called fantasy in fiction, because it almost invariably seems far less fantastic than real life —but here's the rare exception. *Log* may even be a parable, but you can't prove it by me. It doesn't contain a single windy or pretentious line and you don't have to do any simultaneous translation to enjoy it.

The prose is ripe in both diction and rhythm, but it is never precious. It is always talking to you—yes, you!—in its eccentric way. The imagery is far-fetched, but brought near. For example, Mr. and Mrs. Unguentine live on a large ocean-going garbage scow and they have covered over the garbage with dirt and turned their home into a floating botanical garden. It boasts more than forty trees, in addition to shrubs, flowers, lawns and freshwater ponds. But though the trees have grown so tall that you can't see past them from the pilothouse, I haven't the slightest desire to take this as a symbol for blind sailing on life's alternately smooth and turbulent surface, etc., or as a garden of Eden, an ecological microcosmos—or anything but what Mr. Crawford says it is. A barge. With a man and a woman on it who like to lie naked on a private little patch of lawn in its center.

"Unguentine was a man who grew nauseous upon land." So, on their barge, they steer clear of land, Mrs. Unguentine missing her former society at first, brooding over "oil smears iridescent of all that might have been," admitting that her fury "went into tossing huge salads." Still, she came to love it, all but her husband's silences. Though he had smatterings of fourteen languages in order to get the weather reports, he did not care for speech. Space was the language of his choice. If explicit communication could not be circumnavigated, he preferred to insert a terse note in his wife's sandwich or in the spout of her kitchen faucet.

Starved for words, Mrs. Unguentine would scan the water for bottles with messages in them, but her husband snatched them away. If they saw people, it was always dead ones, victims of an aircraft disaster, floating bloated beside their burst luggage. Such tragedies furnished all their needs: clothes, linens, silverware, jewels. In the early days of their travels, Mr. Unguentine would imitate urban sounds as he worked, for his wife's entertainment, but he had a thick, iguana-like tongue that soon gave up even this.

She would put typed notes on his breakfast plate, begging him for "anecdote or two . . . the juicy peccadillo, say." From such small beginnings, she felt, "we could start working our way toward the heart of the matter, on the way engaging in many a colorful argument, discussion, seminar . . ." To provoke his attention, she covered her habitual nakedness with an ancient evening gown. She "ransacked his gestures for a hint of exegesis." When he took the figurehead down from the prow to repaint it, she leaned out in its place, arms outstretched, breasts bared to the horizon.

She asked for a child, but when her husband gave her a son, he swam away as soon as he was able and his rejected mother and father went on sailing toward whichever season their garden required. Unguentine built a greenhouse dome three stories high to protect the plants, and they would lie atop it, sunbathing. He installed floodlights, salvaged from a wreck, and at night they saw their amorousness multiplied in the panes a hundred times. When the barge was too much with her, Mr. Unguentine would send his wife away for a vacation, out on a raft at the end of a three-hundred-yard line.

Mr. Crawford insidiously suggests, however, that this may all have been a drunken dream, that Mrs. Unguentine may have kept her husband landlocked and unhappy until he built his ship in a bottle and beat her for all the things he could not be. I don't know which was actually the case, and I don't care. I like to try it on both ways, comparing, weighing the alternatives, seeing double, balancing one anguish against another, this human triumph or failure against that. On Mr. Crawford's barge, I feel rocked in the cradle of the deep, and that's good enough for me.

Marshmallows in the Embers

During a rap session with some "revolutionists" in their apartment, John Stickney discovered that he was hearing three different records playing at once. "Yeah," his host said, "the walls are paper-thin . . . I wish just once we could get together behind one album." It's that way, the author finds, with their revolution too. There are so many "different drummers" all playing at once that people are having trouble finding the beat. Anarchists, Marxists, Jesus Freaks, Hare Krishnas, White Panthers, Women's Liberationists—there's a psychedelic supermarket of ideologies and many of the young are wandering confusedly up and down the aisles, trying to find something that will nourish their indefinable hunger.

Bored by rhetoric and repetition, unwilling to go backward and unable to locate "forward," the youth movement seems to be grinding to an uneasy halt, to be boiling down to a skeptical "What next?" For many, the trip is over and they haven't arrived at a destination. They are like hitchhikers who have been let out in the middle of nowhere.

During the summer and fall of 1970, the author traveled all over the country to the nerve centers of the radical movements. After talking endlessly, crashing wherever there was room, sharing scenes and drugs with every sort of clique, going to rallies, festivals and communes, Mr. Stickney brings back both good and bad news. Too many of the kids, he finds, are hooked on the idea of a Hollywood-style apocalypse, a fantasy Russian Revolution. Events like the disturbances at Kent and Jackson State have become "media trips that radicalize kids into a profound indefinition." There is rarely any ideology, any plan, any education, anyone willing to take seriously the responsibility of running his community. The revolution lacks any kind of unanimity, the mass base that Marxists found indispensable to social change.

For some, the movement has become a "carnival." When the Bank of America was burned in Isla Vista, Calif.—simply be-

149

cause it was there—one girl said: "Such a beautiful fire, the flames went so high! There was a huge crowd of people in a circle around the bank, just watching it all go down. Everyone went home and came back—dropped acid, smoked dope, drank wine, pulled out their stereos and began to play records real loud . . ." Someone else said: "People had brought hot dogs, you know, and marshmallows and they were just roasting them and toasting them right there on the embers . . ." And then the girl added: "There are so many people around now who are fascinated with . . . burning, you know, anything!"

Two relatively new influences are splitting the movement into even smaller factions: women's liberation and occultism. One articulate informant feels that "in the race between revolution and religion, the occult is winning." Another commentator says, rather grandly: "Factionalism is the luxury of irrelevance." Another: "Street-fighting is a kind of therapy which is self-perpetuating." Days of activity, nights of escaping into drugs is the latest formula, for "how long can you stand the intensity of constant action?" Some few are still on the road, never pausing long enough to get involved. For them, the trip is the thing, an end in itself, a *reductio ad absurdum* of the peripatetic philosopher. Perpetual motion is their answer to a question that won't fit into the trunks of their cars.

Mr. Stickney describes a character he met on the road, a technologist of the drug culture. "What we used to do," this hip pharmacist says, "was to shoot some acid and peak, right, wait for that cosmic flash, and then shoot some smack (heroin) in behind it—that was the ultimate . . . up, down, in, out, back and forth, oblivion, universal contact." How many revolutions, the author muses, can dance on the point of a needle?

The good news Mr. Stickney found is the fact that the youth movement has matured enough, here and there, to see itself with an unprecedented degree of irony and perspective. Noticing a young man reading a book during a rock concert, the author asked him what it was. It turned out to be nothing less than the collected poems of Wallace Stevens. The young man knew his way around in it, too. Flipping through the pages, he said: "Here's what's happening." The title of the poem was "The Revolutionists Stop for Orangeade." "The trouble is alienation,"

he went on. "I mean how many alienated people can one culture
stand? The creativity has waned . . . the direction lost . . . I'm
beginning to wonder just what hip is."

All through his travels, Mr. Stickney found a hangover feeling, a morning-after disillusionment, a nostalgia for the high,
halcyon days when everybody believed a new world was really
in the making. Exhausted or exasperated by aimless action, young
people are beginning to think, to reconsider their positions. One
of those the author talked to went so far as to say: ". . . we have
lost sight of the real enemy. The enemy seems to be ourselves,
not Nixon, not Agnew, not racism, sexism, capitalism . . . What a
drag!" And what a difference! That must be the orangeade talking.

More Commercial than Lively

In 1961, New York's theaters offered five plays featuring prostitutes. A survey of the twelve best performances by Broadway actresses concluded that half of them involved prostitute roles. Since World War II, each Broadway season has had at least one play featuring a prostitute. American films and novels have shown an almost equal interest in the subject. All this reflects a fascination with a woman who has one of the world's most peculiar jobs, who sells to strangers something most Americans still feel inhibited about sharing with intimates.

In popular imagination, the prostitute is seen as attractive, provocative, an expert in the "mysteries" of sex. (It is a common thing for inexperienced girls to envy her this knowledge.) She understands men. She is more "honest," less hypocritical than other women. She is a rebel, a sexual guerrilla, fighting for freedom. She is wise in the ways of the world, a sibyl of sorts. She makes a great deal of money, and spends it as profligately as she earns it. As evidence of the powerful pull of her role, many respectable women have fantasies of being a prostitute.

Now, in *The Lively Commerce*, Charles Winick and Paul M. Kinsie offer us a less subjective picture. They are well qualified to do this. Winick is professor of sociology at City College and Kinsie has been a prostitution investigator for more than fifty years. Both have worked for the American Social Health Association and have had access to its extensive files. The first full-scale study of prostitution in half a century, their book draws on more than two thousand interviews with prostitutes, their associates and clients, with judges, probation officers and others. They made a ten-year study of this nationwide industry that grosses more than a billion dollars a year and involves between 100,000 and 500,000 women.

Here is what they found: Most prostitutes are physically unattractive; some of them have flagrant physical defects. In the last three decades, many prostitutes apprehended by the police tend to be overweight and short, with poor teeth, minor blemishes and untidy hair. Some of them are tattooed with legends like "Keep off the grass" and "Admission 50c." Far from understanding men, they are usually indifferent to them, regarding them simply as "trade." Rarely are they rebels in any conscious or deliberate sense; most are unaware of their real motives in choosing "the life." (Foremost among their reasons is an urge to mock parental love.) In contrast to the dramatic coloration they are given on stage, in films or novels, the majority have relatively uninflected personalities. In describing her work, a typical prostitute said that it was "a little more boring" than her former job as a file clerk. It is about equally well paid: at three $10 "tricks" a day, six days a week, the average prostitute may gross about $9,300 per year and net from $5,000 to $6,000.

Their suicide rate indicates a high degree of alienation and unhappiness. Seventy-five percent of a sampling of call girls had attempted suicide, and fifteen percent of all suicides brought to public hospitals are prostitutes. Though "baby pros" between twelve and sixteen are increasing in number, the median age for the life is twenty-five to forty. While folklore has them going directly from defloration to the trade, there is usually a two-year gap. Their three tricks a day may reflect the declining vigor of the working class: in the nineteen twenties and thirties, prostitutes averaged between fifteen and thirty. Though it is difficult for them to make a living at it, male homosexual prostitutes are increasing. In 1967, when San Francisco police arrested thirty-three streetwalkers in one night, twelve of these turned out to be men in "drag." The experience of European agencies indicates that female prostitutes have a thirty-three to seventy-five percent chance for resocialization, when properly treated.

If the prostitute fails to live up to her billing, the pimp comes off even worse. An occupational disease of the prostitute, the pimp is her punisher or flatterer, her superior or inferior, as the occasion demands. He may be her lover, or he may be impotent. Helping her feel human, spying out the land, dealing with drunks, supplying drugs, breaking in new girls—these are just a few of his odd jobs. The madam—that larger-than-life personality—is almost as obsolete as the piano player, since most girls are entrepreneurs now and the brothel is only a nostalgic memory.

Enter the client. Drunkenness, curiosity, restlessness, bravado, "perverse" desires, or a need for reassurance may have brought him here. In less than fifteen minutes, he must find whatever it is he is seeking; if he takes longer, he may be handed his money and his hat, which may be all he has removed. His first preference is fellatio, but he may also fancy himself a "lover"—an unpopular type who kisses, dawdles and tries to arouse his partner with "marriage manual" techniques. He probably paid for his sex because he can't fuse the tender and the sensual in his feelings, and here he can forget about tenderness. Afterwards, however, he may become more human and talk about his wife and children until his bedmate turns him off. Once in a while, he'll cry. Almost always, his relation to the prostitute is more complex than he supposes. She does not "drain off" his antisocial impulses for very long: statistics show that when prostitution declines, crime does too.

The Lively Commerce comes at a good time. Today, when Americans seem almost obsessed with improving their sexual technique, with increasing their physical sensitivity, with frankness and plain speaking about sex—today it is useful to be reminded just how insignificant and unsatisfying the physical act can be without some sort of metaphysical support. It helps to restore some of Homo sapiens's emotional prestige to show how very symbolic sex actually is—even when bought from a stranger for ten dollars and consummated in as many minutes.

Teaching vs. Preaching Poetry

Poetry is almost as popular as pot with the young these days. In the spring of 1969, at the Poetry Festival sponsored by Lehigh's School of Education, more than a thousand people participated. Out of this Woodstock of poetry came the greater part of this book—eleven essays by ten poets and/or teachers who conducted workshops at "inner city" elementary or high schools.

The festival seems to have created an infectious atmosphere, for there is a surprising unanimity in these pieces. Almost all of them might be described as militant in their approach to poetry. Liberation is the dominant motif and poetry is most often defined by what it is not. A litany of admonitory "cannots" and "must nots" is addressed to the reader, as if all our usual expectations must be swept away before poetry—as unspoiled as the wild boy of Averon—can appear.

Shakespeare is irrelevant; LeRoi Jones is not. Relevance derives not from the human condition, but from conditions as we know them in the parlance of politics. Myra Cohn Livingston, for example, wants to "throw out" the poetry that children cannot "relate" to at first sight. Poetry, we are told, must be written with the heart, not the head. It must not pander to the beautiful. To the inner-city child, form or technique in poetry is akin to oppression. To defy all such rules is one of his civil rights.

Perhaps there should be an asterisk after the statement by Nancy Larrick, the editor, that there is an incredible eruption of poetic activity among kids today, because what she and her collaborators have done is to redefine poetry to include just about anything written down on paper in irregular lines. While it is undoubtedly a good thing to democratize poetry and rescue it from the snobbery of élitism, there is a difference between democracy and anarchy, between turning kids on and turning them loose. These authors appear to be overreacting. In our poetry, as in our politics, we may be doomed to progress mainly in pendulum swings.

One would think that no one had ever expressed any emotion in poetry before, that beauty was beyond the reach of ordinary people, something sold only in Tiffany's. Though many observers have found ghetto children to be quick-witted and alert to nuances, the authors of some of these essays equate poverty with inarticulateness, verbal deficiency and unresponsiveness. As a result, they tend to assume a heavy solicitousness that makes their pupils self-conscious and imposes a pattern on their thinking as well. Shakespeare has been expunged, but the social worker has not. "Who knows from whence I came?/Who knows my name?" ". . . war war/why do God's children fight among each other/like animals . . ." This is not the natural voice of children.

Just as people are said to be in love with love, some of the writers in this book seem to be more in love with the idea of children writing poetry than with poetry itself. Claudia Lewis is disproportionately delighted by a three-year-old who, on first seeing a bunch of blue grapes, exclaimed: "Oh, blueberries on the cob!"

Karla Kushkin is an exception to the evangelical tone of the majority. She is relaxed, undogmatic and in tune with the children, both in her teaching and in her own poetry. Eve Merriam, after squandering several pages on a rather forced analysis of one of her poems, says some interesting things about the ways in which language is undersold in supermarkets and redeemed in the mouths of children. The stereotypical productions of June Jordan's pupils do not support her assertion that "poetry poses an urgent liberation for all children."

"I cultivate my hysteria," Charles Baudelaire said, and this is how Warren Doty and Samuel Robinson approach their pupils —but with very dissimilar results. One of their teenage poets must have John Coltrane blowing and incense burning before he can recite his work. But with all this atmospheric encouragement, he can come up with nothing better than this:

> *Be Be Be Be BeBe Be Be Be Bum . . .*
> *You whiiiite Deeeviiil . . .*
> *You existing projection of artificial*
> *everything, etc.*

One wonders whether all attempts at education need to sound quite so remedial. In his recent *Wishes, Lies and Dreams*, Kenneth Koch, for example, managed to get children from similar backgrounds to write fresh poems without making a Federal case out of it. And it would be reassuring, for a change, to see some of these teachers asking students to rise to poetry, instead of invariably demanding that poetry come down to them.

Still, it is pleasant to see so many people even thinking about poetry, however they define it. And one certainly agrees with these writers that poetry ought to be freed from pedantry. However, to keep from losing not only our perspective but our sense of humor, it ought to be pointed out that there is a pedantry of permissiveness too.

The Writer Vincent Van Gogh

Never has a great painter confided to us so much of what he thought and felt about his work—or expressed it so well—as Van Gogh did. He was such an isolated man that his contact with the world was mainly through letters. He wrote something like eight hundred of them in nine years—to his brother and a few friends—detailing what he was trying to do, how he went about it and what he himself thought of the results. Often in the letters it is as if he is talking to himself while he works or sets up his easel before his subject. Though in some artists this would be principally of technical interest, Van Gogh's relation to his work was so personal—so full of authentic joy and pain—that his "Diary" ought to rank among the most moving memoirs or autobiographies of all time.

Since he worked largely alone, Van Gogh discovered many of the innovations of modern art for himself—unlike those Parisian painters of his time who borrowed constantly from one another. He saw, for example, that it is necessary "not to draw a *hand*, but the *gesture*, not a mathematically correct head, but the general *expression*." After trying formal training in an art school, he wrote: "The figures in the pictures of the Old Masters do not *work*. To draw a peasant's figure in action . . . is the very core of modern art."

It is a miracle that Van Gogh ever found the strength to hold his personality together as long as he did, much less to turn out almost nine hundred paintings and hundreds of drawings. He was sustained by a religious love for people and nature—not a sentimental response, but a perception so intense that it electrified and exalted him. In spite of his suffering and lack of recognition or reward, he said: "I have walked this earth for thirty years, and, out of gratitude, want to leave some souvenir."

Many of his letters describe how something or someone he has seen—a face or a gesture, a combination of colors and shapes—fills him with a genuine zeal to get them on canvas. Yet he is not content to take things simply as they come: almost always, he adds something of his own to carry the picture still further. In a superb painting of giant green beech trunks on a reddish stretch of ground, he has placed a girl in a white dress, as a comment on the majesty and the riotous colorfulness of nature.

In spite of his poor health, he stayed out all night, his hatband stuck all over with candles, to paint the stars. No one has ever painted stars as he has. Sometimes they are of an overwhelming but benevolent brilliance, dazzling us with what would have to be called a heavenly light. At other times, they are like bombs or fireballs, meteors hurtling toward us, third-degree lamps in our faces. Even the serenity of a wheat field can become threatening in his paintings. He describes one as "a mood of almost too much calmness," time and motion come to a stop, somewhere between catatonia and Judgment Day. One feels that it is not overdramatic to say that only a man threatened by insanity could have painted that endless corridor with its suffocating arches at the hospital at Saint-Rémy and its single haunted figure disappearing into an unseen room. Even Van Gogh's good friend, Dr. Gachet, is portrayed with "the heartbroken expression of our time."

Some of the letters quoted in the book refer to the artist's family life and his inability to get along with his father, who was a minister. His father saw Vincent's uncontrollable intensity as that of "a big rough dog with wet paws. *And he barks so loud!*" Van Gogh himself felt some of the truth of his father's aversion: "Like one of the old lepers, one would like to call from afar to people: don't come too near me, for intercourse with me brings you sorrow and loss." With typical self-deprecation, he said he wanted only to show "what is in the heart of such an eccentric, a nobody." In a more positive mood, he wrote: "There may be a great fire in our soul, yet no one ever comes to warm himself at it."

There is hardly another painter in the world who has been so overexposed and sentimentally vulgarized as Van Gogh, yet the editor of this book, Jan Hulsker, more than justifies still another study by the brilliant device of juxtaposing the works and the artist's own comments on them. A good example is "Night Cafe," of which the painter says: "I have tried to express the idea that the cafe is a place where one can ruin oneself, go mad or commit a crime . . . I have tried to express it . . . by soft Louis XV green and malachite, contrasting with yellow-green and harsh blue-greens, and all this in an atmosphere like a devil's furnace, of pale sulphur."

One of the strangest landscapes he ever painted is almost all foreground, with a road running along the left edge and top of the canvas, as if it were trying to wriggle out of the picture. Of this work, he says: "Yes, I must try to get out of here, but where to go?" It is a pity Mr. Hulsker did not include more of Van Gogh's forty self-portraits, which offer a remarkable record of his spiritual evolution. Or his monumental "Wheatfield with Crows," in which an angry deep blue sky presses down on the painter, the horizon threatens to engulf him, all the roads lead nowhere, and the crows float like vultures.

Yet Mr. Hulsker ought to be congratulated for what he has accomplished in this "diary." Just as the paintings in Florence had to be restored after the terrible flood damage there, so Van Gogh—the man and his work—needed to be reclaimed from the flood of absurd publicity that has so long mocked him.

Disguising the Naked Tr

The naked truth plays a very small part in our lives, according to Bernard Rudofsky, particularly in the case of the human body. If we were to take the body as evidence, the human condition would seem to be in bad shape. Eternally bored or dissatisfied with our "divine" image, we are constantly trying to give it an illusion of otherness. We pinch, paint, punish, deform and distort it in the hope of burying a million years' monotony. We "frame" it in psychological, philosophical and religious ambiances, just as some expensive bordellos offer rooms with special effects for jaded tastes. The only animal condemned to be sexually attractive at all times, man is always desperately devising means.

While sensitivity therapists labor to restore our appreciation of touch or smell, fashion has no audience but the voyeur, a notorious eccentric. Rational fashion is a contradiction in terms, as much as rational desire or rational love. Appreciating a woman's dress is almost as complicated as interpreting her dreams. If man in the last few centuries was the plain John of fashion, it was only because it was he who had to be attracted and ensnared into marriage. In exchange for her perpetual novelty, he offered woman permanence. Now that this arrangement is breaking down—under the impact of homosexuality and women's liberation—he is once again becoming the peacock prefigured in nature and echoed in the beribboned courtier of the seventeenth and eighteenth centuries.

No mean voyeur himself, Mr. Rudofsky has traced the history, here and in other cultures, of that much-erased palimpsest, the human body. He shows us the monobosom of the Gibson girl, the steatopygous bustle, the legless and footless female of most of American history, and the ironing board image of the flapper, who had to raise her skirts to compensate for the flattening of her chest and rear. In *The Unfashionable Human Body*, he quotes a variety of thinkers on the vagaries of fashion. Anatole France claims that it tells him more about a particular time

161

than all the philosophers, novelists, prophets and scholars. Herbert Spencer says that "the consciousness of being perfectly dressed may bestow a peace such as religion cannot give." The corset, according to Thorstein Veblen, advertised woman's expensive infirmity, her unfitness for work, making her an example of conspicuous waste, a useless toy in all but the erotic sense, which only the leisure class could afford. Freud comes off rather poorly. Discussing the function of clothes in concealing sex, he says: "The genitals themselves have not undergone the development of the rest of the human form in the direction of beauty."

The Chinese crippled his wife's foot not only because the tiny Cinderella foot was considered beautiful, but because he believed it led to a compensatory development of more important parts. He found her inevitably mincing gait sexually titillating, as well. Walking in America may be a lost art. Our women were militant in their marching stride long before the freedom marches of their politics. No one in the world walks as unenticingly as the American woman. Throwing away her girdle has not given her the "vibrato" walk of the primitive woman—"that brave vibration each way free"—it has only lengthened her stride and reduced her buttocks to the role of a cumbersome cargo. The same is true of the no-bra look: when the bosom is overlarge, it is a defiance more than a provocation, flung in our faces, so to speak. When it is too small, it is a defiance of another sort: a refusal to admit the relevance of female sex appeal.

The excesses of men's clothes in recent history were confined to a utilitarian redundancy. Thirty years ago, a fully dressed man was equipped with seventy or more buttons and about two dozen pockets, most of them useless. The well-dressed man's trousers were wrinkle-proof, never betraying any sign of that which they concealed. When an artist attempted to give a classical touch to a portrait of Washington—showing him bare-chested and swathed below the waist in drapery—the public was scandalized. Austerity and abstraction went even further in the design of monuments to Franklin D. Roosevelt and John F. Kennedy: instead of portrait sculptures, they were represented by "those obstacle courses of cement and stone slabs commonly referred to as playground sculpture."

Speculating on the future of fashion, Mr. Rudofsky finds no

flagging in our invention. He cites a bridal gown by the artist Christo, in which the bride's train—"perhaps the weightiest metaphor on record"—consists of an enormous package made up of four hundred square feet of white satin, attached to her by a harness of silk ropes. How you interpret it depends on where you stand. It may represent woman as a beast of burden; a mystery as yet unwrapped; a bringer of gifts or of heavy responsibilities. Perhaps it would be simpler—and safer—to say that she is, and always will be, a metaphor that passeth understanding.

The Ultimate Souvenir

"My notion of sex, call me old fashioned, was a satisfying and slightly masked and moist surprise, unhurried, private, imaginative, and inexpensive, as close to passion as possible; neither business-like nor overcoy, maintaining the illusion of desire with groans of proof, celebrating fantasy, a happy act the price kept in perspective: give and take, no lies about love." This is Jack Flowers speaking, the hero of Paul Theroux's *Saint Jack* and the most popular pimp in Singapore. Though his is, at best, a despised calling, Jack sees himself as a sort of museum guide to Oriental eroticism, steering his innocents abroad in the direction of their hearts' delight.

Jack is able to read his clients' "obscure and desperate verbal symbols," for as he well knows, "their passions were guesses." When these guesses teeter on the brink of realization, the startled adventurer often panics at his own extravagance—but Jack reassures them, his bulky, deliberately corny, middle-aged Americanism acting as a guarantee of sanity. He believes in what he is doing. In his view, he is helping these travelers to "participate in a cultural secret," to take home "the ultimate souvenir" from this fabled city.

Like the hero of Mr. Theroux's *Jungle Lovers*—a brilliant novel of Africa—Jack is a missionary manqué. Kindness, gentleness, camaraderie, dependability—these and a sort of imaginative elasticity—are Jack's idea of the cardinal virtues. Nor is his job easy. As he sits in the lobby of a hotel waiting for old Mr. Gunstone to complete his assignation, Jack worries about his client's heart, for it has reached that stage in which the pleasure principle and the death instinct are also locked in a passionate embrace. There are risks: when Jack, a foreigner, dares to open his own brothel in Singapore, it is burned down by local gangsters and both Jack's forearms are tattooed with obscenities as a punishment. In a nifty bit of symbolism, he has flowers and a crucifix superimposed on them by another tattooist so that they are almost, but not quite, obliterated.

At first, Mr. Theroux doesn't seem to know what to do
with Jack. He is rather like an odd, slightly disreputable uncle
the author hasn't seen in years and who drops in on him unex-
pectedly. You can see that he's fond of Jack, but he can't figure
him. It is only belatedly, at the end of the book, that Jack
emerges as something more than an amiable sidekick. Meanwhile, however, we are held by a series of brilliant episodes and
by Mr. Theroux's virtuosity in taking us inside the life of a
legendary city.

Just as *Jungle Lovers* was based on five years in Africa, *Saint
Jack* is verified by three years the author spent in Singapore as
lecturer in seventeenth-century drama. His descriptions of a
Chinese family, seen through the iron bars of a window after
supper, husband and wife facing each other impassively across
the empty table under the merciless unshaded bulb, or of an old
man in front of a mirror scraping his tongue with a stick, could
only come from restless backstreet prowling.

There is a fine passage in which a visiting accountant from
Hong Kong dies in Jack's favorite bar. Though neither he nor
any of the other regulars cares for the accountant, they feel
obliged to see him through his funeral because he is an Occiden-
tal. At the cemetery, Jack and his other middle-aged cronies are
outraged by a Chinese family throwing firecrackers into the open
grave of their deceased. A cemetery, to the Westerners, is a muf-
fled place, where one tiptoes in the presence of death, but as one
of Jack's Malay girls who has come along explains, the firecrackers are to "amaze the gods" and make them take notice. It falls to
Jack to telephone the widow in Hong Kong. After a conference
in the bar with the others, he agrees that it would be better to
change the locale of the accountant's death. "Yesterday I was with
your husband at the Botanical Gardens," Jack begins. "It was a
beautiful day . . ."

In a model exercise of irony, Jack sees through a skin flick,
which a client requests, to the reality behind it. The fact that the
man is wearing workmen's shoes, together with his muscled arms
and broad shoulders, indicates that he is a laborer. He must have
lost his job to have agreed to do a blue movie: this is confirmed
as he undresses further to reveal a recent appendicitis scar. The
half-empty bottle on the mantelpiece shows that he had to be
partly drunk before he could perform. He keeps his socks on; it

must have been cold in the apartment where the film was made. Judging from his partner's breasts, she has borne more than one child. From the way she sits on the edge of the sofa, you can tell that it was not her apartment. A glass ashtray full of cigarette butts suggests nervous talk, one or both having to be reconvinced at the last moment.

At fifty-three, Jack is beginning to worry. His pimping and his job at a Chinese ship chandler's are just enough to keep a cigar in his mouth. Because looking into his future is like staring into an abyss—Nietzsche's abyss that stares back—Jack defends himself with reveries of being bequeathed a fortune by a grateful friend or client. His big chance, however, turns out to be less benign. He is offered $16,000 to obtain compromising photographs of a visiting American general in order to discredit both him and the war effort in Vietnam. Jack accepts, hires a photographer and a bugging expert, and puts them to work.

The general has been described as a scoundrel, but in the pictures and sound track he emerges as Jack's kind of scoundrel, a sentimentalist after his own heart. Jack reneges on the deal, choosing his peculiar integrity over a security that would be comfortless without it. It's not so much a noble gesture on his part as a simple tropism. He's too old to change his style of pimping, to go in for another form of prostitution. And so we leave "Saint Jack," sorry to see him go, wishing him luck in his age, hoping he dies before he decays. In the Botanical Gardens, on a beautiful day.

The Man Behind the Myth

Samuel Johnson originally came down to me as a kind of larger-than-life father figure, with his legendary learning raised like a schoolmaster's cane to correct a childish world. Though I, too, admired his *Dictionary*, his delightfully wrong-headed *Lives of the Poets* and his countless celebrated apothegms, I agree with Macaulay that he translated the English language into a "Johnsonese" dialect whose now deflated orotundities still disfigure public speaking and other such pious utterances.

I think Hippolyte Taine was right when he said that Johnson's truths were sometimes a little "too true," and I'm sure Johnson's good friend Joshua Reynolds could be believed when he complained that the Doctor "entertained prejudices on a very slight foundation" and treated "the most light and airy dispute . . . as if his whole reputation depended upon the victory of the minute."

All too often, the books I've read about him have proffered me Johnson rampant, as it were, beyond rebuttal, a rhetorical bully who, as Horace Walpole put it, thought that what he had read was an excuse for everything he said. If Johnson had not been such a wit, he would have been the very quintessence of a bore, going as far as to pontificate, on one occasion, on the semantic aptness of calling a currently fashionable color "stifled sigh."

Though I loved Johnson when he refused as "unfit for a gentleman" the cold sheep's head offered him for breakfast by a rich but stingy host, and when he became so carried away with the refining of his ironies in his famous letter to a patron that he quite forgot Lord Chesterfield's occasional kindnesses . . . though I felt the rightness, for *him*, of his strictures on the metaphysical poets—"Forced thoughts and rugged metres"—Samuel Johnson was rarely, in the books I came across, a warm or lovable figure.

His general unassailability deprived him of humanity, and his pride of pathos. He was not a man, but a machine for making aphorisms and for gold-plating prejudices. He was a giant conversational jock who had to win, to rattle the coffeehouse windows. And worst of all, as far as I could see, his vices were all of the cold variety.

Of course, this impression is contradicted in occasional passages in the ten volumes of the "Yale Editions of the Private Papers of James Boswell," in *Thraliana: The Diary of Mrs. Hester Lynch Thrale*, and in paragraphs here and there of other eighteenth-century memoirs—but the *image* has persisted. And now Peter Quennell gently lays it to rest in *Samuel Johnson: His Friends and Enemies*.

Because the other Johnson is all too familiar, Mr. Quennell concentrates on the great man's foibles and failings. And if the book is to be believed, they were proportionate to his triumphs. While most of us have imagined Johnson as ugly in a majestic way, his contemporaries would say, "Nay, not so!" A number of his admirers were startled at first sight of him. A traveling Irish clergyman who had come expressly to London to see Johnson recorded his impressions: Johnson, he wrote, had "the aspect of an idiot, without the faintest ray of sense gleaming from any one feature—with the most awkward garb, an unpowdered gray wig, on one side only of his head—he is forever dancing the devil's jig, and sometimes he makes the most driveling effort to whistle some thought in his awkward paroxysms." Other contemporary witnesses confirm the fact that Johnson had a whole complex of tics that kept him jerking, kicking and flailing about in his chair.

The Doctor suffered terribly from a dread of loneliness and during the years he lived as a sort of writer in residence with the Thrales, Mrs. Thrale often would have to sit up most of the night with him, as if with a sick or frightened child. Though at twenty-six Johnson married a woman of forty-six and remained happy with her until she died seventeen years later, no one but her husband himself could even conjecture what he saw in her. Johnson's intimates vied with one another in incredulity at this "love marriage."

When he had been a widower for some time, he apparently fell in love with Mrs. Thrale. And though his moral code would not allow him to contemplate the idea of adultery, that good lady's diary suggests that he found a curious way around his scruples. Johnson always felt that he might go—or was going—mad and he insisted to Mrs. Thrale, as his only confidante on this subject, that sternness was the only corrective for his condition. If one can decode the euphemism of her style, she seemed to have hinted that he forced her to tie him to the bedpost and beat him.

Mr. Quennell has quite a bit to say about the women Johnson admired, and in this connection we get a highly interesting picture of the famous "bluestockings" of the period: Hannah More, Fanny Burney, Elizabeth Carter, Mrs. Chapone, Mrs. Desey and others. Considering their talents, these ladies' innovations were surprisingly modest.

Despite the fact that he feared death for most of his adult life, Johnson met it with exemplary bravery. One of his last remarks is peculiarly touching in its uncharacteristic simplicity. When a friend offered him a new pillow, he said: "That will do,—all that a pillow can do." He was in great pain, yet he refused all opiates —it was typical of the eighteenth century's most famous voice of reason that he was "anxious to confront his Maker with a perfectly unclouded vision."

Absurdity with a Small 'a'?

When is absurdity Absurd, and when is it simply free association? This was one of the questions that nagged at me as I picked my way through Donald Barthelme's latest volume of short stories, *Sadness*. I use the word "picked" advisedly, because that, it seems, is what one has to do with this book. A felicitous sentence here, a good but only partly realized idea there, a few apt, antic word choices now and then: it's rather like going to a Chinese restaurant and eating nothing but appetizers.

A reviewer recently referred to what he called the "so what?" factor in judging short stories. If the story doesn't answer the question, it has not succeeded—even if it has not exactly failed either. Most of Mr. Barthelme's stories here leave me with a similar question, which I would put as "and then . . .?" The story, if it is a story, hovers precariously amid its elements without pulling them together, so that all I can feel is the *imminence* of a story, or the possibility of one. I'm left holding a bundle of small packages that threaten to slip out of my grasp.

A philosophical conviction that man's existential situation is absurd does not mean that one need only write down a few *non sequitur*s to create a Literature of the Absurd. It must still be *literature*, which means that it has to hold together in some way that moves us. Otherwise, we are faced with nothing but the Imitative Fallacy, someone holding a dull mirror up to the unnaturalness of things.

In some of his earlier stories, Donald Barthelme was a literary man, a *writer* to a very high degree. His story "The Balloon" is a masterpiece of its kind, a wittier, updated version of Kafka, livelier and less claustrophobically centripetal than many of the master's, richer in language and free of the stylistic severity Kafka imposed on himself. The balloon, which suddenly appeared and hovered over a large section of Manhattan, was a splendid symbol: preposterous, but full, at the same time, of a haunting suggestiveness. Its ambiguities were rich enough to start an exegetical gold rush. The story moved in and out of reality—touched ground and took flight again—with hypnotic ease. We *recognized* it as something that spoke to us, that was charged not only with anxiety, but with a kind of exhilaration as well.

In *Sadness*, the author frequently seems to be merely doodling. More and more I found myself asking, "Why that particular word or image and not something else?" Something equally arbitrary or dislocated, the way a bathtub seems dislocated in a junkyard. The incongruities are predictable; the poking around in dictionaries or library stacks, the lists and scraps of eccentric information, strike one as self-conscious. It is the opposite of Picasso's happy formulation: "I do not seek—I find."

In place of the metaphysical wit of "The Balloon," Mr. Barthelme offers us here a good deal of rather ordinary clowning. Sometimes even he seems out of sorts with his approach to writing. The first story, "Critique de la Vie Quotidienne," comes very close to being cranky. The husband and wife say sardonic, even sour, things to each other and the child comes up on cue with the requisite unchildlike remarks. Gilbert Rogin, who also writes for *The New Yorker*, does this sort of thing better.

Another story, about a city composed entirely of churches, stops right there. Once you've seen the churches lined up on both sides of the street, that's about it, except for a little patter by one of the real estate agents. "Träumerei" has no special virtue other than a species of run-on virtuosity, like a drawing made without the artist's lifting his pen off the paper. "The Genius" lacks the genius of invention and "Perpetua" is just another perpetually discontented divorcee. "The Party" is almost polite, except for the presence of King Kong among the guests. "A Film" is a virtual inventory of missed opportunities. "The Catechist" tempts us to catechize the author. "Subpoena" has one passable, penultimate sentence. "Departures" never goes anywhere. "The Rise of Capitalism" is nothing but literary *laissez-faire*. "The Flight of Pigeons from the Palace" is a bit better. It has pictures, at least, some nice wordplay and an interesting idea: a show that includes among other things graverobbers and a "new volcano . . . just placed under contract." A story about Paul Klee in the German army chins itself up to a certain charm.

"The Temptation of St. Anthony" is the most nearly realized piece in the book. The saint has come in from the desert to live in a small city, where ordinary life is his temptation. But even here, we feel that the author—the Barthelme we used to admire —could have done more with a juicy theme like that. "Daumier," the longest of the stories, is about a man who relaxes from the demands of the self by inventing surrogate selves, who have all sorts of adventures. The only thing I liked about it was the herd of 1,500 *au pair* girls they were driving to market.

The difficulty in contemporary stories of the Absurd seems to be in developing some sort of criteria: When do non-narrative images cohere, and when don't they? How can you tell whether irrelevance is "inspired" or simply irrelevant? How close must you come to an idea or an institution in order to pick its pocket? How many ellipses will the ideal reader absorb? And so on. Mr. Barthelme is so talented that, in the beginning, he just wrote his way right through such considerations. He was one of the best broken-field runners around. But if he can't do this any more, he'll have to work out some other strategy. He may even have to start *thinking* about his stories, like Bellow, Malamud, Updike and guys like that.

Redeeming a Chaos of Ugliness

At a certain stage of puberty, I reached a point where I was ashamed to go out in public with my parents. Overnight, I had become a man of the world to whom they appeared hopelessly awkward and provincial. I even went so far as to imagine people staring at us, startled by our incongruity. This is precisely the sort of vanity and pretension that most American intellectuals feel toward their parent country. Oh, the incredible homeliness —worse than ugliness, which at least has character—of its city streets, its neighborhoods haunting as nightmares, its eating places where a stranger studiously ignores another stranger over Formica, its drugstores piled high with patent medicines for insomnia and despair. Could anything be more damning than a motel, where every detail, every plastic flower, desecrates the idea of home? What is a gas station but an architectural conspiracy to unnerve the motorist? Think of all the small towns forgotten between the city and the frontier, like rubbish thrown from the windows of a speeding train. Imagine the lives of the people in them, as undimensional as clothes hung on a line.

This is the America Edward Hopper (1882–1967) chose to immortalize in his art. To accept him and appreciate him, you must first make your peace with your country, its history and your own. You have to find the beauty in his pictures against your will. You have to stop condescending, give up your prejudices as you would empty your pockets to a beggar whose deformity disgusts you.

Hopper knew all this; he realized what he had taken on. Returning from a visit to France, he found the United States "a chaos of ugliness," which took him ten years to sort out. Only then was he able to see what he describes as "our native architecture with its hideous beauty, its fantastic roofs, pseudo-Gothic, French Mansard, Colonial, mongrel or what not, with eye-searing color or delicate harmonies of fading paint, shouldering one another along interminable streets that taper off into swamps or dump heaps . . ."

More eloquently than anyone else, he captured "The peculiar melancholy of architectural pretension that is no longer fashionable . . ." Just when railroads were beginning to die of our impatience, he painted them as symbols of a terrible lust for mobility, for traveling to a new place indistinguishable from the old, for repeating the irrelevant drama of arrival and departure. One of the first to recognize the pictorial possibilities of a modern city, he rejected the spectacular and concentrated on the ordinary, which, as he said in writing of Charles Burchfield, could be made "epic and universal."

In stark contrast to their swarming character today, his city streets are almost empty—yet the loneliness is not so much of individuals as of settings, as if he was saying that it is not man himself, but the world he has inadvertently made, that separates him from those he seeks. His people are not unwilling; it is simply that their cities deny them the opportunity of one another. In one of his most brooding pictures—"Approaching a City"— we enter at the very place where the train goes underground between high walls; we are swallowed by forms against which we are only so many graffiti.

One of Hopper's favorite subjects is a nude woman in a bleak room standing before a window. Sometimes a night breeze stirs the curtains, or sometimes the woman is pierced by a shaft of sunlight, the kind of light D. H. Lawrence would have thrown on her. We wonder what it is they are waiting for, hoping for, sniffing the breeze like does, opening like flowers to the sun. Perhaps they are waiting for themselves—the self we hear so much about today. The suggestion is strengthened by Hopper. When he was asked about a painting in which there was no woman, only an empty room and a tongue of sunlight searching out the corners, he said: "What am I after in it? I'm after *me*."

In his *Edward Hopper*, Lloyd Goodrich shows him to be almost exclusively interested in the beauty that was hidden below the surface, that could be discovered only through sympathy. The first time he went to the Southwest, he could not paint it because it was already there. His work is rarely pretty in a merely plastic way; there is a bit of the primitive in him that makes him awkward and heavy-handed, given to lumps of homogeneity with little sensual appeal in the pigments. But together with a vision that "liberates subjects from the taboos of their time," there is in him a sense of rueful solidity, of a space and a significance that radiate outward from the canvas.

And, as Mr. Goodrich points out, he is a master of light. Unlike the impressionists who used light to break up forms, Hopper used it to define and model them, to both reveal and isolate his figures. His handling of light was learned from cubism without being tyrannized by it. Though his paintings tend to be static and horizontal, these horizontals, as Alfred Barr put it, "are like the edge of a stage beyond which drama unfolds."

A house, tall, gaunt and excruciatingly stable, stands by a railroad track—its antithesis. In "Sunday," a man sits, arms folded, on the curb, in the enormous vacuum left behind by God. In one of the world's most spectacularly unassuming paintings, Hopper peers beneath a sort of chute to see the side of an old box factory in Gloucester. His captains' houses, all on treeless promontories, are places where sea-loving men end their lives like tropical fish in bowls. An empty barbershop at night is a dark prophecy of the death of that genial institution.

"A nation's art is greatest," Hopper says, "when it most reflects the character of its people." If you read this book, you may not recognize yourself at first, but if you stick at it, Hopper's light may fall on and illuminate you too.

Paris at Its Most Parisian

James Joyce's *Ulysses,* which outraged priggish Gertrude Stein, "fell upon us like a gift of tongues," says Janet Flanner in *Paris Was Yesterday: 1925–1939.* Ezra Pound's learning was "like stony chips whacked off with *hauteur* from the old statuary of the scholarly mind." "Claude Monet, first Impressionist, outlived all of his intellectual generation except Georges Clemenceau, in whose presence he died, as if to use all his friendly contemporaries to the bitter end." He "suffered the ignominy of dying appreciated."

"A young tourist named Captain Charles Lindbergh landed his plane, the Spirit of St. Louis, at Le Bourget." The next morning the event was celebrated in a Paris newspaper by a thirteen-stanza poem, written by young Maurice Rostand at the rate of a minute a line. Jean Cocteau's novel *Les Enfants Terribles* is "a little desert of subtle suffering dotted with stiff events and cactus-like descriptions." In her later years, Isadora Duncan's dancing changed: "As if the movements of dancing had become too redundant for her spirit, she had saved from dancing only its shape." A few years' fame had altered Josephine Baker too: "On that lovely animal visage lies now a sad look, not of captivity, but of dawning intelligence." The American actress Mae West "has elicited praise from Paris that would give her a liberal education if she traced it all down."

Most of this material is taken from Miss Flanner's "Letter from Paris" in *The New Yorker,* written under the name "Genêt." She was, and is, the inevitable person for the job. Nobody has a sharper eye, or a more sophisticated tolerance, for the absurdities that help to make the French such fascinating people. But, unlike so many talented satirists, she *appreciates* her subject too. As acute as it is amusing, her book is a bouquet of epiphanies.

France, she informs us, has seven classes of funerals, not including the three gradations in first class. Despite the fact that Anatole France's in 1924 was "one of the biggest, most pretentious spectacles modern Paris has ever seen," the first anniversary of his death was absolutely ignored, which seems to imply that the French enjoyed his passing more than his books. The Rothschilds are described as "a wildly conservative family." After she died, Sarah Bernhardt's peculiarly bleating voice was not heard again until Marshal Pétain came into power. The resemblance was remarkable.

"Fifteen thousand love letters written on the Isle of Jersey by poor Juliette Druot to Victor Hugo have just been sold for 18,000 francs." Since she was Hugo's mistress for a little less than twenty years, this averages out to something like two letters a day. After President Doumer was shot by an assassin in 1932, newspapers differed over his last words. The popular press preferred "Oh, là là!," while the graver dailies favored: "Is it possible?" Having been told by his aides that he had been struck by a taxi —possibly to spare him any bitter reflections—he was also reported to have said: "But what kind of chauffeur was it?" His perplexity may have arisen from the fact that he was killed at a charity book sale in the Maison Rothschild.

In defending Georges Rème, a thief who had already been convicted seventeen times of that crime, his advocate argued that his client was " 'a character in the best French tradition, on account of his elegance, his imagination and wit. In certain circumstances a man such as Rème has to be invented if he doesn't exist, because in sad periods he is one of those who help to amuse the masses . . .' " When two servant girls murdered and brutally dismembered their mistress and her daughter, they gave as their only reason the fact that the short-circuiting iron had blown out the fuse again. A pair of famous journalists covering the case— the Tharaud brothers—sympathized with them because, when the fuse blew, " 'as jewels of servants who don't like to lose their time they became irritated.' " " 'Many people,' " the brothers added, " 'still belong to early periods of society.' "

Paul Poiret, a great couturier and *bon vivant*, was born a bourgeois and educated in a Catholic lycée, but "nevertheless escaped with his personality." Louis Bromfield's Sunday luncheons were unique for the extraordinary centerpieces he created in perfect imitations of the flower paintings by Brueghel. Léon Blum, chief of France's Socialist party, had ranked for years "as

Parliament's master maneuverer; till now he has even been able to maneuver his party out of taking responsible power—no small feat."

Paris Was Yesterday closes with war clouds darkening the impressionist skies of Paris. Miss Flanner describes the situation with one succinct and one beautiful sentence: "The setup in Europe today is a struggle between the active and the passive . . . No one can know which side's dead men will win the war."

The Irrevocable Reputation

Contrary to popular opinion, a literary reputation is one of the hardest things in the world to lose. Once among the elect, a novelist is as difficult to impeach as a President. There are some who receive large advances on the strength of a string of failures because somewhere, early in their careers, they had a single success. An established novelist is usually given the benefit of the doubt, and since literature is such a doubtful business in any case, this is all the margin he needs. If a book is painfully bad, it can always be praised in words beginning with "r," such as ribald, rollicking, ravaging or riveting. In desperate cases, reviewers can fall back on zany, irreverent or outrageous. When a book seems to make no sense at all, to offer nothing recognizable to the reader, then it is sure to be described as bursting the confines of the conventional novel.

Which brings us to J. P. Donleavy's *The Onion Eaters*. For those who enjoyed Mr. Donleavy's first novel, *The Ginger Man*, and rode along with *The Beastly Beatitudes of Balthazar B.*, *The Saddest Summer of Samuel S.* and *Meet My Maker the Mad Molecule*, here is a real test of character. Clayton Claw Cleaver Clementine, the hero of the book, has not one but two claims to immortality: four alliterative names and an anatomical anomaly to boot. (It will not be identified in this review, a piece of fastidiousness that may well sell out the first printing of *The Onion Eaters*.)

As the book opens, Clementine's great-aunt has just given him a decrepit castle on the Irish coast. After buying a dog—"Hello woof woof. Big bow wow"—he goes to live in the castle. Shortly after his arrival, he is joined by a succession of "zany" characters, beginning with three scientists who specialize in the measurement and classification of random phenomena; who have, it almost goes without saying, developed an aphrodisiac; who propose to infest Ireland with poisonous snakes in order to stimulate the waning alertness of the population.

Erconwald, the leader of the scientists, speaks a polysyllabic pidgin English that defies regional, grammatical or stylistic interpretation. "I entrust you have breakfasted well, good person," he says, and "I would hope that you would agree to save him sufferment of further trepidation." Another character—an Irishman—gets off this sentence: "But when hasn't a man concerned with dignified manners not been enforced upon occasion to employ instant justice when some of your niceties had to become scarce." When a woman says, "You will forgive my husband and I," and Clementine's neighbor uses "extenuating" for "extending," we are not sure whether these mistakes are the author's or the characters'. Here, as everywhere else in the book, one guess is as good as another.

To call the action of this novel free association would be to flatter it. There is a boating party that runs into a storm and a rescue party that has to be rescued. A middle-aged woman named Veronica roller-skates into Clementine's bedroom in the middle of the night. She is nude and carrying a parasol, but her visit occasions nothing more than a sprained ankle. There is a bullfight in which several people are gored. A character called Mr. Lead Kindly Light sets off an explosive at a party. Clementine reminisces on his mother's death. A fire burns up the north wing of the castle. Various people sleep—or are prevented from sleeping—with one another. Someone confesses to a priest that he is homosexual and someone else is accused of "lascivious grass skirt dancing." A force of Irish insurgents occupies the castle.

By the end of the book, everything has happened and nothing has resulted. Any or all of the actions or incidents could be changed, or even reversed, without making the slightest difference. In 306 pages of straining for effect, there has not been a believable character, a meaningful incident, a good laugh, an interesting observation or an admirable sentence. Mr. Donleavy has burst the confines of the conventional novel, all right. In fact, he has managed this so successfully that perhaps *The Onion Eaters* should not be called a novel at all.

Platonic Affair with the Muse

"The function of the contemporary hero is to cancel the affirmations but to keep the setting of what once made him feel like a God." I found this one of the more interesting examples of Alfred Kazin's style in *Bright Book of Life*. The sentence itself has a heroic sweep; it is full of heuristic excitement. I felt a thrill of largeness, luxuriated in the vista offered to me. Yet I had an uneasy—not quite nagging—reservation because I sensed instinctively that the statement is too broad: Not all contemporary heroes can have the same function. Nor am I sure that they always cancel the affirmations (*which* affirmations, exactly?) or keep the setting. And isn't "feel like a God" overreaching just a bit?

In a way, it doesn't matter that all is not quite right with that statement—because it is a grand sentence. And it's close enough to the truth to enable the more adventurous among us to leap across. I certainly wouldn't expect a man to write about American fiction from 1940 to the present without becoming intoxicated to a degree, without occasionally succumbing to hyperbole.

I was pleased to discover that Mr. Kazin is not in the least parochial—as so many big-city intellectuals seem to be. A cosmopolitan Jewish liberal who grew up in Brooklyn, he shows a remarkable empathy for a writer like Faulkner, who, on the surface at least, is everything the author himself is not: a Southerner, a traditionalist, and "the last countryman in America." While I would have expected a politically oriented critic like the author to be primarily concerned with the present and the future, he surprised and charmed me with this: "Man's immortality, if he can be said to have one at all, reaches into the past, not into the future: It lies in a candid sense of history, not in the hope offered by orthodox Christianity." As an extension of this idea, he adds that "the South has produced writers as the Dark Ages produced saints."

Of Carson McCullers and Flannery O'Connor, two more Southern writers, Mr. Kazin shrewdly points out that the strongest character in their work is "nemesis, some primal wrongness . . ." In Miss O'Connor's work "the drama is made up of the short distance between the first intimation of conflict and the catastrophe." I found this idea provocative too: "Faulkner ceased to be an influence on Southern novelists when the South at last had its own worldliness to satirize."

Though we do not really need another essay on Hemingway, there is a good one in the book. It includes this deft line: "The desired clarity of the Lost Generation can now be seen as the last example of the pure tragic sense in our literature." This lust for clarity resulted in literature's being taught "as the Summa of all wisdom to people who still believed that criticism was a counter-culture." Mr. Kazin quotes the late Randall Jarrell's remark that, during this "age of criticism . . . certain married couples depended on a favorite literary critic as they would have depended on a liberal clergyman."

I didn't feel that *Bright Book of Life* added much to what I already knew about Norman Mailer—whose definement, as Hamlet said, suffers no perdition in our time—or James Jones, who is not a rich subject for speculation. Mr. Kazin is acute about John Cheever, though, when he describes his work as "a trying out of freedom in the shape of the extreme . . ." or as "the anecdote of a temporary crisis" rather than "the compression of an actual defeat." I thought this remark especially telling too: "My deepest feeling about Cheever is that his marvelous brightness is an effort to cheer himself up."

Mr. Kazin's chapter on "The Absurd as a Contemporary Style" begins brilliantly with the observation that the feeling of "meaninglessness" that underlines the Absurd is "a middle-class state of mind, a temporary fatigue, that represents the sometimes frolicsome despondency of intellectuals who see no great place for their moral influence . . ." I can't understand, though, why he chose to include Ralph Ellison in this chapter, and I found his reading of *Invisible Man* disappointingly narrow. He says, for example, that the book is "founded essentially on eloquence as redemption through art and as snare to the ambushed minority man . . ." In the same chapter it seemed to me that Mr.

Kazin underestimates Donald Barthelme and overestimates Thomas Pynchon: "The key to Pynchon's brilliantly dizzying narratives is the force of some hypothesis that is authentic to him but undisclosable to us." The author's comment on the late Lenny Bruce—"his sacred rage as a rebel too complex for the times"—perfectly captures for me the pretentiousness of some of the Absurd writers he goes on to praise.

While I felt that Mr. Kazin had straitjacketed Saul Bellow in morality and John Updike in style, his essay on Nabokov struck me as quite indulgent. It even goes so far as to mimic its subject in sentences like this: "Time is the open reality of our senses, space the deception, death a misinterpretation." Mr. Kazin is what I would call an ideophile. He's in love with ideas, but though he generously shares that love with us, I know that I feel a certain lack. I don't mean to be ungrateful, but it's all just a bit too platonic. Mr. Kazin seems to *think* about fiction more than he *feels* it. And though this is an understandable temptation for an intellectual, I believe it is only part of the critical process. Ideally, we ought to let the work enter our blood like a transfusion. Then we might begin to respond to it as if it were working in our veins, in our impulses, as well as in our heads.

Saying Good-By to All That

In 1961, Barbara Norman and her husband bought a house in an obscure agricultural village on the northeast coast of Spain. She was a free-lance writer and he was a concert violinist: they could live anywhere they chose, that dream that is reaching almost obsessive proportions in cosmopólitan people. It used to be only the retired who thought of moving to some out-of-the-way utopia, but today more and more people of all ages are yearning for a "retired" place, some native or foreign retreat where they can put aside the distractions of modernity or technology and turn their attention to themselves.

It is not so much that they want to go to these places in order to do something that they can't do wherever they are now. It is rather that they want to go there and simply *be*. Contemporary big-city life interposes so many abstractions, so many impersonal exchanges, so many pressures, between one and one's sense of identity that the self is often reduced to something like a traffic cop, or a social secretary for a personage who exists only in specific functions.

Miss Norman and her husband bought their house in the town she tactfully conceals under the name of Las Casas del Torrente. He had to go on a concert tour from time to time, but she thought it would be easier to wait for him in Las Casas than in Paris, where they had lived previously. As she puts it: "We had settled in the village seeking the past with its peace and stability. Here in the remote interior of a country long isolated from the rest of Europe by geography, character, and history, we thought the past would last out our lifetimes."

They were attracted to Las Casas because of the "friendly smiles and candid faces of the villagers" and because they loved the view from every house, a view of steep and stony slopes that yet showed the stubborn signs of man. While an untouched prospect offers nothing but romance, "it was the human imprint that made the landscape warm and endearing, that gave a special charm to every roll and lilt of this mountainous northeastern corner of Spain . . ."

"Throughout the day," Miss Norman says, "I was aware of a rhythm ebbing and flowing in the village, from the moment the first mule cart rumbled by our house before daybreak to the last returning for supper after dark . . . I came to feel the rhythm of the seasons and of the work the seasons dictated, a pattern repeated year after year. In a world of change and rapid pace, there is reassurance in that slow repetition." A fixed life pattern develops recognizable character traits. Shapelessness gives way to shape; from the vantage point of Las Casas the Faustian life of the big city seems like a blind crime of passion.

The author of *Requiem for a Spanish Village* is a very good writer and she has so much to tell us about Las Casas as she found it and as she left it after ten years that she almost completely effaces herself from her narrative. She was soon accepted by the villagers because she was not a tourist, but a homeowner, and she spent a good deal of her time talking to the women in their kitchens and walking with the men to their vineyards. As author of two cookbooks, she is well qualified to describe the taste of the "pure" wine (no chemicals added) and the freshly pressed olive oil of Las Casas. She also listened to the dreams of the first girl of the village to leave home for Barcelona in forty years.

Her car became the unofficial ambulance, and one day she looked out of her window to find it completely covered with flowers gathered by the village children. She discovered that though water was scarcer than wine, the women were opposed to installing running water because they treasured their get-togethers at the fountain in the square. She neither censures nor approves the local customs, such as the tradition that forbids widows to go out or otherwise distract themselves. Her favorite informant is "Paco," a "perfect poster peasant"—strong, shrewd and satisfied with his hard but independent life.

Toward the middle of her ten years there, the town begins to come apart at its cultural seams. Formerly, almost everyone was related in at least a distant way: now there is a second town inside the first, composed of outsiders. Many of them came from other villages that could no longer support them. When the tourists arrived in force, it was as if the great dam of the Pyrenees had burst and flooded the land with foreigners. In 1970, there were three for every four Spaniards. With them came the demand for hotels, restaurants, villas, cafés, highways, housing developments and the thousand and one synthetic objects all tourists seem to require. The men of Las Casas deserted their backbreaking farms and the grapevines planted by their great-grandfathers to take jobs in the cities.

The baker left; the olive press was closed; it became apparent even to "Paco" that the small, independent farmer's days were numbered. When the lands he worked on shares were sold to a housing developer, he went to Barcelona to help run his cousin's café. Eventually there were as many houses empty as occupied in Las Casas. If kept up, they would have lasted indefinitely; neglected, their mud and stone walls crumbled with astonishing swiftness. In one abandoned town nearby, Miss Norman found only two elderly men: one blind and the other lame, an ominous commentary on what country life was coming to.

With the village disappearing before their eyes, Miss Norman and her husband boarded up their house and went to live in Ann Arbor, Mich. Now she looks back on those ten years with both fondness and foreboding. Soon, she says, there may be no more villages. Spain, and perhaps other countries too, may be reduced to cities, suburbs, and the ruins of their rural past. If you're looking for a retreat, you may either have to build it or find it inside yourself.

What If I Won't Hate Women?

Perhaps it's naïve of me to expect people to write reasonable books about emotionally charged subjects. But when you have to read and review two or three books each week, you do get tired of "understanding" so much personal bias. You reach a point where it no longer matters that the author's mistakes are well meant. You don't care that he or she is on the side of the angels: you just want them to tell the truth. And I don't think the truth is all that elusive or ambiguous, either. If you're looking for it, and you're not a fool or a fanatic, you can generally find it. But you won't arrive at it if you believe—like so many contemporary authors—that the best way to correct an injustice is to invert it. As I observed once before, American society seems condemned to progress in wild pendulum swings. It's a wonder the clock still ticks.

Now here's Michael Korda come to tell us how men discriminate against women. Though we've heard quite a bit on this subject lately, the problem is crucial to the quality of life in this country and it is still a long way from being solved. However, I don't think a book full of gross overgeneralizations is going to improve things. In fact, it may have just the opposite effect: that of encouraging male chauvinists to turn the author's weapon against him—to assume that if he is wrong in one instance, he too is *all* wrong. Mr. Korda has fallen into one of the characteristic errors of those who write on this particular issue: that of addressing himself almost exclusively to his partisans, an uncritical amen corner, instead of trying to reach the people most in need of persuasion.

The author's exaggerations are so numerous that I don't have room even to list them, much less discuss them. Here's a brief sampling: "The reason men behave the way they do toward the women who work with them lies . . . in men's age-old fear of the demands of the woman, whose sexual demands must be met and satisfied—woman, who knows his [*sic*] strength and weaknesses

187

as no other man can, and can judge his potency and thus, in his own eyes, his value." Now, I can't speak for Mr. Korda's men, but I know a few who, however foolhardy, are willing to run the risk of women's sexual demands.

And quite apart from them, are we to understand all women office workers as pressing their sexual demands on all men? Must all men respond to them, if they are not to suffer the dread loss of status the author keeps invoking? Isn't it a form of female chauvinism to assume that only men suffer from sexual anxieties? Is it true that every woman knows every man's "strength and weaknesses" and can "judge his potency?"

"As representatives of the maternal instinct, they [women] have the terrible power to withhold love . . ." What does this mean? It means that Mr. Korda cannot resist an inconsistency. He refers here to an "instinct" that feminists are furiously repudiating and compounds his error by implying that men, or fathers, have no love to give or withhold, that maternity alone has a patent on it. Women, says Mr. Korda, see men as individuals, while men see any woman as womankind. Dismissing the issue of physical differences, the author remarks that "most men in business are not very much stronger than the average woman, if at all . . ." Yet later he complains about a test of physical strength as having the effect of eliminating women from jobs.

Male Chauvinism! How It Works repeatedly takes it for granted that there is no reason *other* than male chauvinism for a man's behavior toward women. A secretary is always dismissed because she refused to play men's games, not because she couldn't or wouldn't do her job. When a researcher at *Time* magazine remained a researcher for six years—despite her two degrees and "prior journalistic experience"—Mr. Korda does not pause to consider that degrees and experience do not necessarily qualify her for promotion. Nor does he mention the fact that the publisher of Time-Life Books is a woman who rose through the ranks.

Try testing these statements against your own experience. "Most men, in fact, don't much like women . . ." Most men are "obliged" to pretend to their fellow office workers that they are having affairs if in fact they are not. "Our symbols of successful womanhood are still Mrs. Onassis . . . and Ethel Kennedy . . ."

Marriage is "idealized . . . in every magazine and on every television show as a life apart" from "real life." "What every man fears is that women may be *living,* while men continue to exist within the conventions they have invented for themselves." Men "listen to them [women] with our minds already made up . . ." We "just don't want to know anything about them." "It's hard for men to stop being male chauvinists. What else have they got left, what other promise does our society hold out for them, what other rewards?"

Now, I think I ought to make it clear that Mr. Korda does give a number of accurate and well-turned descriptions of how male chauvinism affects women in their feelings, their jobs, their marriages, their social lives. If I have not dwelt on this, it is partly because we have heard most of it before and we shall undoubtedly hear it again. If I have dealt mainly with the negative aspects of his book, it is because I think it is more useful at this stage to try to rescue the women's rights movement from the kind of irresponsible statements that have already begun to fatigue both men and women.

As history has shown us, revolutionary leaders have often ended by cutting off their followers' heads. In a sense, something like this is happening to women now. Reading Mr. Korda's endless accounts of women mindlessly putting up with all sorts of humiliations, I get the feeling that he underestimates them more than most male chauvinists do. When, I wonder, are women going to get fed up with being caricatured by their champions? With friends like these, they don't need men for enemies.

The View from the Tenement

In his new novel, *The Tenants,* Bernard Malamud has rushed in where angelic liberals fear to tread. In exploring the relation between blacks and Jews—and carrying it to its implicit conclusion—he has seized contemporary history by the horns. And because he is one of our better writers, his book is more radical than those who call themselves radicals. Like Saul Bellow in *Mr. Sammler's Planet,* like Ralph Ellison in *Invisible Man,* Malamud goes beyond the rhetoric of the revolutionaries to the very root of the matter, to man's inhumanity not only to others, but to himself. Like them, he has taken a subject that could—and all too often does—degenerate into propaganda and shaped it into art.

Malamud has found the perfect objective correlative for his theme: a tenement about to be torn down to make way for a huge modern complex. This is not the parochial tenement of the author's earlier work, just as the lower East Side is no longer exclusively the home of the orthodox Jew. With its filthy, abandoned rooms, it is the junkyard of our "progress." Harry Lesser, the hero of the book, is a writer and the only person still living in the building. His landlord, Levenspiel, pleads with him and offers him bribes to move, but Lesser is on the point of finishing a book and he is afraid that the displacement of moving will make it even more difficult—if not impossible—for him to arrive at the ending that has so far eluded him, an ending to which he has "invented every step," but which may be "more than he can stand."

One day, in the empty apartment next to his, Lesser finds Willie Spearmint, a black, pounding away at an ancient typewriter. Willie is a writer too and he needs an office, because he can't work where he lives with his "white bitch." Lesser is ambivalent about Willie's presence. He works better alone—the Jew, Malamud hints, likes to hog the limelight, he wants to soliloquize on the stage, apostrophizing himself like Hamlet. But Willie is there to stay, ensconced in the shambles of the ruined flat just as his race is mired in the shambles of history. He sees Lesser's apartment—like the Jew's historical situation—as comparatively luxurious.

Here we have both black and Jew, brothers under the skin, or at least at the typewriter, each working away, on condemned premises, at his destiny. They can't stay there. The building—life as we have known it—is about to be torn down. Each must make a sociological leap. For Lesser, the tenement is the world he knew, a life of work and civilized neighbors, the New York City of twenty years ago, to which he tries to cling. For Willie, the tenement is merely a way-station in his climb out of the depths, another "sit-in" at the Establishment's expense. Levenspiel, the landlord, represents the older, orthodox Jew. Not a loner like Lesser, the alienated artist-intellectual, he is a family man with traditional rather than existential *tsurrus*: heartburn, a sick wife, a pregnant sixteen-year-old daughter, a crazy mother in Jackson Heights, a funeral in Queens. "What's a make-believe novel," he asks Lesser, "against all my woes and miseries?"

Inevitably, grudgingly, Willie asks Lesser to read his work. Lesser, after all, has been there before. He has been searching for his identity for thousands of years. Compared to him, Willie, is, in a sense, not only an apprentice writer, but also an apprentice human being. He comes to Lesser, unwillingly, to pay his rent—because Lesser is a landlord, too. In America now, the Jew is the landlord of literature, at least the literature of self-discovery.

When Lesser reads Willie's work he finds it rich in passion, poor in form. (Considering the excessively primitive and violent content of the stories, Lesser is surprisingly indulgent.) Willie reacts angrily, calling art a dirty word, a circumcision designed to castrate the black writer and make him unfaithful to himself. (The political parallel is obvious here.) Willie repeats the now-familiar argument that whites can't understand black experience, to which Lesser replies: "If the experience is about being human, then you've made it my experience . . . You can deny universality, but you can't abolish it." He advises Willie to "build more carefully" (as the Jew did), "to make black more than color, outrage larger than protest." He wants Willie to go beyond politics and generalized indignation into the lyrical recesses of the private self. "You can't turn black experience into literature," he says, "just by writing it down."

"I am art," Willie says. "Willie Spearmint, *black man. My form is myself.*" He adds: "I want to know what you know and *add on to that* what I know *because* I am black." He wants to stop understudying the Jew and take over the star's role in the drama of American society. In spite of all this, Lesser turns the other cheek. When Levenspiel discovers Willie's "office," he smashes the table and chair—and Lesser, like a liberal foundation giving a grant despite the hostility of the recipient, buys Willie new furniture. He suggests, at the same time, that Willie move down to a lower floor to avoid discovery. He himself lives on the top floor and we feel that his real reason may well be his conviction that Willie's struggle is on a lower level than his own and should remain there. But Willie stays. He has been in the basement too long; he wants the view from the top floor, the cosmic perspective.

When Lesser meets Willie's "bitch," Irene, he is irresistibly attracted to her. She is a Jewish girl who just misses being beautiful, "as though beauty were more of an obligation than she cared to assume." We recognize her immediately, and so does Willie. He says that he has straightened her out. "She had nothing she believed in . . . I gave her an example, that I believed in my blackness." "What does she believe in now?" Lesser asks. "Me more than herself," Willie says, and he is right on, summing up radical chic in a single short phrase.

Obsessed by his writing, Willie neglects Irene, and Lesser approaches and sleeps with her. Now he and Willie are joined not only in their work, but in their woman. While Irene finds Lesser more tender than Willie, he is isolated by his self-absorption, just as Willie is by his anger. There's not much to choose between them. She says of Willie: "The more he writes, the blacker he becomes." For Lesser, it works the other way around: the more he writes, the less Jewish, the more rootless, he becomes. In giving Irene to Lesser, Malamud seems to be suggesting that the Jew reaps the harvest of the black-inspired sexual revolution.

Lesser tells Irene the plot of his book. A man "not yet himself" wants to teach himself "to love in a manner befitting an old ideal . . . He will learn through some miracle of transformation

as he writes . . . Lesser writes his book and his book writes
Lesser." Willie's writing is about learning to hate, and we see
Jew and black at opposite poles: superego and id. According to
Willie, "The way to black freedom is against the Jews."

Malamud only hints at the origin of this paradox, and the
reader has to infer what he can. Apparently, the black sees the
Jew—who thinks of himself as the black's best friend—as an
infiltrator, someone who tries to soften his heart and subvert his
revolution with sympathy, who wishes to convert him to rational
action. This is not the Jew slumlord, the pawnbroker or loan-
shark: it is far more complicated than that. The Jew might well
be hated as an unattainable ideal: rich or cultivated, versed in
the arts and sciences, powerful—the pinnacle of American personality. In this perspective, the Wasp, the more natural
"enemy," is not as relevant.

When Lesser finally tells Willie about Irene, Willie tries to kill
him and is prevented only by the arrival of Levenspiel. (The traditional Jew prevents the liberal Jew from becoming a sacrifice
to the black cause.) What is worse, Willie burns (Burn, baby,
burn!) Lesser's manuscript—his book, his life. Which may mean
that the black has forced the Jew to reconsider his own history.
Has he become too complacent, untrue to his tradition, all head
and no heart?

Lesser begins the painful job of rewriting and finds that some
parts of the book are better—the Jew has learned from the black
—but some can't be recaptured. There is no going back to that
comfortable period in his history. Lesser becomes afraid that he
"can't invent beyond life," can't get past what is merely visible
or palpable. The Jew may no longer be the pioneer, pushing
back the boundaries of the American experience. Between orthodox and hippie, Lesser is lost, existentially adrift. His world, like
his tenement, is disappearing, and he doesn't know where he is
going to be. Like a painter friend of his who committed suicide,
it may be that "he wanted to say more than he could at that
time."

What is the next step for the Jew, now that he has begun to
repeat himself? What is the new handwriting on the wall? This
is the ending of his book that Lesser could not conceive, the
sociological leap he cannot make—or even define. When Leven-

spiel asked Lesser: "What are you writing, the Holy Bible?" he didn't know how close he was. For so many Jewish intellectuals the Jewish novel *is* the Holy Bible, the "truth in unimpeachable form." In today's circumstances, anything else seems hopelessly old-fashioned.

When Lesser finds that he cannot reconstruct his book, he strikes back in a rage by destroying Willie's typewriter with an ax. An eye for an eye. Irene, knowing what to expect, leaves for San Francisco without a fare-thee-well or a forwarding address. Lesser and Willie now have nothing in common but their hatred.

The last few pages are the weakest part of the book. Malamud has a penchant for apocalyptic endings, which sit like a ten-gallon hat on the plain gabardine of his style. The conclusion of *The Tenants* is impossible to accept, either literally or figuratively. But this—and a mild case of symboliasis—rates only a very small, almost apologetic objection. Malamud has given us so much to think and feel about that we are glad to forgive him. This book was wrung out of his bowels, and as he says, from Isaiah, "My bowels shall sound like a harp."

Dirge for Dylan—or for Us?

A few years before he died, I met Dylan Thomas on the corner of Seventh Avenue and Bleecker Street. We were both on our way to the Cherry Lane Theater, where he was to give a reading of his poems. He was with Oscar Williams, who introduced us, and timidly, because I was awed by Thomas, I asked him why he never read any of his earlier works. I named my three favorites: "If my head hurt a hair's foot," "Light breaks where no sun shines" and "After the funeral." He pondered this for a moment, then said: "You know, I think I will." During the reading, even he seemed unusually moved, and you might almost say "there wasn't a dry eye in the house." To each of us in the audience it seemed as if Thomas had arrived in the nick of time, bringing us a message we badly needed. He was like a downpour after a long drought; we were parched with the poetry of our age.

But these are melancholy thoughts after reading this new collection, which is augmented by 102 poems, most of them previously published only in England, some of them not at all. Instead of the goose pimples of fifteen years ago, I felt mainly an impatience to turn the page. True, the best poems are still magical, but there are so many others! Such a fatigue of adjectives, a drone of alliterations, a huffing of hyphenated words hurdling the meter like tired horses. Such a faded upholstery of tears, stars, bells, bones, flood and blood . . . a thud of consonants in tongue, light, dark, dust, seed, wound and wind.

"The nightingale sings badly," said Jean Cocteau, and indeed it does in too many of the poems that Thomas himself had the good taste to withhold. The pieties of scholarship are no substitute for poetry and Thomas has been badly served in having his worst printed alongside his best, pulling them down. It would have been better to put out the poems he excluded from the collected volume in a separate edition, as subjects for specialists, instead of tearing the shroud (one of Thomas's favorite words) this way.

Especially disappointing are the poems written before the poet's sixteenth birthday. For some reason, I had always supposed that Thomas had had the same voice all his life, like Alexander Pope, who maintained that he "lisped in numbers." But, alas, he was every bit as conventional as the next boy, full of the sourceless sadness of adolescence, pimply with phrases such as "vague immensity," "dread wilderness," "pale, ethereal beauty," "cradle-petals of the night," "star-scaled boughs" and "forgotten songs." How much better if they had been forgotten!

To our surprise and dismay, the editor Daniel Jones, who had been a boyhood friend of Thomas's, tells us that even this unwelcome plenty is not complete. "It is still a selection, based on editorial judgment." Grotesquely, he goes on to say: "I doubt whether any reader could tolerate a lengthy account of my reasons for inclusion or exclusion."

But the disheartening effect of the volume is not entirely Mr. Jones's fault. Perhaps, in the winter of our discontent, we no longer care about "seeing the boys of summer in their ruin." Each age demands an image of its accelerated grimace, as Ezra Pound put it, and Thomas's iambic apocalypses sound today like an operatic street singer trying to compete with a political rally in Central Park. "Find meat on bones that soon have none," he urged in one of his poems, and we did. We thrilled to Thomas in his time and now I, at least, feel as if I'm picking his bones.

It seems indecent that really good poems should shrink with shifts in our mood or climate. One likes to think that art is immortal, forever apt, always young. But Thomas traded so wholly in immediacy that it is not surprising if his voice now sounds only a distant halloo. Perhaps we are too uptight to revel in the texture of this "world we breathe," but Thomas does ask a lot with his foxes and ferns, towers and tides, herons and wrens. Push back the question as we may, it is there on the tip of our tongues: "What has this to do with me now?"

Mr. Jones has arranged the poems in chronological order in the hope that this will throw some light on the poet's development. It doesn't: on one page Thomas soars like his omnipresent birds, and on the next, his wings heavy with bombast, he resembles one of those poor creatures who have been caught in an oil slick.

Comparing the *Collected Poems* of 1952 and the present volume is rather like looking at two portraits of Thomas. The first is the famous Augustus John painting that served as a frontispiece in the earlier edition: the poet is young, slim, sensual, almost pretty but for the tension of intelligence in his face. The second is a painting I don't suppose many people have seen. It was done by Gene Derwood, Oscar Williams's wife and a poet in her own right. She pictures a fat, middle-aged, disheveled Dylan Thomas. He appears to have posed in the middle of a New York City street crossing and, to judge from the position of his hands on his hips, Miss Derwood may have meant to show him standing at bay, in a place where he never belonged. The effect, though, is of a man trying to keep his trousers up. It's as if he knew what was coming.

All Her Yeses Used Up

Here is Molly Bloom after the bloom has browned around the edges. Edna O'Brien's Mary is older than James Joyce's Molly, and the title *Night* suggests more than lucubrations about love. There are undertones too of Céline's *Journey to the End of Night*. The unloved are insomniacs, sleepless poets some of them, and Mary's soliloquy is at once more savage and more tender than Molly's. The younger woman ends on "Yes I said yes I will Yes," but Mary has used up most of her yeses. Still, she will not surrender to "no" and the words tumble out of her in search of an emotion, any emotion. For she has reached that sadness at the very bottom of things, that ultimate aloneness of a woman who has dined out all her life on her own flesh and is now facing the need for a new menu.

She is in that limbo between conspicuous erotic attractiveness and the more demanding persona of middle age. Her body bears the stretch marks of an impetuous history. When men look at her now, they are no longer sure what is required of them— nor is she. She knows too much, it shines in her eyes, which seem to say to would-be partners: Come on, let's see what's wrong with you. Here, let me pet your pathos. Her ironical air invites the eccentric, beckons the awry. Born on a farm, she still has a barnyard earthiness, but she has begun to plant artificial flowers in it. She sees her old home as something between a heartbreaking yellowed snapshot and a stage set for a forlorn and rain-drenched Irish drama.

In her earlier novels, one could feel Miss O'Brien trying to keep her passion for language under some kind of control, but now, in *Night*, she throws her arms around our necks. "Flaunched," "seasous," "maraud"—her feeling for words is, to quote her on herself, "a mother's love, like yeast, multiplying, the spores rising up over the lid of the world, too much." But sex and the sweet spasms of language are only overflowings, surplus materials, so to speak. Miss O'Brien has stories to tell, stories

deep as a well, and when she gets down to work she is as crafty
as they come.

Mary's mother's funeral is a tragicomedy of incongruities. The
cortège takes a short cut, leading them through fields of nettles.
Why? Where are they hurrying? Along the path, an unattended
bicycle leans against a yew tree: Where is the owner, everyone
wonders, who has so cavalierly abandoned his vehicle? Is it one
of nature's several urgencies or something supernatural that has
spirited him away? At the graveside, Mary remembers her
mother grieving over her impending death: "She said you could
put all the pleasures that had gone into her life into a little
thimble, and she looked for a thimble, though sewing was not
one of her accomplishments."

Miss O'Brien's stories about men are funny and sad at the same
time. In a restaurant, Mary makes a date with a waiter who has
been pirouetting for her inspection while her escort is in the
men's room. Dismissing her companion, who is not suited for her
purpose, she preens herself and waits for the waiter, crooning,
doing exercises "to get into a more strapping condition." But
when he arrives, in mufti, he is another man. He begins to tell
her his troubles: "His room was cold, his walls were damp and
devoid of pictures or engravings, he had no wardrobe and only
two metal hangers . . . His savoir-faire decreased as his life
story unfurled . . . He spoke of his father, deceased . . . He had
come with one set of thoughts and intentions and suddenly,
hark, his father's death loomed."

Perhaps the finest part of the book is the last section, in which
Mary makes a pilgrimage back to the farm to visit her widowed
father. She has prepared a speech, crammed for the occasion
"as if I were taking an exam." "I am sorry, I haven't written, I
neglected you." She pictures her father sitting before the fire, a
rug or shawl on his shoulders, flecked with dandruff. But his
opening words are "What an hour of night to come home and
what a fright he'd got and how long was I staying."

The next day, at their wits' ends with each other, they decide to
visit a cousin whose sister has just died. They can go in a hackney car. The cousin greets them in the kitchen, where there is a
litter of six puppies. "He said he should have drowned them only
that we came and took up the time." In the hackney going back,

she and her father press their faces each to his or her own window, looking out at their forever-separate lives. When she leaves him, she has "that nice feeling that one has after a convalesence; the joints are weak and the head inclines to reel, but the worst is over, the fever has been passed."

Unlike Molly Bloom's, Mary's soliloquy is something of a peroration as well. One feels her more flamboyant flights of rhetoric as a kind of molting, a throwing off of a gaudy outer covering in order to emerge new and naked. In the space of a single night, we see her dying as a "girl" and being reborn as a woman.

Last of the Cathedral Builders

During the building of the Cathedral of Chartres, noble men and women joined the general populace in harnessing themselves to wagons to pull the huge stones to the site. At Notre Dame, the lowermost blocks of the foundation were just as carefully dressed as those above ground, because every inch of the building was equally holy. At the dedication of the new choir of Canterbury Cathedral in 1130, the text of the liturgy was "Awesome is this place." In planning the Cathedral of Seville, the builders resolved among themselves that "it shall be so great posterity shall think us mad." Antonio Gaudí, the architect of the Expiatory Church of the Sacred Family in Barcelona, belongs to this tradition, and his masterpiece, which was begun in 1883, may well be the last on this spiritual scale. The cathedrals of the future—if we are to have any—will probably be more in the spirit of Lincoln Center or the Astrodome in Houston.

Gaudí was only thirty-one years old when he was given the commission as a result of a quarrel between the architects originally chosen to plan the church. Although he had worked with another architect on the monastery at Monserrat, he had done little on his own except for decorating a pharmacy and planning two private homes. Here was the kind of opportunity architects dream of, and Gaudí seized it as such, devoting the rest of his life to the Sagrada Familia.

As he saw it, the cathedral was to be the world's tallest church, towering over the hot-blooded city of Barcelona as a visible reminder of its sacred duty. The portal was to be "large enough for all humanity to pass through," and the interior was designed to seat 13,000. Despite the enormous scope of the building, however, the pews were to be very narrow. It was typical of Gaudí that he wanted to make it impossible for people to cross their legs in church.

The Sagrada Familia is in the Mudejar style—a combination of Christian and Mussulman influences—but it is such a depar-

ture from everything that had ever been done before that it
might be more correct to say that the manner is Gaudí's alone.
He had no very definite plan, but virtually improvised the building as he went along. As one of his admirers expressed it, the
architect "tried to put into effect each day what the Virgin Mary
had revealed to him the night before."

"Architecture will be soft and hairy," Gaudí said to Le Cor-
busier, and indeed his forms do look as if they had been melted.
Dali's description— "the way an angel cooks a cathedral"—is less
fanciful than it seems. Because he believed that art should remain close to the life of the people, Gaudí softened the sublimity
of his cathedral by covering it with homely decorations such as
fruit and vegetables, turkeys, ducks, geese and rabbits, snails, sea-
weed and sea urchins, a saw and a T-square, a boat and an
anchor.

Though posterity has handsomely compensated him, few people liked Gaudí's work while he was alive. His Casa Milá in
Barcelona is a secular masterpiece whose beetling facade earned
it the title "the Quarry." The Casa Batló, an extraordinary
anticipation of art nouveau, pleased neither its owner nor his
wife. The canons of the Cathedral of Palma felt that the tribune
he designed for their choir looked like a streetcar. Gaudí replied
that "a streetcar can be a very beautiful thing."

Even as early as the nineteenth century, people were no longer
willing to support cathedrals, and the funds for the Sagrada
Familia ran out long before it was completed. Today it is only a
hollow façade, like a "gigantic decayed tooth," a pilgrimage
place for tourists and students of architecture. And though there
are said to be plans for completing it now, this seems, without
Gaudí to supervise it, almost as sacrilegious as leaving it unfinished. An age that for years allowed Gaudí's lovely mosaic terraces and sculptured grottoes to decay in the Parque Güell seems
unlikely to do justice to the infinitely more demanding Sagrada
Familia.

Gaudí the Visionary is a beautiful book—perhaps too beautiful. The pictures by Clovis Prévost may attract more attention
to themselves than to the buildings they portray. The essays by
Salvador Dali, Robert Descharnes, Joan Alavedra and Francesc
Pujols all suffer from the characteristic overripeness of syntax

straining after visual effects. But these are funeral orations, after all, and Gaudí enjoyed little enough hyperbole in his life.

He died in 1926, at the age of seventy-four. Somnambulistically dreaming of the next step in his work, he was struck down by a streetcar—the vehicle he had described as "very beautiful." Because of the shabbiness of his clothes, he was taken at first for a vagabond. And perhaps he was, in a sense. With his life work still only a façade, he might have felt like a homeless man.

Struttin' Some Sociology

Until about a year ago, I used to ride the New Haven every afternoon from New York to Westport, and often, especially in the summer months, the train would stop for inscrutable reasons in one or another part of Harlem. At these times, while the other passengers pored over their newspapers or magazines, I would gaze out of the window and wonder whether we weren't being invited to inspect, at close hand, before going on to our lawns and swimming pools, the squalor of the tenements on either side of the tracks. But then, when I looked down into the streets, it struck me that the picture was altogether different. There an almost carnival spirit reigned. Children ran, played ball, screamed with laughter, gasped with pleasure under an opened fire hydrant. Adults stood about in small, close-knit groups, and I could plainly make out, even through the dirty window, the stylish gestures of the raconteur, sketching out his story.

On the way to my expensive and inconvenient isolation in the exurbs, I would feel a pang of nostalgia, because, as a boy growing up in Brooklyn, I had once known myself the feeling of such a street. It was a *neighborhood*, and today in New York City this seems to be something only black people and Puerto Ricans enjoy. For them, the street is a place where you can play, laugh, talk, dance, beat a conga drum—where you can *live*—while for whites it is mainly a no man's land, a bleak and dangerous passageway to somewhere else. It always seemed to me, remote in my window with the dirt like an editorial scrawled across it, that those people down there were *at home*—in a city where nobody else was.

It is feelings like these that have made me two or three months late with this review of Albert Murray's *South to a Very Old Place*. I hesitated because I mistrusted my sentiments: I wondered whether they weren't oversimplifications, the easy rationalizations of someone who didn't wish to face unpleasant truths. But it wasn't just the streets in Harlem: The evidence was all around me. I'd heard Northerner Norman Mailer on TV talking, not so much like a Southerner, but like a black—and Marlon Brando too, even when the part didn't call for an accent. I've heard ten thousand hairy kids in New York and other places talking black, even trying to strut—to walk and move black. I've watched them trying to think black, act black, *be* black, as if they felt that they had been deprived of some "primal" experience.

Now here's Albert Murray, who's been black for fifty-five years, formulating what I felt, confirming what I saw. He's saying that the majority of blacks have something most whites who write about them don't seem to have noticed. They have an instinctive sense of self and place that no amount of sociological double talk can change. The most concrete people in the world, they are the victims of a diarrhea of abstractions. You'd have to turn from the editorial to the sports page of your paper to see what Mr. Murray means, to read about the style, elegance and mother wit of Willie Mays or Walt Frazier. You'd have to switch from Channel 13, from the fulminations of a black poet who sounds as if he or she were born yesterday, to Channel 9, where you would see Walt take his world in his hands and toss it gracefully through the hoop or watch Willie belt his over the wall.

Mr. Murray resents the white assumption that the Negro (his word) was so simple or ignorant—until he was "enlightened"—that he didn't know he was miserable. If I'm so miserable, how come you're always imitating me? would be his answer. If he agrees with black militants that white liberals don't understand him, that's about the only time he sees eye to eye with them. Because he would say that black militants don't understand *him* either. For the last ten years, he's had the dubious privilege of listening to them tell him how he feels—based on nothing they ever saw for themselves, but something they read in a book.

To test his theory in the only way that means anything, Mr. Murray took it to the people. He went on the road with it, went back to Mobile, Alabama, where he was born; to Tuskegee, where he studied; to Memphis; to New Orleans; to Atlanta and to Greensboro, North Carolina. He talked to the historian C. Vann Woodward, to the novelists Robert Penn Warren and Walker Percy, to editors of Southern newspapers such as Edwin

Yoder—but most important of all, he talked to folks, down-home folks. He traveled back into himself too, where he heard the "slow-dragging circus-tiger vibrato trombones," the creamy contralto warmth of the Southern mammy, and felt the crazy mixed-up "mulatto" quality of American life—the kinship behind the "aginship."

Taking Duke Ellington for his model, he has turned out a riffing, up-tempo stomp of a book. As Kenneth Burke, one of Mr. Murray's white mentors, said: The symbolic act is the *dancing* of an attitude. The Negro's true symbolism is not to be found in the black militants or the white sociologists, the author implies, but in the blues, in the funky and improbable affirmations of Lester Young, in the mammy-crooning of Johnny Hodges, in Louis Armstrong's triumphant "laments," in Duke's whole band wailing a siren song of "Be yourself, baby. Be dark and deep." Until you can feel this beat, Mr. Murray says, don't clutter up the floor. Stand back and watch. Listen and learn. It's *his* Amen corner, not yours.

The Beauty of Terror

I think that the less portentously you write about the late Marilyn Monroe, the closer you get to the truth of her. Judging from Norman Rosten's firsthand account of Miss Monroe, she wasn't so very complicated, and to make too much of her is to lose the woman in the myth. She had all the classical insecurities of an illegitimate child brought up in foster homes, and her fame was a caricature of her needs. She was much too down to earth to be satisfied with being a symbol. It was like offering caviar to a starving peasant girl. This is not to say that she didn't enjoy her star status as a bastard form of emotional security, but everybody knows that this is the most precarious security of all. In another sense, her image as a love goddess was like a childish revenge on her past.

Mr. Rosten and his wife, Hedda, knew Miss Monroe during the last seven years of her life. Although stardom, like scar tissue, had already insulated her against intimacy, she was attracted to the Rostens because they were such homey people. She probably knew no one else with whom she could play house and take off the padded bra of her iconology. The Rostens were remarkably tactful, too, and knew how to ride with the unconscious egoism that famous Americans so often develop, the drop-what-you're-doing-and-come-over syndrome—even though you are three thousand miles away, and she only wants you to see something she has just bought, and it is three o'clock in the morning where you live.

There are moments in *Marilyn: An Untold Story* in which Miss Monroe comes vividly alive for me, although she never did in any of her movies except *The Misfits*. The author has a poet's eye for detail, and it is in these details that his subject emerges. Mr. Rosten points out, for example, that the actress was constantly changing or rearranging the furniture wherever she lived, as if she could never get her home "right." As he puts it, "the completed home eluded her to the very end."

In one of the book's best scenes, Miss Monroe has just bought a bronze copy of a Rodin statue depicting a man and a woman in a passionate embrace. On the way home with it, she begins to have doubts about the statue and insists on going over to show it to her analyst. "What about it?" she demands. "What does it mean? Is he screwing her or is it a fake? I'd like to know. What's this?"—she points to a spur attached to the casting that seems to pierce the woman's body—"It looks like a penis." Her voice grows shrill, and she keeps repeating: "What do you think, Doctor? What does it mean?" In a calmer mood at another time, she accuses Mr. Rosten of being a "lousy friend," because he never came to swim in her pool when he was in Hollywood. Her ability to provide a pool for her less affluent friends was, to her, like a mother giving milk to her child—the child Miss Monroe never succeeded in having.

Though the author is very much on Miss Monroe's side—making too much of her "poetry," among other things—he shows us her tough, unreasonable face, too. When she was in London, making *The Prince and the Showgirl* with Sir Laurence Olivier, who also directed the movie, she decided that he was condescending to her and gave him a very hard time. It must be admitted that he was not very diplomatic: he suggested, for example, that she whiten her teeth with baking soda and lemon because they came out yellow, he said, in the rushes.

Though she was often silly, and I can find no evidence of any sustained intellectual interest, Miss Monroe was capable of making some shrewdly witty observations. After her nude scene in her last unfinished movie, she said, "I hope they give me some good nude lines to go with it." She is affectionately mocking too when, after dancing with Robert F. Kennedy, she reveals to Mr. Rosten that he asked her who she thought to be the handsomest man in the room. During the filming of *Some Like It Hot*, she writes sardonically to Mr. Rosten: "We are going through the Straits of Dire. It's rough and choppy, but why should I worry? I have no phallic symbol to lose."

I would surmise, from the evidence of *Marilyn*, that Miss Monroe married Joe DiMaggio because he was an "ordinary" guy raised to a heroic level—and perhaps too because baseball was such a *popular* game. To her, he might have represented "real life," simplified to batting and catching a ball for the pleasure of the American people. Her marriage to Arthur Miller could be traced to the new image of herself as an artist that she was trying to create in studying with Lee Strasberg at the Actors Studio. For all his angst, however, Mr. Miller was a very *hamish* man, always trying to grow things on their country property.

The Misfits, Miss Monroe's last and best picture, was practically a prescription for suicide, given her kind of history. About to be divorced from Mr. Miller, she plays a divorcee—in a script written by him. One can see all the wreckage of their love and tenderness in the writing and acting of the movie's best moments —but there was bitterness, too, and we find the star "ordering" the writer to discard a speech she did not like.

Though Miss Monroe was little better than attractive to the naked eye, she achieved a kind of beauty, when she was already past her prime, in *The Misfits*. I think Mr. Rosten describes her quality very well in these lines from Rilke:

> *For Beauty's nothing*
> *But beginning of Terror we're still*
> *just able to bear . . .*

Going Nowhere with No One

I remember a table in *Barchester Towers* that had more character than the combined heroes of three recent novels I've read. Trollope spent perhaps half a page describing that table—its shape, size and patina—and then it existed for me. It had meaning, though it was made of nothing but wood and wax. The characters in the novels I'm thinking of are supposedly made of flesh and blood. Like all human beings, they have histories, memories, dreams, hopes, plans, fears, desires and anxieties. They have brains, eyes, ears, mouths, hands, skins and sexual organs. And what do they do with them? One watched television all day and tended a garden. I never learned what sort of programs he saw and what he made of them. I have no idea what grew in his garden. Another character, also a recluse, usually passed the time lying in bed or standing on his head.

And now, in *Going Nowhere*, I'm faced with a hero who simply hitchhikes. For ten years, he hitchhikes up and down the East Coast. Aside from two or three tales he invents to entertain the people who pick him up—plus the fact that he sometimes works at washing cars—I'm totally ignorant of how he spent those ten years, or why. I don't know what sort of human contacts he had, how he got through the day, what he thought about, hoped for, or regretted. As far as I can make out, he's merely a manikin to hang a metaphor on, a flimsy plastic toy with a single idea instead of a rubber band for a motor.

William Blake had a phrase—"wailing along the margins of nonentity"—but I believe that even this is too vivid for Mr. Greenberg's character, Arthur. He doesn't even wail. Arthur is a brilliant physics student, who, just before graduation, loses a leg through a highly improbable— i.e., "symbolic"—accident. Abandoning his career, for which he seems to feel that he needs two legs, he takes up hitchhiking, which of course requires only one. After ten years, Arthur is approached by his former professor, who has kept track of him all this time through an electronic device implanted in his stump. The professor has secretly perfected a flying saucer and now he wants Arthur to get into it and impersonate a creature from another planet in order to bring the earth a message from a superior civilization.

Why has he chosen Arthur? Why not? is the currently popular answer. Unteleology is the message. Teleology being "the movement of life toward a distant goal," the professor wants to promote the opposite notion that "nothing is going anywhere." Unteleology will free people, will enable them to stop struggling toward that distant goal and simply float in purposelessness as they would in a swimming pool. For various vague reasons—the author has as little patience with plotting as he does with characters—the plan fails. The professor is jailed and Arthur is back at the roadside.

The protagonist's further vicissitudes are so pointless, so picked out of a hat, that they don't deserve to be described. I'll just mention one for whatever it may contribute toward a symptomatology of this school of fiction. Arthur is run over by a train and loses his remaining leg. Why? Perhaps it struck the author as funny: first one, then the other. He may have been unable to resist the sheer symmetry of it. On a "deeper" level, we may discover that Mr. Greenberg is reading us a lecture: Arthur's continuing dismemberment may signalize the progressive diminishment of modern man.

When I finished *Going Nowhere*, I found that it had prompted some observations. (A reviewer has to eat the *plat du jour*.) It seems to me that novelists used to be men or women who were either fascinated or disgusted by people, who couldn't let them alone and irresistibly fell to apostrophizing them in fiction. Now I get the feeling that there are any number of novelists who aren't interested in people at all. They don't know how they talk or act, and they don't care. If they cause their characters to do anything, it's either a gratuitous act or a "symbolic" one, not the gratification of a recognizable desire.

Why, then, do these people write? I imagine they do because there's a picture in their minds that needs straightening . . . a vote throbbing to be cast . . . a large gesture settling like arthritis in their joints. What they need, these novelists in spite of themselves, is not the tyranny of the typewriter, but a café. A café with watery beer and Bob Dylan in the jukebox. Fat waiters and thin, adenoidal girls smoking Cigarillos. And people like themselves, talking too and not listening either.

Adverbs Are Deadly Weapons

He cursed silently, steadily, bitterly, helplessly—this is what Helen MacInnes's heroes do when things take a bad turn. For years, I've been wondering what these silent, steady curses are. I've even tried cursing silently, steadily, but I can't seem to work up a coherent sequence. I might manage a short stream of curses if I hit my finger with a hammer or barked my shin painfully on an object someone had wantonly left in my path—but that's about it.

Though I've never met a CIA man or an espionage agent, I've always imagined them as poker-faced characters who are trained not to show surprise, curiosity, eagerness, disappointment or any other emotions. I think of them as speaking in a matter-of-fact way, either because it is intended to disguise what they are thinking or feeling, or because they've seen so much duplicity, betrayal and cynicism that their emotions are too sophisticated for any but the most complicated expression.

Yet in Miss MacInnes's books, they look, and speak, bitterly, angrily, coldly, icily, sharply, sourly, acidly, bitingly, curtly, warningly, worriedly, caustically, cuttingly and grimly. Their spines tighten (whatever that involves). They are chilled by danger, their eyes grow wary, they barely repress groans—or don't repress them. They speak of—or to—their political opponents with unconcealed contempt.

When Ian Ferrier, an air intelligence official, fumbles for a light in a strange room, he can't manage to turn it on. "Was it twist or pull?" he asks himself—helplessly. When he goes to bed, he says, "Oh shut up!" (angrily) to the mosquitoes, then compares them to the questions biting his mind. After dragging a friend to safety, the athletic Ferrier wonders how he was able to pull a man twenty pounds heavier so easily, even in an emergency.

A high government official glares at a door someone has just closed behind him. A KGB department head who trains assassins strikes a heavy door—twice—with his fist after discovering that it is locked. Evaluating the security of his hiding place, he appraises the threat of a nearby museum that contains "things of old Spain—wood carved and painted, silver-work, iron screens, leather, lace, embroidery and furniture." He worries about its proximity. "Arts and crafts, he thought. Always popular. People everywhere. Could be dangerous."

People are always keeping clear of windows, adjusting louvers, refusing to turn on or turn out lights for fear of revealing themselves. "I'll see you out and lock the back door after you," a CIA agent says, in one of many such sentences. An apartment is criticized because its terraces are an invitation to unauthorized climbing. Everything is explained; like silent screen actors, everyone pantomimes what he is thinking or feeling.

In all this, Miss MacInnes is diametrically opposed to the new suspense movies, in which nothing is explained; in which there are no transitions and the actors never change expression. In these films, everything is fast—cut, cut, cut—and the burden of interpretation is squarely on you. In Miss MacInnes's book, everything is slow—talk, talk, talk—and the burden of carrying all these groceries is on you too.

It would not be unreasonable to say that Miss MacInnes—who may be thoroughly acquainted only with her husband, Professor Gilbert Highet—ought to avoid portraying desperate men who will stop at nothing. But her women are not much better. Tavita, her heroine, is a flamenco dancer whose eyes blaze with anger or flash with determination, and whose head is held ever higher under duress, until, near the end of the book, she "seemed to add three inches to her height."

Miss MacInnes's forte—her intimate evocation of the glamorous cities of Europe—is so overlaid with her characters' clichés that we see them as if through a chill rain. The setting of *Message from Málaga* is both Málaga and Granada, and though the author obviously knows these places well, we can't enjoy them in the company she has given us.

The plot of the novel has to do with a KGB official who is playing a double game, with the help of a couple of CIA traitors. They intend to infiltrate and train the militant groups in the United States for a revolution in 1976. But I'd better not say any more. I wouldn't want to give away the suspense of who said what most cuttingly to whom.

Add One Epiphany and Stir

There's a certain type of short story that achieves a kind of virtuosity by distilling a large, embracing symbolism from the smallest possible detail. The more remote, seemingly arbitrary or circumstantial the detail, the greater the degree of virtuosity. *The New Yorker* magazine is famous for this type of story: John Updike, John Cheever and Gilbert Rogin are three of its practitioners who come to mind—and perhaps Paul Brodeur's name should be added to the list, a bit lower down.

In *Downstream*, "Angel of Death" is a good example. Adam Foster is shoveling toadstools from the yard of his cottage when his mother arrives for a visit. She is a widow in her sixties, but she still has youth, sweetness and serenity in her face—derived, Adam supposes, from her religiousness. When she sees what he is doing, Adam's mother tells him that toadstools and mushrooms are regarded by mycologists as synonymous, that there are edible toadstools and poisonous mushrooms. She had been reading up on the subject, but Adam is worried about his fifteen-month-old son, who can't be expected to know the difference. Both he and his wife have heard of "experts" who die from eating poisonous mushrooms, and he doesn't feel that they're worth the risk. "You mustn't close your eyes to things," his mother admonishes, before going off for a walk in the woods.

A half hour later, she returns and tells Adam that she wants to show him something. It turns out to be a large, snow-white mushroom, eight inches tall, standing solitary in a patch of bare, wet earth. This is an Amanita virosa, she says, so poisonous that its toxin can be disintegrated and destroyed only by boiling acids. Specimens of Amanita virosa have been known to retain their poison for as long as nine years. Because it is both deadly and beautiful, it is called the Angel of Death. Adam wants to stamp the mushroom under his heel, but he doesn't because he can see in his mother's face that she accepts it, she believes that "everything in God's universe was as it should be."

On the basis of this little epiphany in the woods, we are led to contemplate a surprising number of things: the unexpected esthetic application of religion; the inseparable horror and beauty of death; the capacity of a serene mind to embrace large perspectives; the poverty of our harried pragmatism; the shallowness of our mere picnicker's relation to nature; our habitual, condescending underestimation of the generation before ours.

Though it works in "Angel of Death," the risks inherent in this sort of approach are all too apparent in "The Proposal." Arthur and Valerie have loved each other for a year, but each of them feels that "getting married might disrupt the delicious balance between domesticity and license" they've been enjoying. Eventually, however, Arthur feels himself impelled to propose. His desire to bind Valerie to him legally is based on an anxious feeling that "she retained some secret reserve or fascination, which, even beyond the sheerest intimacy, was not to be yielded up."

During a weekend in the country, he does propose and she refuses him because, though she loves him, she feels that marriage will condemn them to an incessant clash of prides. When he attempts to deliver an ultimatum, she dashes her drink into his face. He slaps her, she runs out into the night and he watches her through the window, debating whether to follow her. Then he sees that she is crouching in the tall grass watching three deer come out along a path he had earlier pointed out to her. She turns her face in his direction, "as if imploring him to watch," to share the "magic" of the moment with her. He goes out when the deer have passed, bends down and touches her hair—and leaves the story hanging where we first found it.

The deer are supposed to be the key that will unlock the barrier between these two people, in much the same way that the Amanita virosa modified the relation between Adam and his mother—but they don't. The implied sharing of a moment of epiphany, together with its re-establishment of harmony between Arthur and Valerie, seems to be only a passing thing. The deer are too insignificant and peripheral to unravel their difficulties. A whole herd of deer will not alter their mysterious and unexamined prides, their peculiar ambivalence about independence. Instead of a structure, sustained by the symbolism of the deer, we have here nothing but a chronology, a series of events that lead not to a resolution but a frail, temporary and irrelevant equilibrium.

Of the thirteen stories in *Downstream*, seven are quite good. They take us a long way out of ourselves and give us something that fully justifies the journey. Three or four of the remaining pieces are negligible, but the others are worth reading for their originality even in failure—for, as anyone who loves literature will tell you, a venturesome failure is worth a dozen complacent successes.

Notes of a Master Novelist

I've always read that Ford Madox Ford was a difficult, if not impossible, person. I never believed it. Until I read *Return to Yesterday*, I used to think that the man who could write *The Good Soldier* and *Parade's End* must have at least a hundred redeeming qualities. In any case, out of gratitude for these two books, I would gladly have forgiven him all the peculiarities ascribed to him, and more. But now that I've read these reminiscences of his, which have been out of print and hard to find for more than thirty years, I can't imagine why he wasn't loved by everyone he met.

The kinds of things Ford notices and writes about and cares about in this volume make him seem just the opposite of what so many people said. For a literary genius whose talent was well above the average reader's head, he comes across as almost amazingly human. Just to see him forgive Henry James—who always patronized him—is to trust and like him. At one time they lived two miles apart in the English countryside, and although it seems unlikely that either cared for the other, they were intimate for a long time. Ford apparently accepted the intimacy because he believed that James was a great writer; James because he valued Ford's advice in any number of practical matters as if this other great man were his bailiff.

James, says Ford, detested what he called Bohemianism and singled out Swinburne as the age's worst offender. He was so determined to see Swinburne as decadent and sickly that he steadfastly refused to believe that the poet could, for example, swim—while Ford assures us that Swinburne was famous for his swimming prowess, and a remarkable ice skater besides. There's another delightful scene in which Ford, John Galsworthy and James are walking along the Rye Road to Winchelsea. James's dachshund, Maximilian, liked to run sheep, so his master, in order to allow him to exercise in this way, had provided the dog with a leash at least ten yards long.

At one point in his discourse, "in order to round off an immense sentence, the great man halted." While he pursued his thought, Maximilian pursued his own enthusiasm until he had wound the leash so intricately about their legs that they could not move. Typically, James blamed this comic Laocoön on poor Ford. In another place, Ford gives a brilliant explanation of James's later style. "Having found that his limpidities, from *Daisy Miller* to *The Real Thing* . . . suggested less than he desired," James gave them up. After that, says Ford, "I fancy that his mannerisms, his involution . . . were due to a subtle conviction that, neither in his public nor in his acquaintance, would he ever find anyone who would not need talking down to . . . so he talked down to us, explaining the ramifications of his mind . . . as if he were talking to children."

Ford was even more intimate with Joseph Conrad, with whom he collaborated on three books. Why two of the greatest writers of this century should have felt a need for collaboration remains a mystery. How this collaboration could have resulted in largely forgotten books is a still greater mystery. About his part in the collaboration, Ford is most modest, though Conrad gave him more credit. Actually, Ford saw his more important task as the buoying up of Conrad's spirits. He was forever finding ways of beguiling him into writing.

The author of *Return to Yesterday* was so far from regarding himself as a literary giant that he wanted to be a farmer. In Paris, he studied "kitchen gardening" at the Sorbonne under the great Professor Gressent, and we find him sitting for hours at the Café des Deux Magots planning—not *The Good Soldier*—but the ideal kitchen garden, in which every bed radiated from a dung-well in the center and could be reached by a hoe.

Stephen Crane was another friend, playing cowboy and dying of tuberculosis in the English countryside. We find Emile Zola sitting on a bench in Hyde Park, exiled during the Dreyfus case. On seeing Ford approach, he said: "What was one to think of a country where nursemaids dressed the hair so improvidently that he had found as many as eighteen hairpins on one morning in front of one park bench?"

Ford has a wonderful ear for dialect, and uses it lovingly to describe the peasants he knew—or hilariously to parody the speaking and writing styles of his age. Out of pure personal necessity, he and Conrad were revolutionizing the English novel form, which they considered a pastiche of stale conventions. What the literary Establishment hated above all was the *mot juste* but the collaborators needed it because their ambition was "above all to make you see."

While he wrote more novels than any of his acquaintances and even became famous for some of them, Ford considered, at the time he wrote these reminiscences, that he had written only one. That was *The Good Soldier*, begun on his fortieth birthday. *Parade's End*, written ten years later in the nineteen twenties, is another masterpiece, yet he takes no pride in it in these memoirs.

For several years Ford was so depressed that he went to nineteen "nerve specialists" and received treatments varying from a diet of one grape every quarter hour for sixteen hours to boiling shampoos and freezing foot baths. But while he willingly suffered every sort of absurdity in his desperation, he never despaired in print. *Return to Yesterday* is as rich in charity, humanity, wit and acumen as any memoir I've ever read. If Ford had any fault that put people off, it could only have been that he was too honest, too faithful to himself, for most people's taste. Without that quality, he could never have written his two great novels—or this warm and moving memoir.

Norman Writes a Dithyramb

It is just as easy to ridicule Norman Mailer as it is to admire him. In his unselfconscious way, he advises us to do both: it is good advice. He is at once more primitive and more sophisticated than most writers, and the reader has to keep this in mind. Even in print, he is usually speaking off the record, confiding half-formed feelings that should not be taken too literally, but tasted, so to speak. The beginnings of his books—when he is clearing his throat of his ego—are likely to put readers off. He seems to be daring us to misunderstand or underestimate him. *The Prisoner of Sex* is no exception. It begins as if Mailer had just woke up from a night of disastrous drinking and staggered over to his desk to scrabble blindly among his papers, muttering, "Where am I?"

The book was originally conceived as a reply to Kate Millett's blistering attack on Mailer in her *Sexual Politics*, but as he points out, all the themes of his life had gathered here: revolution, tradition, sex, the family, the child, the shape of the future, technology, the ethics of the critic, the male mystique and the rights of minorities. After some introductory maundering, Mailer turns to an examination of the male's alleged emotional callousness. Not true, he says. Men are delicate too; the roles are equally difficult. A man's sexual force is not luck, but "his finest moral product . . . an adventurous juncture of ego and courage."

The main burden of the book is that the revolution of reason and technology is a form of scientific vanity that threatens our naturalness. Though this is not new, it cannot be said too often. Mailer is worried here about the "technologizing of sex," which reduces it to the mere currency of power—who is adored by whom. His often-cited dislike of contraception is rooted in the notion that conception keeps sex serious, insures it against becoming a casual transaction. And while there are obvious objections to this, there are equally obvious objections to the stripping of all consequences and all "mystery" from the sexual act.

Mailer feels—and Germaine Greer agrees with him in *The Female Eunuch*—that the new emphasis on clitoral orgasm is a push-button approach to sex. What has happened, he asks, to Blake's most lovely idea that "Embraces are cominglings from the Head to the Feet"? In this same passage, he offers such a good description of the possible range of female response that one wonders why, in his novels, women are not given greater opportunities to enjoy them. In trying to explain why nature placed orgasm "in the midst of the act of creation," he says "when a man and a woman conceive, would it not be best that they be able to see one another for a transcendent instant . . .?"

When Mailer turns to Miss Millett's attack on Henry Miller, it quickly becomes clear that she is only half right. While it is true that Miller depersonalizes women, it is also true that she cuts out all his tenderest passages to make him lie in her Procrustean bed. Mailer sees Miller as a smockless Dr. Masters, a researcher into the deserts of dreary lust, where man is sometimes driven by a sense of alienation from the nature that brought him forth. Miller's lust—and he recognizes it himself—is an attempt to get back into nature by force, by will alone. A pertinent passage from Miller is so exquisitely written that any woman not in a polemical mood would be tempted to forgive him. Mailer ends with an eminently reasonable summation, pointing out that Miller sought a tonic antagonism, while today we are looking for an accommodation of the sexes.

D. H. Lawrence "could not have commanded two infantrymen to follow him." A part of him was "like a little tobacconist from the English Midlands who would sniff the smoke of his wildest ideas . . . and hack out an irritable cough." But with all his eccentricities and limitations, Lawrence wrote more sensitively about women than any woman. As Mailer puts it, "we would not know how to try to burn by such a light." Lawrence "reminds us of the beauty of trying to be a man, because he was not much of a man himself." He knew his lungs would not let him live very long, and so "he saw every serious love affair as fundamental do-or-die: he knew he literally died a little more each time he missed transcendence in the act." He wished to go even beyond love, to what Mailer describes as "the existential edge" of becoming.

Speaking in his own voice, Mailer says that sex must have a meaning that goes to the root of existence—but "give meaning to sex and one was the prisoner of sex—the more meaning one gave it, the more it assumed, until every failure and misery, every evil of your life, spoke their lines in its light . . ." While Miss Millett sees the differences between men and women as nonessential, excesses of emotion to be conditioned out, he finds in their "asymmetry" a contrapuntal richness of choreography that no other formulation can offer. Her revolution, he concludes, could be the first bureaucracy of sex.

The Prisoner of Sex is Mailer's personal self as against his public one, if they can still be distinguished. His recent books have all been testaments of a sort, and this one is the most intimate, inclusive and deeply felt of all. It says more about love and sex than *Armies of the Night* said about politics—and today they may be even more important. While he is not always right in these pages, it doesn't really matter, because "beauty is truth, truth beauty." What Mailer has tried to do here is to write a love poem. Let us hope that women never become so liberated that it is impossible to write love poems to them.

Maunder in the Cafeteria

If Allen Ginsberg's introduction doesn't turn you off Jack Kerouac's *Visions of Cody*—now published for the first time in its entirety!—the book itself soon will. The introduction is one of the silliest pieces of writing I've ever seen. It is below even Ginsberg's usual level in prose, for I get the feeling that he wasn't entirely happy about writing it. He too may have outgrown *Visions of Cody*, or if that is too ambitious a word, let's say grown away from it.

The book does seem terribly dated, in the sense that it deals not with a particular period, but with attitudes that have not survived the period, that were soon recognized as the emotional and literary debris of that decade, doubtful even then. Evoking that time is like rehashing a teenage binge, complete with drunkenness, delusions of grandeur, the requisite trip to the whorehouse, and the final act of vomiting, which is an involuntary confession that it was all a mistake, more than anybody should be expected to stomach.

Never a man to indulge in understatement, Ginsberg seems to have trouble sustaining his rhapsody over Kerouac and Cody, who stands for Neal Cassady, "the great experiencer and Midwest driver." Our attention is reverently directed to Kerouac's "hair consciousness . . . sung in prose vowels," and here I think the author of the introduction has stumbled inadvertently on an accurate observation. Kerouac's books often do sound as if they were written without benefit of consonants, mumbled, so to speak. But at other times, Ginsberg seems a trifle uneasy: apologetic, defensive, ambivalent. Of the 128-page taped conversation set down unedited in the center of the book, he says that "despite monotony . . . it's real," confusing, as Jack Kerouac did, literature and reality.

The irritating thing about both Ginsberg and Kerouac is their habitual assumption that only they and a few of their friends have known reality, and the rest of us will have to find it in their books. This approach, of course, completely begs the question of art or literature. And since each member of their clique unabashedly asserts the "greatness" of the others, their characters or actions are never put to the test either, never made to measure up to any sort of criteria, any more than their "reality" is. It's an airtight system, something like a pot party, where all critical impulses go up in smoke.

After the ungrammatical litany of the introduction, the first pages of *Visions of Cody* come as a relief. They are simply descriptions of cafeterias. As Franklin P. Adams, of all people, once said, nobody can describe a guy eating a plate of beans better than Jack Kerouac. What a pity Jack didn't stick to that. As an offshoot of the beans, he was pretty good on cafeterias too. They were his "living theater" and gave him a chance to do what he does best: to observe the theatrical minutiae of a stranger's behavior and guess at what they meant.

At the top of his form, Jack Kerouac was a cross between a poor man's Thomas Wolfe and the early Henry Miller—but he didn't have Wolfe's intense involvement with life or Miller's ear, his sense of irony and his eye for beautifully unpretentious epiphanies. There's a faint whiff of the painter Edward Hopper in Kerouac too—that god-awfully ugly loneliness of small towns and impersonal places, a vision of America struggling toward an excruciating ineffability somewhere between past and present, a mood growing out of a random and runaway history whose final drama no one can remotely conjecture.

Kerouac can describe people and places, but what he *cannot* do is find anything meaningful for them to do in those places. Usually, they get drunk or high, have maudlin conversations and leave for another place where exactly the same thing happens. Regarding these conversations, I would like to propose, once and for all, a pox on "spantaneity" in fiction: spontaneity is a psychological, not a literary, quality. Though it may sometimes be pleasant to experience spontaneity it is almost never interesting to read, and while I'm at it, I'd like to point out that there are all kinds of spontaneity, good and bad, and the notion that what comes naturally is naturally welcome is one of the great idiocies of our age.

What is *Visions of Cody* about? Well, I've read it, and I'm damned if I know. I'm pretty sure, too, whose fault it is that I don't. The book has something to do with "pure-souled" Cody—Ginsberg calls him "heavenly" Cody—and the hero Jack Duluoz's need to get together and reminisce with him. It is about "the mystic rippling clothesline" in somebody's backyard and "enormously dark chocolate cake (gleaming scatological brown)."

There is a place for a book like *Visions of Cody*. I think it ought to be displayed in hockshop windows, below the "sad" or "ancient" trumpets and saxes of undistinguished men who gave up music and searching for the sound only they could hear, in order to buy a bottle and a dream of peace.

It Ain't Necessarily So

Somewhere under all these affectations there's a promising black author named Charles Wright. He says he's about forty, which means he's pretty old to be promising. You would think with two highly praised books already to his credit, he would be further along in the evolution of his style. He should have outgrown, for example, lines like "pierced with cut crystal sensitivity"; "the uric sperm of those years has flooded my mind"; "hoarded prejudices beget slaves who impale their masters on the arrow of time"; "mankind prepares not to scale the summit but to take the downward path into the great valley of the void"; "life's eyedropper is being sterilized with ant [urine]."

Can you imagine trying lines like these on, say, Miles Davis or the late Charlie Parker? Picture Joe Frazier's expression, or Willy Mays's, if you came on like that. When is the last time anybody speaking his own language ever talked about scaling summits? Has any black man outside of politics or the church used the word scale in that sense in the last fifty years? What is life's eyedropper, anyway, and why is it being sterilized with ant urine?

If Mr. Wright can mention Henry Green, Malcolm Lowry, and Nathanael West, he ought to know better than to mix their names with such nonsense. Why, Sonny Liston had better lines, on the average, than you'll find in *Absolutely Nothing to Get Alarmed About*. As an uneducated prize fighter like Liston proved, there *is* a rich black idiom, but so few black writers use it. Here and there, Mr. Wright shows that he has a good ear for genuine speech rhythms, but he keeps falling instead into a forced, amphetamine splutter or a drone of Cadillac oratory. In the middle of a nice blues-like scene with an ironic obbligato, he'll remember that he has read Faulkner and start bopping.

When he's relaxed and moving naturally, Mr. Wright can bring life—sad, bleak, painful, embarrassing or funny life—to the drug, wino, East Village and Bowery scenes that are his territory. (Much of this book appeared as separate essays in *The Village Voice*.) Sometimes he's so good-humored in these unpropitious environments that he makes it sound as if being black were a form of entertainment. And perhaps it is, under certain circumstances. Perhaps the human comedy is even funnier when your laughter has a touch of hysteria in it.

At other times, though, Mr. Wright sounds all smug and buttoned up. Although he rarely *is* alone, he's always telling us how much he *wants* to be alone, how sufficient unto himself he is, how far beyond the blandishments of poor, deluded humanity. He pontificates as if meditation was his thing, yet he's always popping dexies or drinking enough for half a dozen Madison Avenue executives.

As you read on in *Absolutely Nothing to Get Alarmed About*, a question is likely to arise in your mind. Why do many black writers deal only in extreme experiences? It's too easy: the drama is already there, and all too often it is the *same* drama. Don't any blacks lead bourgeois, or even ordinary working-class lives? Mr. Wright's cards are so stacked that, even when we know the elements of the scene are real, we feel that the characters are self-consciously posing too. The first to protest against stereotyping, many black writers seem determined to create one of their own.

The day has come, also, to reconsider one of their fundamental propositions: that "whitey" will never let you forget you're black. In Mr. Wright's case, the patent leather shoe is on the other foot. A further assumption that needs re-examination is the notion that a life thrown away constitutes a tragedy, a "horror," as the author would say. If a man shoots heroin into his arm, or a woman takes up prostitution, it is still possible that he or she, individually, is responsible and not "society." They are not always "forced" into it. If we take that line, who shall we blame for forcing the forcers into *their* special brands of unhappiness? Are we seriously to suppose that all American society is a hierarchy of imposed unhappiness with President Nixon at the top, a *primum mobile*?

Mr. Wright is at his best in his throwaway lines, like the time he described two junkies trying to sell him a pair of ice skates. When he sums up a particular kind of white girl as having "a ban-the-bomb-air," we feel that, yes, we've met her. We're even willing to forgive him his dangling clauses when he goes down to the Chelsea health center to show up a busy surrealist day at the V.D. clinic. We want to like him—he's appealing in his cranky way—but he keeps fading out of focus on us. He insists on blowing both hot and cool, and the two don't jive.

At one point in his hot phase, he says that blacks have nothing to lose but their lives—and it ain't necessarily so. Mr. Wright, for example, can lose his audience, his talent, his dignity, his sense of humor—oh, any number of things.

Fare for the Ideal Audience

T. S. Eliot once remarked that his ideal audience would be made up of illiterates. Presumably, they would receive his work with open minds, uncluttered by preconceptions. Unfortunately, only children's books are read this way—and we can see what Eliot meant. If we remember nothing else of our reading, there are always those first few stories, like first loves, never to be forgotten. How do we use this unrivaled opportunity? Not as well as we might, says Selma Lanes, and she goes on to show how difficult it is to do justice to a child's imagination.

Some of us err in the direction of sentimentality. After lavishing infinite care on our children's diets when they are infants, we are content to feed them nothing but sweets when they are old enough for books. Some of us are too didactic. The books we choose for our children are about as much fun as toilet training. Nor are "emancipated" parents invariably wiser: Mrs. Lanes tells of an otherwise sensible mother who preserved the remains of her child's umbilical cord, so that she could paste it in a memory book and present it to him when he was fully grown. Here is the ultimate "realism" in a children's book.

Energy, versatility, sensibility. This is a large order, but it's what we should be aiming for, says Mrs. Lanes in *Down the Rabbit Hole*. And some writers are. She describes a story by Uri Shulevitz that imaginatively joins the old and the new—the escape from reality and the affirmation of it. It is called "One Monday Morning," and in it a king, queen, prince, knight and palace retinue—all in full panoply—proceed along a shabby street to a rundown tenement, where they huddle in a hallway to look for the doorbell of the little boy they inexplicably come to visit each day of the week.

In a story by Isaac Bashevis Singer, Princess Nesika rejects her latest suitor "because his boots are foolish." Maurice Sendak has a story that begins where most leave off: its dog heroine, Jenny, has everything and is discontented, because, as she says,

"There must be more to life than having everything." When she gives up all her comforts in idealistic renunciation, she discovers that "There must be more to life than having nothing."

In a witty review of the old versus the new, Mrs. Lanes betrays her own nostalgia for that world of certainties that has all but disappeared. Kate Greenaway, her favorite nineteenth-century author, has the artist's essentially tragic view; her books express the poignancy of life's evanescence in the act of recapturing childhood. Mrs. Lanes has doubts about the dazzling pictorial emphasis in some of the new books. They are not books so much as "products," the illegitimate children of advertising and technology. At their best, such books may create a generation that is verbally retarded and visually advanced.

When she praises, Mrs. Lanes goes all out, making Maurice Sendak the William Blake of children's books, and giving E. B. White's mouse-child, Stuart Little, almost as much symbolic significance as Gregor Samsa in Franz Kafka's "Metamorphosis." In her enthusiasm for Dr. Seuss—the Patrick Henry of today's nursery set—she rather glibly rationalizes the unnecessary ugliness of his drawings.

The integration of children's books is very reasonably reviewed. Mrs. Lanes is not afraid to say that—though it will not do now—*Little Black Sambo* once helped white children see black people as sympathetic human beings. And she has an "alas" for the fact that Brer Rabbit and Dr. Dolittle too are rife with white-supremacist attitudes. She comments wryly on the tokenism of simply darkening apparently white children until they look "sunburned," as one black child put it. And then she comes right back with a scarcely concealed impatience for a self-consciously black poem that begins:

> *Afraid of the dark*
> *Is afraid of Mom*
> *And Daddy ...*

Like the old saw about the poet, the author of a children's book is still something of a child himself. Perhaps this accounts for the lack of inhibition that has made children's books—with the possible exception of cinema—the most experimental and inventive popular art medium in our time. Children today don't have to live on candy any more. They can enjoy a precocious anomie in *The Phantom Tollbooth*. They can apostrophize the universe in a lisp if they like: the late 1960's brought a wave of bittersweet books that boldly confront the question, "What is happiness?"

But though literature like this will probably help them get through life, some of us may prefer to go on seeing children's books as author Paul Hazard did: as "insurance against the time, all too soon, when there will be nothing but realities."

Old Age as Life's Parody

You ought to be warned right away that simply reading this book may be enough to age you. Miss Beauvoir loads us with so many depressing examples—from primitive, historical and present-day society—of the predicament of old age that we cannot help cringing a bit under their burden. She has an ax to grind and society is her whetstone. Her writing has an abrasive quality not only for this reason, but also because Miss Beauvoir seems by temperament to be a professional pessimist and tragedian. As if this were not enough, she applies to the already bowed shoulders of the aged some of Jean-Paul Sartre's more obscure existential strictures on the human estate.

If Miss Beauvoir were simply giving us a summary of the condition of the aged in different societies, past and present, *The Coming of Age* might be a useful anthology with the reservation that the quotations strongly reflect the personal bias of the editor. But the author has a thesis, and one often feels that her documentation is determined by that thesis. It is no secret that "learned" quotations can be found to support almost any view.

After citing the customs of a number of primitive people, Miss Beauvoir sums up a variety of practices that anticlimactically appear to balance out. In such societies, the old are killed; they are left to die; they are given enough for bare subsistence; they are provided with a "decent end"; they are revered or cherished. In other words, the treatment of the aged runs the whole gamut of response.

In civilized societies, it is only the "privileged classes" that have passed on the record of their aged members, and these have been valued for their "real" worth: i.e., their wealth and property. The underprivileged or "exploited" aged—whose lives were not recorded—Miss Beauvoir projects into institutions, imagines them "pushed out of the house or even secretly put to death."

In the middle chapters of the book, the author quotes almost compulsively from poets, novelists and philosophers, and insists on taking literally those rhetorical remarks of which famous writers—especially French ones—are so fond. "A very old man's memories are like ants whose ant hill has been destroyed." "Fifty years of reading: and what remains of it?" "Oh, be damned to old age, that hideous thing!" If an aged person should express himself as happy, Miss Beauvoir discounts this as a defense, or asks, in true Gallic fashion: What is happiness?

Even the famous man who has accomplished more than he ever hoped for is seen as successful, not in his own experience of himself, but simply in the eyes of others. "The promises have been kept," the author says of her own life, "nevertheless I have been swindled."

The picture is too negative: "The role of a retired person is no longer to possess one." Children "very rarely" help their parents, the author states, and then goes on to say that one out of three do. Is this "very rarely?" If a home for the aged offers television, "it tires their eyes." Miss Beauvoir claims: "I have never come across one single woman, either in life or in books, who has looked upon her own old age cheerfully." The reader may feel a fundamental conflict between a statement like this and his own experience.

Again and again, the author accuses capitalist society of being interested in people only for their economic potential. She describes the "humanism" of such societies as mere window dressing, as if nothing disinterested were ever done for the aged. Of course, there is some truth—one might even say much—in what she writes, but she adulterates it by overgeneralization. Many of her observations are merely common sense, as when she remarks that the retiree's state of mind goes a long way toward determining the quality of his life after retirement. The only solution to the emptiness of retirement, she believes, is to go on pursuing life in concrete terms, to work at something in order to keep from falling into nothingness.

Senile dementia, she claims, is something like an identity crisis, caused by the condition of the aged persons' life: their isolation, lack of contact with reality, feeling of uselessness and poverty. The depression so common among elderly people is nothing but a mourning over the loss of the ego. Similarly, according to Miss Beauvoir, no one dies of old age, but of some form or another of pathology. On this basis, she conceives of people working—at scaled-down tasks—until death overtakes them, thus eliminating this painful stage of life.

As things now stand, old age is life's parody, a view borne out by the plays of Beckett and Ionesco. And now the author comes to her thesis: "The reason the retired man is rendered hopeless by the want of meaning in his present life is that the meaning of his existence has been stolen from him from the very beginning." "Between youth and age there turns the machine, the crusher of men," which conceals all problems in the mere routine of living.

"Old age exposes the failure of our entire civilization." "It is the meaning that men attribute to their life, it is their entire system of values that defines the value and meaning of old age." Therefore, "it is the whole man that must be remade." Before we can change old age we must "change life itself." The statement has grandeur, all right, and éclat too. One only wonders how much practical or immediate value it has, and whether fashionable sociology ever settles, these days, for anything less than panaceas.

Weeds and Four-Leaf Clovers

Years ago when I lived in the Village and had a nine-to-five job, I used to eat breakfast at a place called Joe's Dinette on West Fourth Street. Most mornings, there was a guy named Dick in the next booth, reading *The New York Times* and chuckling over little items he found in it that amused him. As far as I knew, he didn't work, this Dick, and I wondered why he got up so early in the morning. Perhaps he didn't mind getting up because there was no job waiting for him to buckle down to, or maybe he went back to sleep after he finished chuckling over the *Times*. Whatever his reasons, I know I both envied and resented his freedom. I would have liked to have leisure and the detachment to chuckle over the *Times* too—the news wasn't as bad in those days—but I had to hustle off to work. This is how I feel about Richard Brautigan's stories. In fact, what I've just written sounds like a Brautigan story, right down to the inexplicable coincidence of both characters' being named Richard.

Brautigan sounds like a relaxed observer with all the time in the world to muse over the curious little turns life takes. Overheard remarks, incongruous occurrences, sense impressions, the shapes of buildings or the look of people, the color of the weather—all this mixed in with memories, girls, places, jottings in a notebook, made by a man with nothing pressing on him, no compulsion to put it all in perspective, interpret it, drive it to the wall and ask, "What does it mean?"

He can get sixty-two "stories" into a 174-page book that begins with page 9. The shortest is three lines and the longest is seven pages. As you can see, there isn't much room for deep probing or sustained interaction. No sweat, man, you take it as it comes. Don't look at it too hard or you'll see beyond the moment, the two-penny epiphany, to the fact that these are just postcards, sent by somebody who's on vacation from life, a vacation he took a bus to, carrying nothing but a knapsack.

This doesn't mean that *Revenge of the Lawn* isn't fun to read. It often is. There are lots of nice things. A man who "looked as if life had given him an endless stream of two-timing girlfriends, five-day drunks and cars with bad transmissions." A friend who burns his transistor radio on the beach because his wife has left and the music has gone out of his life. A man who is so fond of poems that he decides to take the plumbing out of his house and replace it with poetry. A sudden sight, on a beach near Monterey, of a group of "frog people," boys and girls dressed in black rubber suits with yellow oxygen tanks, eating watermelon.

There's a pleasant vignette of Brautigan watching a guy in the City Lights bookstore trying to make up his mind to buy one of his books. Finally he tosses a coin and the book loses. A really sweet piece—yes, I mean sweet—describes last night's girl getting dressed in the morning, disappearing, in due time, into her clothes and becoming an altogether new experience. There's another girl "sleeping in a very well-built blond way," until suddenly she starts to get up. "Get back in bed," he says. "Why?" she says. "Because you're still asleep," "Ohhh . . . okay," she says, cuddling up close.

Brautigan has a good feeling for the American past, for small towns and the erosion of life styles, that is surprising in a man only in his middle thirties. But sometimes he's not satisfied to leave these quaint old snapshots alone and tries to tint them with literature. His longest story is about a boy going hunting in Oregon with his Uncle Jarv. They stop in a small town, where Uncle Jarv writes a postcard and the boy stares at a nude Marilyn Monroe calendar on the post office wall. Somebody in the town has shot two bear cubs and a practical joker dresses them up—one in a white silk negligee—and sits them in a car. From this—the death of the bears, the masquerade, the negligee, the calendar in the post office—Brautigan reaches all the way out into left field for Marilyn Monroe's suicide, years later, while she is still a cuddly little cub too, dressed up in death like a practical joke.

He does this too often for comfort. A story about a "crazy" old lady who fills her house with vases of flowers ends with a sententious bit of irrelevance: "This was a month or two before the

German army marched into Poland." Out hunting one day because he "just wanted the awareness of hunting," the first-person narrator is shocked to come upon an ugly shack, erected in what had always been virgin forest. Four small children without shoes come out on the porch of the shack to stare silently at him. It is raining and they are getting soaked, but they stand there, staring, silent. The author then nails up this heavy sign on their porch: "I had no reason to believe that there was anything more to life than this."

He wins some and he loses some. Once in a while a piece will rise to poetry. Others never get beyond easy vignettes, light enough to blow off the page. At its worst, *Revenge of the Lawn* sounds, simultaneously, like a clumsily written children's book and a pretentious piece of avant-garde impressionism. At his best, Brautigan is one of those odd-looking guys with long hair and granny glasses who sees, hears, feels and thinks things that may make some of us believe he's found a better answer to being alive here and now than we have.

The Ecology of Fiction

Why should it be so hard to write a readable novel? All you need is a couple of believable people trying to do something conceivable with a perfectly natural degree of emotional investment. Then you just throw in an impediment or two—something circumstantial or peculiar to the people themselves—and see which way the matter falls out. A believable character will have a particular way of speaking and acting; he will have strengths and weaknesses; a share of both appealing and repugnant qualities. Most of us are sufficiently addicted to our species to follow its members through all but their most routine activities.

We do this every day, in listening to the stories and anecdotes of friends, relatives, co-workers or lovers. It's nothing short of marvelous—all things considered—how willing we are to contemplate our fellow man. It may be positively paradoxical, but we still appear to find him more fascinating than the riches of museums, the charms of landscape, the seduction of music or the rewards of meditation. Our predilection for him borders on the perverse.

With all this in his favor, you would think that a writer only has to put something down on paper, to tell it as it is—as the current phrase goes—in order to produce a readable novel. Not good, but readable. Certainly, our earlier novelists knew how to do this: they crammed in page after page of reality and used art only sparingly, as a condiment, so to speak. In fact, one may justify a generalization: the evolution of the modern novel has been in the direction of a remorseless substitution of art for reality. Today there are novels being written with no reality whatsoever, as if art were actually all that long and life so woefully short.

I'm driven to these reflections by the number of novels I come across that I would classify as not readable—in the sense that page 1 does not create an appetite or curiosity for page 2, and that this effect is intensified rather than lessened the further I go. Often, instead of feeling that life is being transmogrified into art for my pleasure and improvement, I get the uneasy sensation that the novelist is trying to work on me *directly*, as if he and I were the only protagonists of his work and his theory of the novel the only plot. The ecological crisis has infected fiction, too: the waste products of technique and experimentation are threatening to choke out the organic.

On the dust cover of *Suddenly Tomorrow*, I see four quotations from respected critics praising P. M. Pasinetti's first three novels. They contain phrases like "meaningful action" and "full of life." In receiving an award from the National Institute of Arts and Letters, Mr. Pasinetti was described as in "the grand style of tradition but with a probing modern imagination." In *Suddenly Tomorrow*, that probing modern imagination seems to have been his undoing. Indeed, the book seems more like a probe than a novel. "So-and-so probes the predicament of contemporary man."

I don't see how I can summarize the book without boring you. It has to do with an international "group," sponsored of course by an American, which buys control of a number of Italian periodicals and begins to "restructure" them according to the newest American conceptions of efficiency. This efficiency is expressed in a vocabulary that sounds like an unconsummated marriage of Pentagon prose and McLuhanese.

Dissension follows and the group divides into two factions: a "scientific" one manipulated by an "organization man," and a "creative" one magnetized by a writer. In the creative camp, everybody makes love; in the other, generalizations. No one utters anything resembling human speech. Cause and effect, those old friends of "the grand style of tradition," are forgotten. The characters change only in their locations. The original issues, such as they were, rot away into a rubble of symbols.

What all this means should be left to people who like to do crossword puzzles. I suppose it would be safe to say that *Suddenly Tomorrow* contains the suggestion that the integrity of things is threatened by the depersonalizing trend of modern life. If Mr. Pasinetti has not succeeded in dramatizing this idea, the moral is not yet lost—for he has *illustrated* it only too well. I believe his book suggests still another moral: if the reader can't get his teeth into a novel, he ought to be forgiven for fastening on the author.

Much Ado about Very Little

It's a poor reflection on Regency England that Lady Caroline Lamb was able to cut such a conspicuous figure in it. Regarded as a romantic heroine and a raiser of even the most jaded eyebrows, she strikes one in *Caro: The Fatal Passion* as little better than an impostor. Her behavior was so stereotypically neurotic that it hardly left room for a personality. Her beauty was not remarkable; she had no particular talents; and without her great family name, she might never have surfaced in society.

Her notoriety grew chiefly out of her "affair" with the poet Byron, yet the evidence strongly suggests that there never was, in fact, any affair. She boasted of being Byron's mistress; wrote him hundreds of letters, both adoring and vituperative; forced her way into his carriage and his rooms; waited on other people's doorsteps for him; fell in and out of "fevers" on his account; grossly mistreated a husband far too good for her; and generally made a nuisance of herself. Yet she and Byron actually saw each other for only a few months.

He was being lionized in London for his *Childe Harold* and his famous profile. Quite a few women of the smart set offered themselves on the altar of literature, but Caroline threw herself like a pie in the poet's face. For his part, Byron couldn't seem to decide whether or not to duck. A snob and social climber, he was also monolithically conceited. Though he seemed to have no desire for Caroline—her thinness reminded him of butterflies or spiders—he found her irresistible as a feather in his cap. You might say that he wanted to have his cake without eating it.

Neither of these notorious "lovers" appeared to have any taste for the activity that the word implies. Byron most unpoetically believed that "one must make love mechanically, as one swims," adding that he never indulged "till almost obliged." Caroline, who was married to William Lamb, by all reports a handsome and strongly sexed man, recoiled in dismay from her wifely duties, though at the time she believed herself to be in love with her husband. Byron seemed comfortable only with compliant older women. Caroline cared only for the rhetoric and the agony of passionate posturing.

On the lawn of her country home, Brocket Hall, she burned him in effigy in a curious dramatic performance written and choreographed by herself and acted by a score of young maidens dressed all in white. He wrote scurrilous accounts of her to a number of people she knew, but sent her sentimental love letters by the same post. She also had the distinction of inspiring some very doggerel-like lines when her antics outraged him beyond prose description.

The genesis of *Caro: The Fatal Passion* seems reasonable enough. Caroline's great-great-grandniece put at the author's disposal the unpublished sketches, diaries, commonplace books and other memorabilia of her celebrated ancestor. Unfortunately, Caroline was such an exhibitionist during her lifetime that there was very little of this material that she herself hadn't already publicized out of all proportion. And twenty years of hysteria based on six months of unconsummated "love" is bound to grow monotonous. Mr. Blyth has not ennobled the occasion, either. He hovers between homilies on the dangers of permissiveness and far-fetched pornographic speculations concerning Byron's sexual proclivities. His attempted reconstruction of the poet's wedding night—he married another woman for her money—is a masterpiece of inadvertent comedy.

Even so, Byron comes across as a cad, condemned in his own words. The great lover not only was a reluctant obliger, but also disliked sleeping in the same bed with a woman. Even eating together disgusted him, he said, adding that "lobster salad and champagne" were "the only truly feminine and becoming viands." Byron's famous pallor, attributed by female admirers to his poetic exertions, was caused, says the author, by a habitual use of laxatives.

In a fit of pique, Caroline wrote a novel called *Glenarvon*, in which she again demonstrated her almost total lack of taste by misrepresenting her husband, backbiting her friends and adding fictive substance to her apocryphal affair with Byron. Not to be outdone, the poet noised it about that he and his half-sister Augusta were lovers, thereby ruining her reputation without even affording her the pleasure that a bad name usually implies.

It all ended anticlimactically enough. Exiled in Greece

because incest was the one indulgence the Regency could not condone, Byron died of "a fever" at the age of thirty-seven. According to the serving woman who laid out the corpse, it was "white like the wing of a young chicken." The Greeks tried to claim his body, but were allowed to keep only his lungs. Caroline, his wife and his half-sister all tried in vain to learn whether their names had been among his last words. After much debate, his memoirs were burned. The author hints in his heavy way that Byron's friends and intimates were trying to keep from the curious world the poet's own confession of certain perversities. Caroline died soon after of dropsy. She was forty-one.

For all its sound and fury, *Caro* is only a tempest in a teacup. Not a very pretty cup at that. It turns out that Byron was only a man, after all, not a myth. And all his poetry was in his pen.

The Star-Crossed South

In her second collection of short stories, Shirley Ann Grau shows
an impressive range: her stories stretch from fairly good to pretty
bad. She is very much a Southern writer, with many of the virtues and flaws this description implies. Southern fiction, for
example, seems to have a soft spot for the freaky, the sort of
thing Tennessee Williams is famous for: ladies who are spiritually on their last legs, who "imagine" things, who look as if
they've been tenderly brought down from the attic, and are
given to talking to themselves in a rather "dicty" way.

Hot nights, moss hanging from the trees, the heavy scent of
magnolias, snakes in the hollows, a nostalgia for feudal living,
an elocution that encourages bombast, a need to outdo the
North—all this may have influenced the Southern style of writing. And a history of intimate domestic contact with black people may have encouraged the development of a sort of white
voodoo, which is the Southern writer's equivalent of the Absurd.

Faulkner and Flannery O'Connor were good enough to salvage something out of this tattered anachronism—at least in
their best work. Less talented authors tend to fall into the bayou
or swamp, into inscrutable wisdom of the South. All too often
in fiction, the South seems to be looking back. "Immemorial"
was Faulkner's favorite word, and characters in Southern books
are always gazing off into the pathos of distance and remembering. People grow older by hungering for what they have left
behind. The cornfields are always ripe for picking. Every night
you can hear the dying cry of the field mouse as the owl swoops
down. The stars are invariably crossed.

In their favor, Southern writers have an environment that
might still be called heterogeneous. They have a sense of tradition that is useful as a contrapuntal line. If their language is
sometimes debased, the corruption is of their own making—not
"the media's." They believe in mystery, in refreshing contrast to
the quiz-kid omniscience of too many Northern writers.

Of the eighteen stories in *The Wind Shifting West,* the best and the worst are those which are most typically Southern. "Stanley," the last and longest story, shows us a forty-six-year-old black butler watching a rich white man almost twice his age reminisce in his wheelchair. The old man sits in a greenhouse especially built for him—to keep him from drying up?—and the huge cage of tropical birds beside his chair is constantly replenished, as if to deny such a thing as death. The old man has had a colorful life—one of his last remarks is about the condors of San Ysedro—but the butler already feels that his own is over. His experience has not rejuvenated him. All he looks forward to is going *back* to the town where he was born, to sit on the porch and recall his childhood, the only part of his life worth reviewing.

"Homecoming" is a bitter blow at Southern sentimentality and love of ritual. A girl is notified that a boy who gave her his ring before going to Vietnam—a boy she hardly knew—has been killed in action. Her mother, who has all too coincidentally lost her husband in another war, treats the occasion as a widowing of her daughter and invites her friends to a "wake." The girl is galled by her loveless bereavement, and her last words to the memory of the boy are almost an emancipation proclamation for Southern writing: " 'Good-by,' she said in a very light whisper. 'You poor bastard.' "

In "The Thieves," an aging girl waits for her lover to propose to her. One night, his indecisiveness so annoys her that she helps a thief, who was trapped by the police in her backyard, to escape. This is her rebellion against the convention and the "safety" of marriage. When her lover does propose, it is too late. She has already seen beyond him, into an unfillable void, and answers with "Go away, little boy."

"Beach Party" is a very deft story about a good-looking woman of forty who is seduced on her brother-in-law's boat as they go to pick up her husband, who has foolishly—symbolically?—splintered his mast in showing off. Though it begins promisingly enough, the story settles for mere deftness and an imposed pessimism. After making love, the woman says ". . . that's all there's left . . . some weed on the anchor and some salt dried on our skin." The brother-in-law replies with "There isn't ever much left, when it's done," and the reader wonders why not? Why isn't there much left? And, in fact, after a moment's reflection, anyone can see that the truth of the story has been sold short for the price of neatness, so the author can quit while she thinks she's ahead.

"Last Gas Station" is pure backwoods Beckett. A family that runs a gas station progressively diminishes by desertion, traffic mysteriously increases, abandoned cars clutter the roadside, and so on. "Pillow of Stone" is a broken-English slander against Creoles, a folk opera in which a pregnant daughter braves heavy seas to reach her dead father's bedside so "he can rest" once he knows that she has "come with one to take his place."

There are a few more O.K. stories and a few inconsequential vignettes, snapshots that didn't develop well: like one of a young teenager absorbing the death of a skindiver at a beach party with about the same degree of discomfort and understanding that she might feel if she swallowed her chewing gum. Miss Grau has sharpened her tools, but they cut too easily through her characters. Her formal preoccupations sometimes have the effect of cramping their style, of keeping them from being fully themselves. *The Wind Shifting West* would be a more interesting book if they all broke through the plotted trajectories of her stories to the incalculable reaches we sense in them.

Overtime at the Office

Perhaps every unmarried woman is a bit of a sociologist, majoring in men. If she works with them, listens to their troubles and sleeps with them too, this ought to entitle her to some sort of Ph.D. God knows her life will need all the philosophy, all the doctoring, she can give it. No man is a hero to his valet, someone said: this is equally true of his secretary. And imagine how much less a hero he is when he sleeps with her too, gets staggering drunk with her and cries on her to boot.

And this, apparently, is what the brilliant executives of one of our most brilliant New York companies do with their female co-workers, according to the fifteen women Jack Olsen interviewed in *The Girls in the Office*. How Mr. Olsen got them to tell so much—"to lay the brain upon a board and pick the acrid colors out"—is a mystery, but one never doubts that they are telling it as they have experienced it. Or, at least, as well as they can, subject to the possible distortions of disappointment. And it's not only the brain they lay out, but the heart and everything else too.

Anyone who has ever worked in a large, sophisticated New York office will find hundreds of home truths here. And anyone who runs such an office could learn more by reading this book than by hiring management consultants to tell him what's wrong with his operating procedures. Here are just a few of the "girls' " observations: There are two kinds of workers, those who work too hard and those who don't work at all. Most of the work is done by a "nucleus of martyrs." "The greater part of many employees' energy goes into bitching." The members of the new generation don't get emotional about the company or its product: They're only interested in getting ahead. They are mostly "engineers, with no poets." And the new companies are killing their employees with kindness, undercutting their sense of responsibility with an ever-increasing permissiveness.

Mr. Olsen simply lets his anonymous women talk—and how

they pour it out! Bitter truths spurt from them like blood from the severed artery of someone who has slashed her wrists. The subjects of his interviews range from a jet-setter of fifty to small-town virgins in their early twenties. These last usually come to New York not so much because it appeals to them: they are simply fleeing their hometowns and their parents. After a while, most of them become hooked on the city, like addicts. As one of them put it: "New York is where I *have* to be. I wish I knew why."

Their outpourings range over four subjects: their lives and backgrounds, their jobs, their men and their feelings about the city. Some of them come out with remarkable lines. One woman, speaking of the brutality of today's muggings, says: "You can't even be robbed gracefully in this city." Referring to the police, she says that they have turned into "statisticians" of crime rather than preventers or punishers of it. Describing the locks on her door and the bars on her windows, another woman remarks: "Pretty soon I'll be as safe here as any person in solitary." Still another points out that middle-class people in New York live in lower-class housing; upper-class people live in middle-class housing; lower-class people live in "caves."

There is a great deal of sex going on at the company, most of it with married men. It is almost inevitable, one of Mr. Olsen's informants feels, because of the intimacy of working together. You're "producing a product in close conjunction with brilliant men, just as married couples produce children." Because the men at the company make other men seem dull or ordinary, many of the women in the office can only be satisfied by having affairs with their bosses or other colleagues.

Some become the permanent "other woman"; for many, life is "wall to wall men." Few of them are happy with their roles by the time the novelty wears off, and on the morning after, they have some caustic and telling things to say. One warns that when a man cries on your shoulder, it takes away his masculinity and then he is forever trying to get it back—at your expense. Another complains that the men in the company make sex carry such a heavy load, using it for everything except what it really is.

One "religious" executive promised God he'd give up something important if he got the promotion he wanted. The "something important" turned out to be his office mistress. A jilted woman gives us a harrowing description of her situation: "When you're in hell, you can see *everything* that your survivors do; you are *forced* to see . . ." A more philosophical observer feels that sex is the best and most available "counter-irritant" for a messed-up life. One of those who have been turned off believes that "love requires a better setting than New York City." People in New York don't love, she says—they copulate.

There's enough pathos in some of these monologues to melt all the company's typewriters. One fifty-year-old former belle simply "refuses" to age and talks wildly about science-fiction fountains of youth. Another is so insecure that she exclaims in genuine anguish: "How I must have bored people in my lifetime! I keep telling myself to say less and less . . ."

After listening to these fifteen women, one gets the impression that adultery is as necessary to the running of the company as electricity or air-conditioning. One might go even further and say that it is as much a part of the office's functioning as the company's product itself. It is tempting to wonder what would happen if these women—who are treated as if they were something between a wastebasket and a vase of flowers on the boss's desk— were to say no to the ever-present propositions. Or if the men never made the propositions. The mere idea of rechanneling all that energy is enough to drive one to drink.

Prix Fixe Passions

Of all the writers who have been generally accepted as geniuses, Balzac seems to me to be one of the least readable today. Though he was highly praised by such redoubtable figures as Henry James and Marcel Proust, it is difficult to see how they could forgive him his prose style, which ran to sentences like these: "Our passions, vices, our inborn extremism, our pleasures and our pains are torrents of the mind flowing through us. When a man concentrates on violent ideas at any given point, he is destroyed by them as if he had been pierced by the point of a dagger." Apart from their pedestrian tone, these statements are not even true. Paralleling his life, which was a series of financial schemes and scrapes, Balzac's novels often resembled a marathon of moral bookkeeping. Though it was a Frenchman who called the English a nation of shopkeepers, I think his own countrymen are better qualified for this compliment, including their writers. No one is fonder of wrapping up human nature in little prose packages.

The maxim, a manufactured profundity, differs from a homily or a Chinese proverb only in its delusions of grandeur. For centuries, French literature has staggered under its burden. This prix fixe view of the passions is probably an impoverished descendant of the celebrated conversations of court life and the salons, where discourse had displaced the jousting of feudal times. In life, Balzac was obsessed with furniture, bric-a-brac, carpets, knickknacks, gimcracks and gewgaws; in literature, he was not very different. Mr. Pritchett says that, near the end of his life, Balzac was "becoming a fantastic scrap merchant," and this is not an unfair description of his novels.

When we learn that most of Balzac's precious purchases were worthless, that fake paintings and antiques were frequently palmed off on him as originals, that his taste throughout his various houses was execrable, we are naturally inclined to wonder about his alleged omniscience regarding his era. He was, after all, anything but an ivory tower artist: the stuff of things was supposed to be his forte. In a letter to his haughty fiancée, trying to impress her with his financial assets, Balzac even reckoned the value of his house furnishings by their weight alone. It seems to me that critics tend to apply this same criterion to his artistic worth.

One finds the word "fecundity" frequently popping up in their appraisal of him, but this word has more to do with quantity than quality. Even if we take it to mean richness of invention, the kindest construction, this is still insufficient. If he invented a thousand situations, they dealt with only a dozen themes: greed, power, money, jealousy and a few other staples from Les Halles. A hundred minor novels will not make a major writer. Balzac was like a sheepdog, trying to herd all humanity into his fold, his prose a monotonous bark of explanation, for as Mr. Pritchett observes, "He was a born explainer and lacked the gift of omission and suggestion." The author chooses to praise Balzac's "ubiquity . . . the spry, pungent, and pervasive sense that in any scene he was *there* and in the flesh." Such a statement seems to me more of an indictment than a compliment.

All this, however, does not prevent *Balzac* from being a diverting book, for its subject was a better character than any he invented. Short, fat, gap-toothed, uncouth, absurdly affected, he was so alive, so sincere in his insincerities, that people—especially women—found him irresistible. When he was in love, he wrote so many interminable letters that they constituted a kind of rape by attrition. One can see his prospective mistresses weakening under the assault of this lyrical third degree. Any one of them could easily have stuffed a mattress with his correspondence.

From Mr. Pritchett's account, it would appear that Balzac's reputation as a libertine was exaggerated. Considering the fact that he overdid everything, his consumption of women was proportionately modest. He preferred older women, because they served the dual purpose of satisfying him sexually and supplying him, out of their experiences, with material for his novels. According to the author, Balzac worked best when he was sexually satisfied, which would seem to discredit Freud's view of art as sublimation as well as a widespread story which has Balzac emerging from a brothel exclaiming, "I've lost a book!"

Born in a bourgeois family, Balzac began as a law student, then worked as a hack writer of Gothic shockers for about ten years before he began what was to become *The Human Comedy*. In his incessant plunges into debt, he seemed to invite difficulties so that he would have to write his way out of them. He went to bed at eight every evening, awoke at midnight and wrote until six in the morning, with incredible facility. But as an English wit remarked: "Easy writing's curst hard reading." Balzac did revise his work but only in galleys—sometimes three successive sets of them—so that as much as a third of his royalties often went into printing costs.

When all his moneymaking schemes, including a pineapple plantation outside Paris, had failed, Balzac clung to his dream of marrying the wealthy Polish countess he had pursued for seventeen years, waiting for her elderly husband to die. When the obliging count finally vacated his side of the bed, the countess cruelly teased Balzac with one excuse or another. Here again, his life was a finer tragicomedy than his fiction, for she married him only a year before he too died. He had characteristically bought and furnished a mansion in her name in Paris, and though he was already enfeebled by fifty years of frenzy, this incurable bourgeois wrote repeatedly to his mother from Poland to see that the rugs were brushed, the furniture dusted, the lamps cleaned and the curtains covered in calico to keep them from fading.

When he and his bride arrived at the mansion, he half-dead, she with her feet so swollen with gout that she could not walk, they found the gates locked and a locksmith had to be sent for. Inside, the house was a wreck, everything smashed by a servant who had gone mad. As if he recognized an irony that could never be revised on the galleys, Balzac took to his bed and died.

The Real Casanova at Last

It is ironic that Casanova's memoirs are popularly known chiefly for their sexual content, because he is the least pornographic of writers. In contrast to the characters of so many contemporary authors, he is so completely satisfied during his encounters that he feels no desire to talk about them afterward. In the twelve volumes of his *Life*, there is hardly a single mention of a sexual part, or an "explicit" description of love-making. In this most concrete of contexts, he is at his most abstract, speaking only of "charms," "fires," "happiness" and "bliss." Often it is like parsing a difficult Latin sentence to discover exactly what happened. Instead of priding himself as a conqueror of women, Casanova sees himself as a bearer of gifts. His enthusiasm and his gratitude for "favors" received are so uncool that today's sophisticates would consider him corny. And in our promiscuous age, his long sieges, his labors in the lists of love, seem quaint at best, an antiquarian study, a minuet, you might say.

He describes his successes as one would describe a chess game: a series of strategies, of moves and countermoves, that lead to victory. Though he seems to have an extraordinary capacity for sexual pleasure, he never writes possessively of pleasure, as if he had pioneered in it, or was planning to take out a patent on it. For all his experience, he offers few recipes or how-to-do-it formulas. If he had, it would not have helped, for his technique was inseparable from his temperament. More than his wit, his talent for intrigue, his good looks, Casanova's strongest point as a lover was an almost hypnotic ability to project his appreciation. He made women see themselves magnified in his eyes: to look into them was an unexpected plunge into autoeroticism.

Casanova differed in several important ways from other heroes or high priests of sex. He never derides women as Henry Miller does; he doesn't feel obliged to deify them as Lawrence must; he rarely turns away in disgust like Boswell. They were a pleasure, a sport, a vocation, an art form—but always realistically perceived. Like William Hickey, another great diarist of the eighteenth century, he enjoyed women as such, with a fullness and a naturalness that puzzles our self-conscious age. He wasn't trying to prove anything except that it is wonderful to be alive and to have an opposite sex to celebrate it with.

With Volumes 11 and 12 of his *History of My Life*, we find Casanova in his forties, seducing, charming and intriguing his way through Spain, France and Italy. He was as irresistible to men as he was to women; when he could not secure a patron with his social gifts, he fell back on his talent as a con man. Posing as a magician-necromancer, complete with "oracles," he gulled the rich in order to live as they did, because luxury, like love, was indispensable to this lowborn son of Spanish-Italian actors.

What makes Casanova so unusual is the contradictions in his personality. Though his poems, historical essays and mathematical treatises were respected in his own time, though he was accomplished enough to impress the Pope, Frederick the Great and Voltaire, he was also capable of shady dealing when driven to it by necessity. Yet, somehow, he never lost his integrity or his sense of dignity. When he was sleeping with a man's wife, he was capable of resenting the smallest slight or breach of manners on the husband's part. Though sometimes a thief, he was a Robin Hood, too, helping impoverished friends whenever he could. For example, finding the chambermaid in one of his innumerable lodgings to be disfigured by a glass eye that was far too large and of a different color from the other, he took her out and bought her a superior one—before he even suspected that he would sleep with her.

Casanova was as interested in the world as he was in women; he anatomized it even more closely. Manners, conversation, gossip and intrigue all fascinated him, and he reported them with the detail and accuracy of a dry-point etching. Because his personality was such a well-defined complex of contemporary tastes and discrimination, we see the eighteenth century through the prism of one of its own best.examples. Thanks to his penchant for getting into trouble—politically or sexually—he is always being banished from one city or another, and the reader is continually treated to new places and fresh adventures.

This double volume concludes the twelve-volume set of Casanova's *Life*. Though he lived to be seventy-three, the memoirs break off when he is only forty-nine. And perhaps it is just as well, for he was nearing the end of the kind of life he loved best. His last fourteen years were spent at Dux, in Bohemia, where he was reduced to complaining that dogs barked in the night, disturbing his sleep. Poor, lonely, bored, he was librarian to Count Waldstein, the last of his patrons. In the isolated castle, he began his memoirs as a means of occupying himself. The vividness of the *Life* derives in part from the sad circumstances, for Casanova put the last flickerings of his passion into it. It meant everything to him—his salvation and his sanity. We feel him reliving in his loneliness each of the episodes in these volumes. He had no difficulty remembering them: they were fixed in his mind by constant retelling. When he was a penniless guest, he had often paid with his *Life* for his bed and board.

Now, after 160 years of neglect, mutilation and misunderstanding, the *History of My Life* can be had in its original form—to the disappointment of the prurient and the delight of everyone else. In this handsome edition, we too can have Casanova under our roof, and without worrying about whose bed he might be straying into.

Keeping Up with Updike

I think it's time we started praising John Updike, when we do, in different terms. He's no longer a boy prodigy; he has outgrown his Little Lord Fauntleroy suit. It's condescending to keep calling him "clever" and talking about the delicacy of his prose, the subtlety of his insights, the poetry of his perceptions. Though these are all partial truths, they do more to distort than illuminate what he is doing. What he is doing is growing, a kind of growth that can't be simply quantified, because he is not giving us more of the same but something different. In *Museums and Women*, as in *Bech* and *Rabbit Redux*, his former preciousness has toughened into precision. His gaudy intelligence is less intrusive, more at the service of his talent. His language, which was once as self-indulgent as a cat licking its fur, is now an instrument rather than an end in itself.

If there is anything that reminds us of the old Updike in his short stories, it is his fondness for a form that he seems almost to have invented. This particular form is not so much a story, but a meditation. Sometimes it borders on being a kind of prayer. In such pieces, the characters may be hardly more than the valets of an idea, for the idea absorbs most of the attention, most of the life, on the page. But even here, Mr. Updike has both relaxed and intensified his vision. If we look back to the title story of an earlier volume, *The Music School*, we find metaphors modulating into what is essentially an atonal tour de force. In the title story of *Museums and Women*, the author has traded in the remoter brilliance of atonality for the seduction of melody, for the recognizable extensions—like a delicious stretch—of theme and variations.

In this mood, Mr. Updike's piece is easier to feel, less tempting to merely think about. Yes, we say, nodding our assent, museums *are* like women to a certain kind of man. In both, he is pursuing an ideal that can never satisfy him for long because he has the unappeasable hunger of a being who is dissatisfied in himself.

The beauty he finds in a museum, like a woman's beauty, is someone else's. After a while, the *otherness* of it can just as easily make such a man not happy, but sad.

The longest story in the book, "I Am Dying, Egypt, Dying," fails in my opinion precisely because of its length. Clem, the protagonist, cannot support his controlling idea, the cross he has to bear, over such a distance. The author hasn't given him the strength for it, and as a result he becomes an innocent bystander on the periphery of his fate.

To come back to the prose, one finds every few pages a sentence one would like to keep for company, to write down in the notebook one had always meant to maintain. "He had drawn a straight line from that night to the night of his death, and began walking on it." Looking at his several children, a character feels that "the traces of his own face in their faces troubled him with the suspicion that he had squandered his identity." "Slowly he had come to see that children are not our creations but our guests . . ." "She had nothing to give him but bereavement and a doubtless perishable sense of his existing purely as a man." "Our task had been to bring a society across a chasm and set it safely down on the other side, unchanged."

My favorite story is "Marching Through Boston." After years of marriage, children and comfortably apathy, Richard finds his wife, Joan, reinvested with the original promise of excitement he had seen in her. She has been rejuvenated, her blood quickened, by a cause. Civil rights, a movement peculiarly attractive to the very young, has made her young again. Richard does not share her enthusiasm, but he is jealous of its magic, and in spite of an oncoming cold he joins her in a march to hear Martin Luther King and other leaders of the movement.

He is disappointed in the speeches, confounding them with the magic of sheer involvement, of feeling intensely about something. His cold is worse, and he finds his wife possessed by a passion he cannot share. In an ambivalence so complex that I haven't the space to describe it, he begins, in a parody of self-pity, to speak of dying of his cold, which has now turned to fever. And his language, as he apostrophizes his imperturbable wife, is the broad dialect of the plantation "darky." It is at once an attack on, and an attempt to feel, the rhythm of the black experience.

In several of Mr. Updike's stories, men revisit—in actuality or imagination—the women they have loved. They do it not out of sentimentality, but because these experiences have been landmarks or milestones in their emotional history. Without them, these men would have to look back into a flat and featureless past. Some of Mr. Updike's men are scholars whose whole life's study has been to discover woman's loveliness to herself. By conferring this knowledge on their mistresses, they create them in a sense and are somewhere between artist and lover, reluctant to give up to the public a revelation that was intended only for the two of them.

Though women today are more in a mood to discover or create themselves, it seems to me that Mr. Updike is saying that they can best do that, if not necessarily through, at least with, men. Perhaps, in his next volume of stories, or in the unfolding story of American life, each sex will do it for the other.

Coroners of Dead Cultures

In nonfiction books now, there seems to be a whole new genre devoted to the passing of a way of life. Divided between alarm and elegy, a kind of wistful anthropology, these books assess with varying degrees of sophistication the pros and cons of progress. Modern medicine is usually the only pro that receives unanimous approval. But even this cannot heal "the sickness unto death," these authors contend, for the destruction of a way of life leaves its people with damaged souls, stripped of personality. Survival techniques and the acquisitive instinct are their only remaining qualities. Alienation is their tent, hut or hovel, anomie their landscape.

The passing of a culture usually means that its inhabitants are weaned away from the land to the formula-feeding of the cities. Nature is now suffering the fate of so many other mothers: she is a stranger to be visited occasionally on Sundays. Once, she was awe-inspiring, a goddess alternately fierce and gentle. Now, like a dentist, technology has pulled her teeth.

What these coroners of dead cultures seem to dread is the loss of diversity, the creeping impoverishment, each passing occasions. Already, they are articulating the effects of an esthetic claustrophobia, an anxiety arising out of the thought that one day they —or their children—may see every other face as redundant, converged in a single race.

William R. Polk, the author of *Passing Brave,* is one of the more reasonable of the anthropological undertakers. He knows that, while picturesqueness comes cheaply to the tourist, it can be very expensive for the native. It may mean hunger, disease and a nearly animal existence. He is also aware of the paradox of technology: that it cheapens in the act of enriching. Mr. Polk has no pat answers, only poignant questions. His best argument is what he himself experienced when, together with a photographer, William J. Mares, he made a 1,300-mile trip on camelback, under the most archaic conditions he could contrive, across the Arabian Desert.

As a former professor of Middle Eastern studies who had previously traveled extensively in the area, Mr. Polk was well-qualified for his project. "Like the sea," he writes, "the desert has attracted and even mesmerized those who have come within its orbit . . . removed from the encumbrances and barriers he has constructed around himself, man is forced to feel, to taste and even to suffer the full onslaught of an ungentled nature. Unblurred by filth, undistracted by noise, unsheltered by roofs or trees, he sees and senses the stars, the moon, the sun and the wind as nowhere else."

"Many travelers have felt it to be an almost mystical experience." For Mr. Polk, it was to be, at least partly, a poetic one, for in their trip he and Mr. Mares "sought to share the experience of one of the greatest classical poets [Labid] . . . to gain a deeper understanding of his magnificent description of life in the desert in the sixth century." In this approach, the author was being more realistic than the reader may imagine, for Arabic poetry, according to him, is the key to the Arab character. In the world of the desert Arabs, it is not *an* art, but *the* art, a repository of social form and cultural value in which the Bedouins concentrated most of their intellectual and artistic energy. Not exotic or esoteric like so much Western poetry, theirs is remarkable for the brilliance and clarity with which it evokes a life style. Even the ordinary Arab, he found, knew enough poetry to engage in verse-trading "duels" with his companions around the campfire.

After long correspondence with the Saudi Arabian Government, the two Americans arrived in Riyadh, where they were immediately informed that camels were almost impossible to procure, that even Bedouins no longer rode them, that the old wells in the desert had not been maintained, that the caravan "highways" had long been obliterated by sand—in short, that they had better travel by truck. It was only by parading his command of Arabic poetry that Mr. Polk was able to impress the Government with his seriousness. Even so, the travelers were forced to accept the services of a delivery truck each night for the first week of their trip.

The author was forty-two years old and, in his own words, rather pudgy; Mr. Mares, a younger man, was in better physical condition. Without any preliminary training or toughening up, they left Riyadh and headed for Amman, Jordan, accompanied by a maddeningly inefficient Government "guide" and three Arab helpers. In *Passing Brave*, the pleasures and vicissitudes of the trip are interspersed with acute observations. Though the Arabs could see objects on the horizon that even his binoculars failed to pick out, Mr. Polk has a fine eye for small distinctions and the corrosion of social change. Among other things, he remarks on the ecological extravagance of the mechanized Arab wells, which use up centuries of water in a few weeks.

Flowers suddenly springing up out of nowhere after a rare rainfall, the low horizon of life in some of the desert towns, the warm generosity of their hosts, the amazement and nostalgia that their party evoked, the sandstorms that scoured the desert like steel wool, the intense revival of almost-forgotten sensations—the book is full of good descriptions. Mr. Mares's photographs, taken under the most difficult conditions, are fine.

In summing up his wish to hear "the last gasp of an antique civilization," the author warns that we are witnessing the "mass death of human creativity." For our age, he says, diversity may be "the one luxury beyond the dream of avarice." Or, as one of the Arabs in his party put it: "You were right about the truck. It has killed us all."

The Body Brooding on Itself

The female nude in art is a spiritual and sexual reflection of her original in life. If we trace her evolution, we find her moving in the direction of a greater variety of roles and an increased consciousness of self. You might say that she began as little more than a navel in the fertility symbols of prehistoric art. Early Egyptian nudes were poised, self-confident and beautiful, but there was relatively little psychological suggestion in their portraits. Indian temple carvings rarely ventured beyond a dancer's grace and a robust eroticism. Classical Greek nudes were generally bland, healthy-looking and reasonably proportioned—a geneticist's "golden mean." In the Middle Ages, the stingy breasts, swollen belly and artless posture of the nude suggested the expulsion from Paradise, and childbearing rather than beauty as a rationalization for being undressed.

By the Renaissance, the body had commonly become chic and stylized, narcissistically flaunting an improbable perfection of geometrically flawless curves. Rubens and Rembrandt revolutionized the nude by broadening and humanizing the image of woman. In their work, we can see at last what Lord Clark calls "the accidents of the flesh," the actuality of the body as it is altered by movement, use and age. In spite of their voluptuousness, however, these women suggest rather domestic qualities: predictable pleasure, comfort, affection and understanding. Their appeal is more Apollonian than Dionysian, and it is manifestly finite.

The impressionists were perhaps the first group of painters to investigate on a large scale the novel idea that the female body might say just about anything to us. In their work, the nude began to come increasingly into her own as a highly complex subject, one whose body and attitudes were colored by her experience. She was somewhere between a case history and a visual poem. Now we could see the accidents not only of the flesh, but of the soul as well.

Though Egon Schiele lived to be only twenty-eight and died in

1918, just as art was embarking on what amounted to an incessant, almost frenzied seeking, he was already one of the nude's greatest interpreters. The 228 drawings, watercolors and paintings in Rudolf Leopold's *Egon Schiele* leave no doubt of this. It must be admitted, though, that Mr. Leopold himself does not seem fully aware of it. In his comments on the nudes, he impassively analyzes their compositional logic, and more often than not, says only a tepid word or two about their intense expressiveness as *women*.

Faced with the astonishing variety and vitality of Schiele's conceptions, he remarks that the "decadent" Vienna of that time was given to moods of "lust and death." He tends to prefer the relatively static, more sentimental oil paintings to the drawings, when it is clear that oil has the effect of stilling the turbulent waters of Schiele's temperament. Mr. Leopold also considers the landscapes equal to the nudes, though they plainly fail to stir the artist's draftsmanship to the same degree. What he sees as "maturity" in some of the later works looks instead like a waning or subduing of Schiele's ferocious originality. And though he is voluble about dates, places and other minutiae, Mr. Leopold tells us very little about Schiele himself, leaving us to wonder what it was that enabled him to perceive and project such a reach of meaning in a pair of clasped hands, an averting or a lowering of the head, the jut of an elbow, the delicate incurving of the knees.

The twentieth-century nude incorporates in her posture the close attention she has been accorded throughout the centuries. She has progressed from an object of contemplation to one who contemplates herself. In Schiele's drawings, a mere lift of a shoulder can conjure up everything questionable in the condition of woman. An outthrust hip is at once the most provocative and ambiguous of parentheses. No one understands better than Schiele the theatricality of a woman's back, the implicit plea of the shoulder blades, the suspense of the spine, the brash insouciance of the buttocks. Though Mr. Leopold tells us that the artist was accused of pornography and corrupting the morals of minors, the sexuality of his women is at least as pensive as it is carnal. His habit of pulling up a model's clothes to expose only her lower body suggests a fascination not so much with genitalia as with genesis, with sex as center and source.

The adolescent girls in particular seem seized by a wild, shy surmise, not unlike Mary's in the Annunciation pictures of the Renaissance. These virgins too are pregnant with portent. They sense that sex is both a burden and a privilege, a threat and a promise, pain and ecstasy, common as life and incomprehensible as death. Commenting on a nude girl clinging to her mother in this mood, the author notes "the awkwardness and immaturity of a young girl's over-slender body."

Schiele is a master of elongation, using it to evoke spirituality, precariousness, a wasting passion, sexual erection, the sheer physical tension of stretching, the dominance of line and idea over volume and fact. Sometimes he compresses the female body too, kneading it into a form as economical as a mollusk, a folded bud or a closed hand. These cryptic attitudes are riddles, teasing our conjecture.

Schiele's nursing women are among his most original conceptions. "Young Mother" shows a kneeling woman flinging her arms up as if she were flaunting or abandoning herself in an orgiastic dance. Her nursing child twists around her from behind, and she looks over her shoulder at him with a mixture of surprise and amusement. Motherhood is obviously only one—and not necessarily the most important—of the many ramifications of her femininity. In "Female Nude with Infant at the Breast," the woman is lying on her back, sulkily ensconced in her sexuality, as if she was unaware of the suckling infant, who lies not on, but alongside her. Breastfeeding is no longer an embrace, but an incidental or parallel function in which the child must satisfy himself as well as he can. His avid pursuit and her erotic egocentricity offer a prophetic hint of future sexual patterns, some fifty years before the women's liberation movement.

When Mr. Leopold quotes a few scraps of Schiele's poetry and his occasional comments on art, we discover that they are disappointing. All his genius went into interrogating and solemnizing the most inexhaustible image that art—or life?—has to offer. He treated the female body with an intimacy born of thousands of years of interdependence and with something like awe as well, a sense of the mysteriousness of the spirit brooding on its substance.

Mulchpile to Megalopolis

It is one of the paradoxes of American literature that our writers are forever looking back with love and nostalgia at lives they couldn't wait to leave. The feeling seems to be strongest in those who grew up in neighborhoods, small towns or on farms. Every day, everybody, everything they did or felt was so vivid, so palpably *there*—this is what they keep telling us. The reassuring rituals of a conventional or circumscribed world, the security of unambiguous beliefs, the powerful family ties of love or hate, the simple pleasure standing out in such bold relief against hard work or discipline, the almost animal relation to the land or the block—these are the reiterated themes, as in a blues song, of those who can only go home again as tourists or autobiographers.

America has changed so rapidly and so radically that nostalgia is becoming our national anthem. Where once our writers ran to Paris and congratulated themselves in cafés, now many of them are looking back over their shoulders and reconsidering the Faustian bargain that made them artists or intellectuals. Children of an economic depression, they are the adults of a moral one. Staring about with an amnesiac air, they might be wondering whether they got off the bus or train at the wrong time or place. As William Empson remarked in one of his poems: "Earth has shrunk in the wash." In *We Have All Gone Away*, Curtis Harnack implies that it has faded too.

This is a short book, but it takes us a long way—all the way back to a farm in Iowa, where the author grew up as one of seven children jointly raised by his widowed mother and her married sister. Barely middle-aged, Mr. Harnack seems to be straight out of the nineteenth century as he describes the barn built by his grandfather. A large, cross-shaped building, it is a school, slaughterhouse, breadbox, armory, playground, trysting place, ballroom—and, yes, a cathedral too, whose tower is a fancifully hand-carved cupola.

Uncle Jack is a large, powerful man who had dreamed of being an engineer before necessity hobbled him to his farm. The author's mother, widowed at thirty-eight, put aside her life in favor of the lives of her children. Mr. Harnack remembers her for her "fidelity to sanity," her determination that her children should not simply be, but *do*. They were Germans, intermarried with Danes and Swiss, and their family feeling was so strong that every year they drove two hundred miles for a reunion that filled an entire state park picnic ground.

One of the oddest passages in *We Have All Gone Away* is the portrait of Uncle John, a half-brother of the author's mother. At sixty-three, on the death of the last of his uniformly ill-fated wives, Uncle John came to visit the family after having been "lost" for years. It was clear that he was trying to find himself, but everything had altered, people had died, the tie that binds could not be knotted again. For all their goodwill, people had forgotten him. When he couldn't see himself reflected in their eyes, he grew vaguer and vaguer, until he just drifted back to where he'd come from.

In the pure zest and detail of Mr. Harnack's descriptions, one can feel the solidity, the deep satisfactions, of life on that Iowa farm. Where else could an elderly aunt die with the words *"Lord, here I come!"* But for Mr. Harnack, his sister and his brothers, the future was a ladder to achievement, with his mother at the bottom urging them on. Though she was of an earlier, earthier generation, she too behaved as if she were only making the best of it in living close to the land. She was determined to push her children out of the nest, and the effort drove her insane: she died in a psychiatric ward when she was just past fifty. After the success of her children, there was nothing for her to do—and she had never learned simply to be.

Mr. Harnack has gone back to visit the farm—a risky enterprise. He found Uncle Jack there alone, decaying as all organic matter does. In his enforced leisure, the old man has realized a small part of his engineer's dream: he has patented two inventions, one of them a device for freeing jammed ears of corn in a picker. He talks about tearing off the porch, too, in order to build a carport, a notion that makes you wonder whether he ever looks out over the land any more, or whether the TV set on its plastic wheels is all the porch he needs now.

The author pays his respects not only to Uncle Jack, but to "the mulched dead matter of agrarian life," which accounts for so much of our vitality. It's a curious kind of alchemy, from mulchpile to megalopolis, but since he himself has undergone this transmogrification, Mr. Harnack ought to know what he's talking about.

A Truly French Tragicomedy

Nothing could be better calculated to bring out the absurdities under the surface of French sophistication than the case of Gabrielle Russier. She was a thirty-two-year-old teacher of French literature in a Marseilles high school, who, in 1969, had an affair with a sixteen-year-old student and was arrested for it. The boy, Christian Rossi, was a big, bearded, militant Maoist who looked at least twenty-five. Mrs. Russier was tiny and frail, like a child with an unusually grave face. After an orgy of public controversy and months of preventive detention, Mrs. Russier was tried, fined and given a suspended sentence of twelve months. However, within thirty minutes of the verdict, the public prosecutor moved for a retrial—a most unusual action—asking for a stiffer sentence. Before the retrial could take place, Mrs. Russier committed suicide.

The case was a tragicomedy that surpassed anything in French literature. Christian's parents were not only teachers—steeped in literary parallels and psychological perspectives for their son's behavior—they were also doctrinaire Communists, the last persons one would expect to appeal to the "enemy," the bourgeois police, to prosecute a colleague who was also one of their former students, and who was guilty only of practicing "free love."

Gabrielle Russier was divorced and a mother of nine-year-old twins, who lived with her. Though she was an emotional teacher who rebelled against the archaisms of the typical French school, she was also a rigid disciplinarian of her children, forbidding them to leave their two separate rooms without permission, to make "unnecessary" noise or help themselves to food when they were hungry. And she had the kind of mind that impelled her to write a paper on the use of the past tense in contemporary French fiction, complete with charts, graphs, diagrams and word-counts. Her lover Christian's only distinction, as far as one can tell from the book, derives from the fact that he once battered a hole in the door of her home. His parents went to court because they were afraid that Mrs. Russier would take Christian away from them. After subjecting him to sleep cures and psychiatric treatments, they were desperate enough to suggest that he join the navy.

Mavis Gallant's introduction gives a nicely balanced picture of the issues, the ironies and the facts. She points out the intensely antifeminist nature of the case, noting that when the sexes are reversed, the charges are usually dropped, if they are brought at all. A man who "deviates" a minor—the French equivalent of "corrupts"—is simply acting natural, making the inevitable response to a consenting female. A woman, however, "should know better." Mrs. Russier would have received more sympathy, too, if she were simply "having a fling" with Christian: the fact that they proposed to live together made the matter "unreasonable."

Raymond Jean, a professor of French literature and a friend of Mrs. Russier, contributes another long essay, both more and less interesting than Miss Gallant's. His taste for paradox leads him to say: "In my opinion, this is the type of behavior that cannot be judged, that first must be thought of as a fact, a hard fact." He is fond, as well, of those typically French sentences that hover between philosophy and poetry and defy interpretation. However, he does say some penetrating things about Mrs. Russier, including a remark about her "destructive hyper-lucidity which makes relationships with other people difficult and occasionally impossible." This can be translated into a masochistic dogmatism, for Mrs. Russier refused to compromise on anything or accept any of the pragmatic solutions of her difficulties. Mr. Jean also quotes a fine passage from an article in *Le Monde*: "The sickness of the family is the fear of risk. Its credo is economy of the self, out of which comes the prohibition of all intense emotional activity."

In publicity, Mrs. Russier's case may have outdone even Dreyfus's. Her letters were read—or rather performed—on the radio by actresses. Newspaper and magazine articles went into paroxysms of rhetoric, as if in a national contest to see who could write the most profoundly Gallic exegesis. Moralists and metaphysicians of passion had a field day. Even President Pompidou entered the lists. Questioned by a reporter, he fell back on his own experience as a professor of literature and quoted a poem by Paul Eluard that, after a frenzy of speculation, yielded almost nothing.

After the two long introductions, Mrs. Russier's letters are anticlimactic, to say the least, full of brave resolve and literary bits and pieces in the beginning and self-pity toward the end. Even allowing for her unhappy situation, they are not distinguished. And one is not warmed by her concern, when it is too late, for her children. The impression one gets is of a self-willed martyr—a woman who sacrificed herself, ostensibly for love, but actually on some more mysterious altar. There is a strong temptation to trace her tragedy not to her principles or her affair with Christian, but to her paper on the past tense in contemporary French literature, with its charts, graphs and diagrams. You might say that she died of a certain kind of literal-mindedness that is the other side of the famous French élan.

A Case of How It Strikes You

I never found *Lucky Jim*—which launched Kingsley Amis—all that funny, but *Girl, 20* is. It's one of those deft comedies the British seem to specialize in—a story that makes us laugh without being outrageous, manic, obscene, antipatriotic or ethnic. It satirizes society without trying to bring it crashing down around our ears. It does not smear the Absurd like catchup on everything in sight. There is no gimmicky situation to set you thinking of Alan Arkin or Woody Allen. Its effects are derived mostly from its characters, who are all recognizable contemporary types. Their actions are funny not because they are inconsistent—the famous *non sequitur* syndrome invented by American wits—but because they are *not*, because these people keep plugging away, with varying degrees of ingenuity and success, at their peculiar but not unusual stratagems for getting what they want.

At fifty-four, Sir Roy Vandervane is a successful symphonic conductor, a second-rate violinist and composer and a man looking for a new lease on life. He finds it in a girl, who is actually nineteen—a creature named Sylvia who makes our bomb-concocting militants seem both bland and mannerly. Sir Roy is a first-class character, possibly Amis's best. As the author puts it, "rage at absent, or largely imaginary, foes was part of his lifestyle."

To advertise his democratic convictions, Sir Roy slurs his speech—accent still being an index of class in England—and Amis has an infallible ear for catching this sound. Tim peaches, corm beef, moce people, nongconformist, thack girl, foam book and hambag are just a few of Sir Roy's demotic effects. His speech is further enriched by "obscenity-savers"—expressions he has always disliked and now uses in place of the standard expletives. School of thought! Sporting spirit! Christian gentleman! Pucklike theme! Statesmanlike act! As you can see, they are much more expressive than their alternatives.

Sir Roy's hair, of course, is long and he wears wide-lapeled, double-breasted jackets that "set up uneasiness in the beholder by looking very nearly as much like a short overcoat." It's Sir Roy's underpants, however, that get him into trouble. Never particularly fastidious about them under ordinary conditions, he always betrays his latest affair by stockpiling a new supply, which steadily dwindles.

His wife, Kitty, appeals to a young friend of the family, Douglas Yandell, music critic, to help her endure the latest run on underpants. He is at a disadvantage in sympathizing with her, because she is the type of woman who makes an equal show of tragedy when the dog food fails to arrive. She is always gazing at him with such a rich mixture of emotions that he can't tell which of her many classes of appeals is being made. Yandell is also concerned about Sir Roy's infidelities because he is in love with his daughter Penny and worries about the effect on her of her father's behavior.

It is Yandell's appointed task to try to "reason" with Sir Roy, which he does as well as his Hamletlike disposition allows. You know, he tells the errant husband and father, that any man in his senses would find Sylvia insufferable. But Sir Roy is less interested in his sense of dignity or loyalty than in other senses, for which Sylvia has an unfailing appeal. "Of course she is impossible," he says, but then, referring to their affair, he adds, "You can't imagine how it makes me look forward to each day, and really want tremendously to work . . . ."

As they talk, in a taxi, Sir Roy takes the small folding seat, "perhaps in the hope of suggesting a cultural frontiersman's indifference to comfort." It is also a device for advertising his humility, part of a ploy that Amis describes in a sentence as convoluted as Sir Roy's tactics: "He had planned to be helped to feel how deeply he was affected by the case against what he wanted to do before going off and doing it anyway."

Yandell's relations with his editor, who happens to be Sylvia's father, illustrate the kind of difficulties some critics have with their superiors. "How can a Japanese write music?" the editor asks. "I mean real music, not bloody pots and pans." "You can't change a whole culture overnight," he adds, as a clincher. Yandell is no luckier with Penny, who, when he arrives at her house, "looks at him with slightly less curiosity than one passenger in a lift will normally show another." When she goes to bed with him, in payment for a favor, "she started undressing with the speed and conviction of someone about to go to the rescue of a swimmer in difficulties." In a few minutes, though, she is warning him: "Letting you talk soft isn't in the contract . . . until breakfast I'm at your disposal" and that's it.

Because he is the one who is most inspired—the only one, in fact—Sir Roy has his way. Trying to explain Sylvia once more to Yandell, he says: "As you get older you'll find that absolutely straight-down-the-middle sex doesn't strike you in quite the same way as it did when you started off. It *is* the same when you get to it, in fact it may be rather better, because you'll probably have picked up a few tips over the years, got better control and so on, but it doesn't strike you as the same . . ." and there's no denying sex "as a side of life where how things strike you matters at least as much as what things are really like. Whatever they are really like. Everybody spends much more time being struck by it all than actually on the job."

Though he may not have covered the moral aspects of his case —whatever they are—Sir Roy has put his enthusiasm, at least, in a nutshell. And his wholehearted pursuit of it, in our halfhearted time, makes for an uncommonly lively book.

The Androgynous Ideal

Androgyny, as Carolyn Heilbrun uses it, "defines a condition under which the characteristics of the sexes, and the human impulses expressed by men and women, are not rigidly assigned. Androgyny seeks to liberate the individual from the confines of the appropriate." "Because," the author says, " 'masculine' traits are now and have for so many years been the dominant ones, we have ample evidence of the danger the free play of such traits brings in its wake. By developing in men the ideal 'masculine' characteristics of competitiveness, aggressiveness, and defensiveness, and by placing in power those men who most embody these traits, we have, I believe, gravely endangered our own survival." If we go on as we are, she adds, "we can look forward to continued self-brutalization and perhaps even to self-destruction."

I have quoted this much of *Toward a Recognition of Androgyny* to illustrate a curious and disturbing phenomenon: that so few women seem to be able to write without hyperbole on this subject. Mrs. Heilbrun is no furious militant—a word that everywhere haunts our history these days. She is not in the front ranks of the women's liberation movement, but a professor of literature at Columbia University. And she describes her book as not a polemic, but a search into myth and literature to trace a concept that has run, like "a hidden river," from its source in pre-Hellenic myth through the writing of the Western world.

Another melancholy circumstance in connection with the book is the fact that, *after* reading it, I felt *less* sympathetic toward the idea of androgyny than before. The title, *Toward a Recognition of Androgyny*, is more persuasive than anything that follows it. Less stress on "sexual polarization and the prison of gender" seems to me an unarguable good. Each sex would surely benefit by borrowing a cup of sugar from the other. But haven't quite a few of us been doing this all the while? Is it likely that the "hidden river" of androgyny could have run so persistently through myth and literature without running into all our lives rather more than Mrs. Heilbrun alleges?

If androgyny has no more appealing arguments than the author advances, then I'm afraid we are doomed to that "self-brutalization" and "self-destruction" she foresees. Who will be persuaded by reading that "the androgynous overtones of *Oedipus* . . . suggest that the destiny of murdering one's father and marrying one's mother might perhaps refer to strong inner impulses toward the rediscovery of one's 'feminine' self"? Isn't Mrs. Heilbrun contradicting herself in asking us to see the "feminine" part as the brutal murderer?

I found this reading even more improbable: "Hamlet . . . a beautifully androgynous individual, must eschew androgyny and destroy Ophelia, who represents his feminine self, if he is to murder Rosencrantz and Guildenstern and run through poor old Polonius with a sword." A more "brutalizing" reading of that play is difficult to imagine. In connection with Shakespeare, the author also treats us to a relentless analysis of the identical-twin-in-drag theme that struck me, at least, as a perversion of scholarship.

I don't know how Mrs. Heilbrun arrived at the generalization that "eras of extreme sexual polarization are also eras of great prudery." In the early stages of the Russian Revolution, when sexual intercourse between male and female "comrades" was considered as natural as "drinking a glass of water," an alarming falling-off of heterosexual enthusiasm was reported. The evidence clearly suggested that sexual desire was depressed by the absence of polarization.

The author sometimes seems to go out of her way to weaken her own case, as when she says that "for a period of nearly fifty years such major writers as Ibsen, James, Shaw, Lawrence, Forster were to find that, at the height of their powers, it was a woman who best met the requirements of their imaginations. The woman hero, in this period, became the embodiment of the male writer's artistic vision." In spite of the formidable talents of James, Shaw, Lawrence and Forster, I don't believe that many men—or women—would consider them ideal sexual models. Nor does Lytton Strachey, another of Mrs. Heilbrun's favorites, strike me as a happy example.

Some of us may be startled to hear that in the ideal androgynous world, "marriages accepted as 'successful' doom their members." A quotation from Virginia Woolf is no less cavalier, if one may use such a "masculine" word: "Love—as the male novelists define it . . . has nothing to do with kindness, fidelity, generosity or poetry." When Mrs. Woolf says that, by the turn of the century, men were writing "only with the male side of their brains," Mrs. Heilbrun adds that they are still doing it. I wonder which side of *her* brain wrote this sentence: "The novelists of the post-World War II years, including Roth, Malamud, Mailer, Bellow, picture the universe as one in which men are escaping women, demeaning them, or exploiting them."

If this is the voice of androgyny, I can't see it luring the guys out of the locker room.

Books, and What Ails Them

John Aldridge has always seemed to me to be some sort of an organ transplant at *The Saturday Review*, one that never managed to revitalize the arteriosclerotic old body but that, paradoxically, continued to thrive by itself. His mind is independent enough to seem almost perverse, at times, and perhaps that explains his willingness to appear in its pages. It might help to explain, too, his watering down of what could have been a fairly provocative new book with ancient pieces on the writer in the university, on Hemingway, James Farrell and John Dos Passos. Reading about Farrell and Dos Passos today is rather like watching old movies on *The Late Show*.

Age has not withered, nor custom staled, Mr. Aldridge's finite variety, if I may take liberties with Shakespeare's line. He gets better as he goes. He has some trenchant things to say about literary celebrities being examined as phenomena rather than for their quality as artists. He damns William Styron—who was knighted, in our equivalent, when Jacqueline Kennedy called him Bill—with some of the faintest praise I've ever read. Mr. Aldridge describes his style as "the traditional language of our native form of modern genius. It is rich, reckless, bombastic, melodramatic, poetical, rhetorical, metaphorical, and sentimental." It is secondhand as well, "a big sprawling house of language, crammed with antiques . . ." In *Set This House on Fire*, Mr. Aldridge says, Mr. Styron alienated the old-fashioned critics without succeeding in pleasing the new-fangled ones.

Mary McCarthy is taken to task for itemizing instead of analyzing, for allowing herself to be seduced by an egalitarian dream that doesn't belong in the same bed with her conspicuous élitism. Because she has a terror of appearing ridiculous, she swathes herself in petticoats of sophistication and refuses to take the kind of risks that could make her a major novelist.

Occasionally, Mr. Aldridge himself is seduced by the hairy-chested pipe-smoker pose, the man's man behind all this book learning. He actually admires those conversations in the bar with the whore with the heart of gold in Hemingway's *Islands in the Stream* and seems not to notice the almost hysterical self-consciousness of the final chase scene.

Though he is pretty good on Norman Mailer, he is capable of saying that the monotonous obscenity of *Why Are We in Vietnam?* is a device "to help alleviate the psychological pressures that have driven us to commit the atrocity of Vietnam." He is much closer when he says that Mr. Mailer's natural subject was not other people but himself. "He did not want to invent: he wanted to confess, to display himself as the sole recorder and protagonist of significant contemporary experience."

There are some mischievous and amusing half-truths in his claim that Saul Bellow's *Herzog* is "a wonderful, absurd, adorable Jewish Uncle Tom whose predicament is that he is finally too pure for this world." He adds that Herzog "emerges, in fact, as the Waste Land cliché irrigated and transformed into the Promised Land."

Mr. Aldridge is very good on John Cheever, praising "his power to infuse the commonplace and often merely dyspeptic metaphysical crises of modern life with some of the generalizing significance of myth." Then he gets tougher: "Somehow the nightmare tonalities of his work come to seem after a while a little too coy and cloying, the postures of psychic torment a little too much like the smartly macabre décor of some Fifth Avenue shop window."

Aldridge describes black humor as "the cliché of anticliché . . . capable of registering only the histrionics of a ritual angst, a merely ornamental because creatively unearned absurdity, a sleek couturier note of apocalypse." He accuses the black humorists of abdicating their responsibility to deal coherently with events and quotes W. H. Auden's beautiful remark that "the expensive delicate ship that must have seen something amazing, the fall of Brueghel's Icarus into the sea, had somewhere to get to and sailed calmly on."

Shifting from the subject of literature to "civilization in the United States," Mr. Aldridge finds that "we are the most housebound and house-proud of nations because there is so little worth leaving the house for . . . no village life or pub life or cafe life or

market square." In traveling across our country, he feels that
"destination is the lone reality in this vacuum." "We always
move," he says, "through a present we don't care to experience
toward some future time and place at which real life will finally
begin."

Young people, Mr. Aldridge sighs in another essay, "have
become so used to thinking of our society as a corporate entity,
afflicted with bureaucratic inequities and manipulable disorders,
that they seem to have lost sight of the agonized individual faces
in the lonely crowd." "They appear to be most aware, not of
qualities, but of conditions . . ."

Though Mr. Aldridge is deeply and personally concerned
about life and literature in our country, he is not too discouraged
to turn an elegant phrase or tool a neat formulation. Compared
to some of his colleagues, he is as bracing as the plunge in the
snow that is supposed to follow the sauna.

"Daddy Quit," She Said

It's interesting to see how a good writer can make us care about a "bad" character. I mean bad in a moral sense. Talent, it seems, can find the humanity behind the inhuman, the pathos that comes from being out of step with the world, the loneliness, like death, that is the wages of sin. In spite of our increasing disillusionment in fiction and in the social sciences with Homo sapiens, he is still all that we've got and only the most obdurate misanthrope can resist him when he is presented in the round, when even his imperfections pulse with life and hope.

An evil character brilliantly portrayed will awaken our empathy—even sympathy—more readily than a good one in a pedestrian description. It seems that we hunger for vividness, that we are afraid of being engulfed in a gray anonymity. Give me character of any kind is an unspoken plea of our age, to which the "charismatic" craze bears witness. I think, for example, that the unprecedented hostility shown to President Nixon is not a response to his character or his politics, but to his insistence on concealing his character in his politics.

I suppose that Ballard, the protagonist of Cormac McCarthy's *Child of God*, is evil, but I hesitate to call him that. It is not a philosophy of permissiveness or any diabolist leanings that inhibit me, but the fact that he is so real, coupled with the further condition that all of his actions flow so naturally from what he is. He murders, rapes, vandalizes corpses, sets fires and steals—yet Mr. McCarthy has convinced me that his crimes originated in a reaching for love. Now ordinarily such a statement—and there is no shortage of them—would make me feel very impatient with the person who made it. But art, apparently, hath charms to soothe the indignant breast.

I cared about Ballard and very nearly forgave him his sins because the author seduced me into feeling that he was someone I knew very well—so well that I felt like a reluctant neighbor being questioned by reporters about the fellow next-door who had just committed a lurid crime. That's the magic of art. It can make you contradict yourself, surprise yourself, discover charities you blush to confront. When Ballard lugged a dead girl several miles to his freezing shack and thawed her out in front of the fire so that he could vandalize her, I felt not disgust but pity. "He poured into that waxen ear everything he'd ever thought of saying to a woman." Well, I temporized, it seems to be the best he can do.

When he goes out and buys clothes for the dead girl, so he can dress and undress her—first going outside so he can steal a look at her through the window—I could see the perverted poetry of it. It was the same sort of feeling that induced him to carry everywhere with him two huge teddy bears and a stuffed tiger he had won at a shooting gallery. When he began wearing the clothes of his other female victims as he went out to commit murder, his character took on still another dimension. Though it was harder for me to trace and identify Ballard's motive here, I felt that his gesture was still comfortably within the author's conception of him.

Mr. McCarthy has the best kind of Southern style, fusing risky eloquence, intricate rhythms and dead-to-rights accuracy. I've often wondered whether this kind of writing—William Faulkner is the classical example—isn't partly a result of the black influence on Southern speech, a stress on sonorousness and musicality. Whatever its source, the author uses it to splendid effect in several flawless scenes. In one of them, Ballard is sleeping in his shack when a pack of hunting dogs, close on the trail of their prey, follows its scent through the doorless entrance and out the window, while he, first terrified, then enraged, strikes out at them.

When Ballard finds a rusty old axhead and takes it to the blacksmith to be sharpened, the smith croons a beautiful elegy to the lost instinct of workmanship, describing, again in infallible rhythms, each step of the process. "Some people will poke around at somethin else," he says, "and leave the tool they're heatin to perdition but the proper thing is to fetch her out the minute she shows the color of grace. Now we want a high red. Want a high red. Now she comes." While the blacksmith's speech is a perfect example of an author *finding* the poetry in a character, Mr. McCarthy does not fall into the familiar error of forcing all of his people to talk "poetically" simply because they live in the rural South. In fact, Ballard is taciturn, as we might expect. He knows that talking won't help him and he doesn't fool with it. His silence is in tense counterpoint to the tumult of his actions.

There aren't many authors who know how to use silence or terseness, who can strip a character's speech down to bare necessity, so that his whole personality becomes a kind of aposiopesis, a breaking off for dramatic effect. In another scene, Mr. McCarthy again demonstrates what I am tempted to call a voluptuous economy. A father catches his daughter behind the barn with a boy and chases him off. But then he finds sex so strong in the air that before he realizes what he is doing, he has taken the boy's place. His daughter's response ought to go down in the annals of Southern history. "Daddy quit," she says.

To demonstrate that he is human too, Mr. McCarthy makes a few small mistakes here and there. He ought to resist words like strobic, palimpsest, mutant and inculpate, as well as inversions like knew not. And there's an apostrophe to fate on page 156 that belongs in somebody else's book. But these are overflowings, mere spills, from a brimming imagination. Child of God is no idle title. Ballard is one, like you and me and the author too, and this book isn't going to let us forget it.

Franz Kafka Reconsidered

I was both startled and aggrieved to find myself bored by a number of these stories. Like almost every other critic—with the notable exception of Edmund Wilson—I had always regarded Kafka as the uncanny voice of our age. He stirred us as no other writer ever had; he was our grandest nightmare. In the late forties and early fifties, every quarterly published several articles on Kafka and many devoted entire issues to him. When *The Great Wall of China* was out of print, I tried unsuccessfully to buy it at any price. People just wouldn't part with it.

But now I find that, except for "The Metamorphosis," "In the Penal Colony," "A Report to an Academy" and passages here and there, many of the stories are heavy going. Everyone knows the theme of "Metamorphosis"—Gregor Samsa turns into an enormous insect—and most serious readers are familiar with "In the Penal Colony," where a harrowlike machine inscribes the victim's crime in blood on his back. "A Report to an Academy" has never received the attention it deserves, as one of Kafka's most tightly structured, poignant and resonant pieces. It is the story of an ape who, finding life in his tiny cage impossible to bear, becomes "human" in order to be let out. He is not at all interested in freedom—which he deeply mistrusts—simply in getting out of an impossible position.

The other major stories—"Investigations of a Dog," "The Burrow," "The Great Wall of China," "The Hunger Artist" and "The Judgement"—seemed to me, on this reading, to suffer from Kafka's obsessional or paranoid style. Though obsession and paranoia are perfect objective correlatives for the central predicament of modern man, I feel that Kafka sometimes falls into the imitative fallacy in using them: they control him, instead of the other way around. Though it is perfect in its way as a description of the psychological defenses of an insecure person—or even a fussy metaphysician—there is a too-muchness about "The Burrow." It goes on too long; it is like a fugue without much melodic interest. Once we recognize it as a tour de force, it becomes redundant. "The Hunger Artist" depends too heavily—like Kafka's famous parable, "Before the Law"—on its punch line: "I couldn't find the food I liked."

"Investigations of a Dog" shows Kafka's invention reduced to musical dogs and soaring dogs. In "The Judgement," despite the father's inspired outburst, the son's suicide by drowning is bathetic and insufficiently prepared for. "Blumfeld, an Elderly Bachelor" finds the rigid order of his life disturbed by a pair of bouncing balls that have invaded his apartment. In the absence of any sexual reference, the balls are simply too arbitrary or gratuitous to carry much meaning. In "Josephine the Singer" and "The Little Woman," the metaphors are rather too mechanically explored; there is a feeling that they are permutations and combinations of plot, rather than brilliant or witty invention.

These shortcomings, which one notices only in retrospect, after the initial excitement of Kafka has subsided a bit, were precisely the elements seized upon by Kafka's many imitators. Just as T. S. Eliot felt that it might have been damaging to a young poet's development to read John Milton, so Kafka's influence seems to have crimped or crippled the "school" he inspired. To seize upon a minimal premise and harry it to death; to assume that, if you nagged at it long enough, any absurdity would bleed significance; to employ a legalistic style pockmarked with hedges and qualifications: this is what his disciples thought they were borrowing from Kafka. In a typical example, William Sansom wrote an interminable story about a scrubwoman whose world-view never rises above the shoe tops of passers-by.

Paranoia sometimes reaches lyrical heights, as it did in some of the later poems of Sylvia Plath, in Dostoyevsky's *Notes from the Underground* and in passages of Saul Bellow's *Herzog*. But it isn't a guarantee of either literary quality, contemporaneity or truth. Sometimes it's merely paranoid, centripetal and suffocating. Those who most successfully avoided these pitfalls are Donald Barthelme and, to a lesser degree, Jorge Luis Borges.

Unlike the majority of Kafka's legatees, Barthelme is witty—remembering perhaps that Kafka himself used to laugh aloud while reading his work to friends. Barthelme has relaxed the paranoid grip more than Borges, too, developing a looser, more richly textured surface. Borges's bibliomaniac and other arcane ruminations often fall into the fugal pattern of Kafka's less successful work.

At his best—as in his novel, *The Trial*—Kafka astonishes us simultaneously with comedy, pathos and profundity. Joseph K. finds the size of the cathedral almost beyond human endurance: religion is too large for life. The lawbooks of the court turn out to be pornography: the prissy chief clerk is being condemned for not feeling, not living, passionately enough. The advocate, like an old school psychoanalyst, keeps his client writing up the "brief" of his entire life in a dark, womblike room.

I suppose that what I'm saying here is that we have more or less domesticated our paranoia by now, our sulking over the confines of the human condition. It is still there, but it is no longer the tiger at the gates: rather, it is like a pet that is not quite housebroken. These days we have so many particulars to worry about that only a philosopher can afford the luxury of universals. Eventually, ordinary indignation elbows despair out of the way.

War as Opera Buffa

Most of us know something about the tragedy of war: in *Spy in the Vatican 1941–45,* Branko Bokun shows us its incidental comedy. He depicts the desperate improvisation of people in impossible positions, the endless adaptability of the human animal, the absurd domesticated as the everyday. He couldn't have been better placed for the purpose: At the age of twenty-one, he was sent to Rome by the Yugoslav Red Cross to seek Vatican intervention on behalf of Orthodox Serbs, Jews and Gypsies who were allegedly being slaughtered by fanatic Croatian Catholics. Italy at that time was just beginning to play out its pathetic opera buffa and Rome was the principal stage, a city where every other person seemed to be either a spy or a refugee, where the inefficiency of the government and the demoralization of the people combined to turn the traditionally conventional Italians into practicing surrealists.

We find the government melting down church bells into bullets. Enraged with the apathetic bourgeoisie, Mussolini is abolishing sleeping cars, restaurants and first-class travel on all Italian railways. In an attempt to please him, his ministers also propose to abolish riding, golf and sailing. When the war news worsens, a law is passed against unserious behavior in public, such as whistling in the street or the wearing of shorts by men or slacks by women. Telling jokes or laughing is also forbidden as "demonstrations of defeatism." At the announcement of a new German secret weapon, all the foreign diplomatic representatives, who are confined to the Vatican, rush to the library with requests for the books of da Vinci. A group of Rumanian Jews appealing their deportation write to the Pope in Latin in the hope of "speeding comprehension" of their predicament.

When Mussolini's ulcer is at its worst, he goes home to his wife instead of his mistress. After a token bombing of Rome by Allied planes, the Pope parades through the streets in a white cassock spotted all over with red, the biggest spot over his heart. Prepared to flee at a moment's notice, Italians carry all their most precious belongings everywhere in knapsacks; vanity inspires many of them to enlarge their knapsacks with paper. On the black market, leaflets can be bought containing instructions on how to distinguish rabbit meat from that of dogs and cats. Disguised German soldiers are trying to "wander" through the city like tourists. Everyone's bowels are weighted with the sand mixed in the bread by bakers to give it body.

After failing to get to the Pope, Mr. Bokun meets Ivo, a young Yugoslav linguist whose job reading all suspect ingoing and outgoing mail gives him a one-sided intimate acquaintance with all foreigners living in Rome. The author also meets Sascha, a former lieutenant in the Red Army, now a black market mogul. His roommate, Bora, another Russian refugee, is planning to stage Dostoyevsky's *Crime and Punishment* in the old Roman theater at Ostia Antica. Raskolnikov will be dressed in a toga . . . With the help of Ivo, who bribes the attendant, the author is allowed to peep at Mussolini through a keyhole as he paces up and down his office.

After Mussolini renounces his leadership under pressure from his ministers, the author tells of meeting him by accident on a beach on the deserted island of Ponza, where the former dictator is in exile. Mr. Bokun has gone there to visit a friend who is also interned on the island and stumbles on Mussolini sunbathing on the beach while his guards sleep beneath a tree. According to the author's account Il Duce's first questions are "Have you seen me before?" "Don't you think I'm in better shape now?" and "Are you pleased to meet me?" He quotes the Fascist leader as saying that "Italy could never win a war . . . we are too sensitive." Comparing himself to an entertainer in an empty theater, Mussolini occupies himself inventing a new religion, "a religion of grandfathers," which will soften the tyranny of God the Father and mitigate the timidity of the Son.

Mr. Bokun has an uncanny eye and ear for the incongruous. When Marshal Goering visits Count Ciano in Rome, we are informed that the subject of their meetings is Boldini paintings. Ciano's new mistress has a passion for Boldini, but Goering has been able to find only one or two of his paintings in Paris. The Americans are furious because the Pope has received the Japanese in the "Sala di Trono," and our representatives in the "Sala di Piccolo Trono." As soon as the Italians see that the war is indeed lost, they begin "buying" Allied refugees and escaped prisoners of war on the black market—hiding and feeding them to prove to the Americans when they arrive that they are "underground" soldiers for freedom. Because the departing Germans are rounding up all able-bodied men for slave labor, everyone is in disguise. Men walking dogs are never seized, it is said, nor are postmen—accordingly, dogs and postmen's uniforms proliferate. Young men go about dressed as women. Thousands of people put on mourning clothes in the mistaken belief that the death of a loved one will deter the Germans.

Mr. Bokun tells us these stories with the irony and compassion they deserve. His style is unobtrusively brilliant as he compares the expressions of Germans during an air raid to the audience at a Wagner concert in prewar Berlin, or when he describes a partisan guard flicking the ash of his cigar into Mussolini's nostrils as his body hangs upside down in the Piazzale Loretto. Deported and unable to go home, the author escapes to Paris, where he meets his old Yugoslavian boss, who has also been forced to flee. They are both working in the Citroën factory, sandpapering cars. Here, says his old chief, slipping him a coarser grade of paper—it makes the work a little easier.

Visiting the Back of Beyond

In Walker Percy's prophetic novel, *Love in the Ruins,* a character remarks, not altogether facetiously, that our world began to come apart at the seams "when we abandoned the Latin mass." In Brian Moore's *Catholics,* which is also set in the near future, the Roman Catholic Church has gone a bit farther in "modernizing" something that was supposed to be timeless. Not only is the Mass already in English and the priest facing the congregation instead of God on the altar—the Sanctus bell sounds no more, and private confession has been replaced by public confession, except for the most extreme cases. The Catholic Church is also working for an *apertura,* an opening up, toward Buddhism.

Out of these rather special materials, Brian Moore has made a moving novel, one that sends a quiet thrill of portent through even the secular reader. In it, he pleads not so much for religion as for an attitude of mind, a resistance to remorseless change. He seems to be saying that, though the innovations of our technology continue to proliferate, though we are daily liberated from one or another restraint, the result seems to be a continuous shrinking of the social structure, a streamlining or homogenization of anything that obtrudes itself in a highly particularized way.

Mr. Moore has found a very satisfying image for his theme. The monks of Muck Abbey in Kerry, Ireland, have continued to celebrate the Mass in the old way, and it has come to the attention of the Father General, as the Pope is now called, through newspaper and television accounts. It seems that pilgrims are flocking by the thousands to kneel in the rain at Mount Coom, where the monks have been forced to move the Mass to accommodate the crowds. Lolling in his Eames chair, looking out of the window at that "monstrosity" (the Vatican), the Father General instructs a representative to go to Muck Abbey and put a stop to this flouting of the Ecumenical movement.

James Kinsella, the agent, is an American priest, but he does not call himself "Father." When he arrives at Cahirciveen, he is carrying "a paramilitary dispatch case, a musette bag and wearing gray-green denim fatigues." He is refused at the hotel, where he has a reservation, until he identifies himself as *Father* Kinsella. Muck Abbey is on an island twenty miles away; a boat is sent for him, but the pilot refuses to believe he is a priest and turns to leave without him. When Kinsella seizes the gunwale, his knuckles are rapped with an oarlock.

Kinsella charters a helicopter, the first flying machine ever to land on the island, as the abbot points out, calling it a "frumious bandersnatch." The island and the abbey are beautifully evoked: though the weather there is usually forbidding and the work hard, the life the monks lead comes across as snug and satisfying. Faith is a roaring fireplace that warms every room. The abbot is a fine character, less a holy man in the old sense than a sort of foreman or manager. Though he wants to be laid down "like wine bottles" with the other fifty-one abbots in the transept, and though he would not leave the island for a better position, he occasionally suffers the doubts of a reasonable and phlegmatic man.

He finds that when he peers too closely at God, when he faces Him directly in prayer, he is seized with a "fear and trembling that was a sort of purgatory presaging the true hell to come, the hell of no feeling, that null, that void." Doubt seized him when, as a younger man, he visited Lourdes. The Virgin was supposed to have appeared to an illiterate French girl in a grotto, and he feels that this "miracle" has turned Lourdes into a "tawdry religious supermarket" of miraculous cures, an ugly clinic for diseased bodies and souls. This vulgarizing of the Church disgusts the abbot, and he finds that he can keep his faith intact only by giving up prayer, by avoiding confrontations with the supernatural.

The abbot is that ravaged man in the middle, for he finds the new mood of the Church equally repugnant. Kinsella's wish to dispense with churches as places of worship and replace them with a more generalized community concept, "a group gathered in a meeting to celebrate God-in-others," would strike him as no religion at all. Though miracles are too much for the abbot, man alone is not enough. Ironically he quotes a new theologian who sees a future for Christianity, provided it gets rid of God.

Why did he continue with the old Mass, against orders? Well, he says, we tried the new way and no one came to church. "Yesterday's orthodoxy," he says, "is today's heresy"—and the reader feels that this is true in more than the Church, that Mr. Moore has chosen it to ring out a general alarm, as church bells used to do in times of emergency. In the end, the abbot risks his own soul for the sake of those who serve under him.

Catholics has the brooding quality of a rainy day. It is difficult to explain why rainy days appeal to poets and so many other people: perhaps they prefer a world with a dark as well as a light side, a heaven with more than one humor. In the neighborhood, Muck Island is known as "the back of beyond": that's Mr. Moore's territory. You ought to visit it next time the world is too much with you.

Tilling "The Waste Land"

It has long been common knowledge that when T. S. Eliot finished the first draft of *The Waste Land*, he gave it to Ezra Pound to read and Pound persuaded him to discard at least half of it. Puzzling over this, I once asked Milton Klonsky, a poet who is a friend of mine, what he supposed Pound had cut away. "All of Eliot's own lines" was his answer and there is a wry truth in it. Now that the original manuscript, which was presumed to be lost, has reappeared, complete with both Eliot's and Pound's annotations, we can see the aptness of the remark. The quotations, paraphrases, evocations and echoes from all the sources cited in the notorious Notes to the poem form its skeleton: what Pound ruthlessly excised was pure Eliot. He crossed out long passages in which Eliot was experimenting with a conception of dramatic poetry in which several voices contributed to a polyphonous effect.

The poem had begun with a long prosy recitative about proletarian pub-crawling; sandwiched between arias, there was a page and a half of brittle couplets in which a woman called Fresca functions somewhat like the Elizabethan clown to relieve the atmosphere with levity. There was an apostrophe to London: "London, the swarming life you kill and breed,/Huddled between the concrete and the sky . . ." and a parenthesis on Highbury: "Highbury bore me. Highbury's children/Played under green trees and in the dusty Park." In "Death by Water" we are treated to a long passage in which sailors run aground on reefs of blank verse, complete with "gaffjaws," "garboard-strake" and "gleet."

A dirge about one drowned Bleistein includes these lines: "That is lace that was his nose . . . (Bones peep through the ragged toes) . . ." In the discarded "Death of Saint Narcissus," "His eyes were aware of the pointed corners of his eyes/And his hands aware of the tips of his fingers." Narcissus was sure that he had been a tree, then a fish, a young girl and finally "a dancer to

God." The poem originally fizzled out not in "Shantih shantih shantih," but in this: "I am the husband and the wife/And the victim and the sacrificial knife/I am the fire, and the butter also."

One could go on, but it's not fair. It was a first draft, after all, and Eliot had put it together—out of old fragments and new material—in the space of several weeks while he was having something like a nervous breakdown in Switzerland. The Eliot who had already written "The Love Song of J. Alfred Prufrock" and "Portrait of a Lady" would certainly have had the taste to cut most of what Pound did.

"Prufrock" and "Portrait of a Lady" were relatively modest in scope: in *The Waste Land*, Eliot had taken on the world—and just at the time when the world was too much for him. In his poor health, he surrendered to the ever-ready Pound a job he probably could have done in time himself. While there is no denying that the poem in its original state was a shambles, this is true of most first drafts. Some years ago, a number of poets, including Stephen Spender and R. P. Blackmur, contributed to a book called *The Making of a Poem*, if I remember rightly. In it, they each reproduced successive drafts of one of their poems, and I recall reading both Spender's and Blackmur's with incredulity. Didn't they know better than to expose themselves so nakedly? To see the clumsiness and poverty of their first and second—even their sixth and seventh—drafts was a sobering experience.

Eliot must have been aware of the weaknesses of the passages quoted to give in so completely to Pound. He was not an uncritical admirer of "il miglior fabbro" and it is interesting to see him refusing many of Pound's suggestions in the surviving lines. Though he surrendered on structure, he was stubborn about texture. He knew the words he wanted. A man who attended a Harvard seminar under Eliot told me he would pause in his lectures for as long as five minutes, searching for the *mot juste*.

Pound was probably wrong in Part IV: "Death by Water," which he cut to ten lines. Eliot wanted to retain more of the original or eliminate it entirely: Pound's insistence resulted in a truncated section that is completely out of scale with the others. Eliot often pays a heavy price, too, for Pound's emphasis on concentration. While the poem does gain in intensity, it gains in obscurity as well. Connective tissue is sacrificed to the demands of the staccato rhythms Pound preferred; everything is essence, heard against what is not said. The hand that wrote the Cantos has left its fingerprints on Eliot's pages. Nor was it only the common reader who suffered with the difficulties of the poem: as Max Eastman pointed out, it was greeted on publication with widely differing interpretations by the critics.

In a sense, this solving of the first mystery—the text of Eliot's original—only raises a larger question. What would Eliot have done if not for the intermediation of Pound? Would the poem have been better or worse—or simply different? It is inconceivable that he himself would not have been able, in time, to bring it under some sort of control. Valerie Eliot, the poet's widow, confines herself in her Introduction to a brief description of Eliot's condition and circumstances at the time he wrote *The Waste Land*, but though she mentions the closeness that existed between the two poets, she says nothing about their differences, or about how Eliot privately felt, after his gratitude, toward Pound's editing. If it is impossible now to get at the real root of the mystery, at least we can reaffirm what some readers seem to have forgotten: it was, after all, Eliot's poem, not Pound's.

On Going Down in Flames

Philip Roth once remarked that reality in America has become so bizarre that it makes the invention of the fiction writer seem pale by comparison. Perhaps this is why so many talented people are turning to nonfiction. For here's where you'll find the most awesome images, the most spectacular ironies, the most terrifying perspectives. Here's where you can snap language like a whip, where prose is bloodstained. This is no make-believe world: that's your fellow man there, squirming on the operating table.

Sometimes it seems as if fiction and nonfiction writers have changed chairs. The stylists have embraced the social sciences like lovers, while so many of our novels now read as if they were written by social workers, Ph.D. candidates or petty bureaucrats. Sharon R. Curtin is one of this new breed of nonfiction writers, full of good phrases and overflowing emotions. Not objective or "scientific," she wants to squeeze inside the experience she's writing about. She gets her hands dirty dragging out her material and then wipes them on you.

In *Nobody Ever Died of Old Age* she exaggerates—but it becomes her. She's not only angry about her subject: she also came to it with all her nerves exposed as the result of the disintegration of her own life. Having just lost her husband, her two children, her home, dog and cat in a divorce, she gives you the impression that she's avenging herself on the world that did this to her by exposing another part of its inhumanity. Just to keep sane, to have something to do, she tackles the question of how we treat the old in a society in which most things reach obsolescence in a few years.

Miss Curtin's own family may have been one of her reasons for choosing this subject. At an advanced age, her maternal grandmother left a husband and five children to see what else the world had to offer. When she reached seventy-five, she wanted to marry again but her children protested, so she decided to elope. At eighty-three, she was killed by a truck while she was running for a bus. Her first husband died in almost the same way and at the same age: he was struck while walking home from a night on the town. The author's paternal grandmother is still preternaturally alive at ninety-six.

The fact that these people were such vivid personalities suggested to the author that old age may—to a large extent—take its coloration from the individual. It need not be an institutional gray, an apologetic shuffle toward oblivion. Aging is more an attitude, a psychosomatic illness, than most of us realize. Above all, Miss Curtin feels it is the shock of displacement, of being exiled from reality. Retired from their jobs, estranged from their scattered families and from neighborhoods or communities that no longer exist, the aged feel disoriented, and no wonder. They *are* disoriented: many of them are faced with social workers for company instead of sons and daughters; with enforced idleness instead of productive work; with patronizing baby talk instead of normal communication.

Like the young, the old are disenfranchised, only with this difference: They are not going anywhere. They have no future, for as the author puts it: "To age is to learn the feeling of no longer growing." Some of the old, like Harry and Al, are merely "professional survivors" who no longer "even experience their life as real." Her description of them would do Samuel Beckett credit, especially their breakfasts together: "Everyone in the diner was in the same state of early morning sorrow, that moment of gathering strength to face a day over which one has no control."

Aunt Jenny was pretty bleak too: "She was angry and asking the questions too late. She was near the end of her life and had never experienced magic, never challenged the smell of brimstone, never clawed at the limit of human capability." Miss Curtin is not sentimental about old people: she is just as impatient with them as she is with everybody else for accepting the situation. Institutions, she implies, are not the answer. "So far, in this society," she says, "we have not discovered how to make *any* institution fit for human occupancy." She may be a bit too hard on institutions: there are some in which the occupants seem both contented and meaningfully alive, and her opposition to shock treatments—which have been quite effective in cases of senile depression—seems merely stubborn. What she suggests in *Nobody Ever Died of Old Age* is that the old band together to form a political force. With twenty million people over sixty-five in the United States today, they could certainly make their influence felt. As a first step in this direction, the author recommends "consciousness-raising groups," a tactic that she borrows from the women's liberation movement. If the traditional roles have been abolished, she says, the aged can articulate new ones for themselves. Anything is better than "rocking the years back and forth," occupying as little space as possible, or crippling oneself with unnecessary humility. If we are soon to be ashes, then let us go down in flames.

Some of our fantasies feature youth taking over the world: Wouldn't it be wonderful to see the tables turned? If the old are eccentric, so much the better! God knows, we could use some genuine eccentricity. If they harp on the past, it might help us to salvage the present. If they insist on *living* until they die, we might each of us shake the queasy feeling that ". . . at my back I always hear/Time's wingèd chariot hurrying near . . ."

Reading Between the Murders

Good mystery writers have always known that man himself is the greatest mystery of all, more baffling than the most labyrinthine plot. And so they are gradually shifting the emphasis from "Who killed X?" to "Who *was* X, and what did he do that drove someone to the desperate and improbable expedient of killing him?" Some of the best British mysteries are mere pretexts for prying into the peculiarities of their people. When someone is murdered, policemen must ask questions—but most of the answers they get have little or nothing to do with the crime and everything to do with the vicissitudes of life in our time.

The crime in many of the more sophisticated suspense novels is often treated ironically, as if it were an atavistic accident, a deplorably ungovernable and ephemeral passion. Its solution brings the—actually existential—questioning to an arbitrary end, just as closing time concludes a pleasant evening of drink and conversation in a pub. Speaking of pubs, it seems that in the better mysteries, a pub and a country town play important parts in providing the "escape" that is still desired by the typical reader of mysteries.

The world weighs heavily on some of us, and serious fiction, despite all its virtues—because of them, in fact—offers us little relief from it. The catharsis of art must be balanced against the persecuting intensification of life that we find in them. Some of us want to get away for a few hours—at least halfway away. We want people, places and events that are real enough to pass our critical threshold and illusory enough to allow us to regard them with a complacent detachment.

There are many ways to escape. In *A File on Death*, Kenneth Giles encourages us to lose ourselves in the venial sins of life rather than in the mortal one of death. His Chief Inspector James is a ruefully thoughtful man whose fastidiousness makes him just as ill-suited to police work as some of us are to our respective jobs. Sergeant Honeybody, his assistant, is a homelier type who contents himself with the perquisites of his toil. He eats and drinks his way through each case as if every dead body demanded an old-fashioned wake. In the wry Mr. Giles's words, the sergeant "labored under the delusion that the world was interested in his entrails." Honeybody comments, for example, on a disappointing offer of tea that "fair curdles the colon" as well as on the surprising savoriness of bull's testicles seethed in champagne and cooked Spanish style.

When Chief Inspector James is put on a ticklish case of recovering documents detailing the scandalous behavior of people in high places, he replies with dismay: "I just catch criminals, civilian criminals." To which the British equivalent of a CIA man suavely replies: "Very good. I shall dine out on that. Well put indeed!" The disaffected clerk who stole the documents is described as the "source of all the scatological remarks" heard in his department. The indispensable Vicar in the requisite country town shoots, stuffs, mounts and sells birds to turn an extra penny. While he explains to James and Honeybody that he has listened to "every kind of prevarication" in his calling, he twists a "Shoveller's beak into a more entertaining position."

The other characters are decked out in a full fig of eccentricities. Sir Hugh Palabras, "magnificent failure, founder of foundered political parties," father of 118 illegitimate children, is a man who "would delight to send this country into chaos." Señor Abajo is, at ninety-three, "the last of the *Castrati*" and bold enough to boast of poisoning the Duke who resorted to surgery to retain his favorite soprano. Asked by the sadistic sister of one General Gould whether he had ever witnessed a hanging, Honeybody gratifies her with a harmless lie: "Seventeen," he says, "including once when the head came off and two when I had to mount a stepladder in order to swing on the ankles as an act of Christian charity." A dismantled pistol barrel hidden in a frozen suckling pig brings us the incidental information that the Spanish are so fond of suckling pig that it is depicted in one of their carvings of the Last Supper.

A Life for a Death, by John Creasey as Gordon Ashe, as the dustwrapper will have it, is everything the other novel is not: pedestrian, humorless, mechanical without attaining even that level of ingenuity. The author stresses all the wrong elements:

as against the incontrovertibility of Sergeant Honeybody's colon, we now meet top police officials who "gulp," "bark" and "match" women's eyes in laughter. We read "the elevator hustled him up" and wonder what purpose is served by such a sentence —quite apart from the fact that it is inaccurate. Coffee "burped and chuckled" in a percolator. As you can see, the writing sounds as if Mr. Creasey avoided the natural on principle.

All the heroic figures are tall, their height being the most tangible quality the author can imagine. Most of the emotions are forced on, rather than drawn from, the characters. Much of the action consists of descriptions of their facial and vocal variations. When a famous policeman is believed dead, hundreds of mourners from all over Europe "flew over at short notice, in deep distress." It's difficult, in reading this last sentence, not to think of "deep distress" as a type of aircraft. But that should be enough: here's a good book and a bad one. If these snobbish criteria mean anything to you, you'll know which to choose.

Rising, Not Falling into Love

"I feel I'm starving to death, have been starving all my life. I need a certain kind of food soon or I'll die." In Robert Granat's *Regenesis*, this is how his hero, Edward, experiences his second breakdown within a year. His whole being becomes "a maniacal search party" for this "food." On sick leave from his job as a high school teacher in Albuquerque, he sends his understanding wife and his two children to her parents in Ohio, so that he can devote all his time and energy to trying to find whatever it is that will save or restore him. He has already tried shock treatment, drugs, psychotherapy. He is just thirty-three, intelligent, in love with his family; his life history is of only average unhappiness. Surely, he pleads, there must be hope for him . . .

He feels that his predicament is "spiritual." Once he annoys his analyst by quoting Jung to the effect that most of the psychological problems in patients over thirty were actually spiritual problems. "Don't you need something to believe in?" he asks his doctor, and the answer is "I believe in growth." When Edward asks what kind of growth, his psychiatrist evades the question by saying that, to be able to help *all* his patients, he must keep himself value-free.

But that is why I am mad, Edward answers. Freedom from values has reduced me to a chaos of possibilities, and like the philosopher's logical jackass who starves to death between equidistant bales of hay, I, too, am starving. There is no logical reason to choose anything—everything being equidistant—but to live is to choose. When the doctor suggests that it sounds as if Edward is holding out for a miracle, Edward denies it. He doesn't expect God to come to him. He doesn't even want God. All he wants is "a sense of Him, a scent of Him, His whereabouts." Though he has "neither expectation nor desire to go to the North Pole or the North Star," he needs to know in which direction North is, simply in order to navigate correctly down here where he is.

He has "lost" his mind, he points out, and cannot even begin to look for it unless he can first get his bearings. He has fallen out of the pattern of his life: the "data-processing mechanism" that regulates his separate, fragmented self—personal, professional, social, secret—has broken down and they are colliding like blind people in a panic. On the brink of suicide, he pauses to mock it: "Not even the suicide kills himself in desperation. Before the step he deliberates so long and so carefully that he literally chokes with thought." Indigestible thought.

Walking aimlessly, passing a church, he gives in to an impulse and enters. But the cross is a thirty-foot plus sign of stainless steel tubing, with no figure on it. The stained-glass window is an abstraction, depicting only "a religious mood." The minister is "tall, slim, thirty, soberly suited and tied . . . He might have been a junior sales executive." The church itself is new, "redolent with the spirits of recently departed architect firms and design associates, color schemers and subcontractors, fund-raisers and bank officers, contract lawyers and building inspectors . . ."

When Edward wakes each morning, the day is "imposed like a criminal sentence"; he watches his inflamed consciousness like someone "watching a wild animal from a blind." He is living at the end of his nerve when temporary salvation arrives in the form of a friend, who, to get away from his visiting inlaws, proposes that they drive to Mexico for a week or two. And it is in Mexico that Edward is able to see man *"dans le vrai,"* in the real, as Flaubert said of the Parisian proletariat. Undisguised by distraction, unfragmented by the contradictory demands of affluence, the Mexican peasants of the small town of Pàtzcuaro are visible, palpable, in their humanity. Not superior or saintly in a sentimentalized primitivism, but simple enough to be unconfused, to be relatively uncorrupted by the disease of contemporaneity. They live not only in the now but in an unbroken chain of being that goes all the way back to the beginning. They have not traveled far enough to lose themselves in the middle of their lives' journey.

Encouraged, Edward goes to mass to see Pàtzcuaro's famous effigy, *Nuestra Señora de la Salud,* Our Lady of Health. And there, like a loveless man ambushed by emotion in a group therapy meeting, he rejoins the human race. He can do it here because the terms of the contract are so simple that even a child, or a man at his wits' end, can understand them. Merely to belong to the species is, in a sense, to believe. Someone on each side of him is holding his sore thumb of a self in their hands. As the author puts it, "the keg of self was springing leaks. The outside did not cease to flow into him, but now he felt a new and strange counterflow—himself outward." "Everything—time-place, here-there, now-then, this-that, I-other, all the landmarks of human awareness—went up in an explosion of light. All emotion incinerated, the waves of sadness and beauty, tragedy and separation, pleasure and pain. Consciousness volatilized in the sun of being, the unthinkable splendor of human being . . ."

As you can see, Mr. Granat's epiphany is well described. It should satisfy even those whose taste runs to the secular. *Regenesis* is spiritual without being in the least dogmatic. The author does not insist. Some readers may even regard its resolution as a "poetic" rather than a religious one. But just as Edward's life could not cohere without this final "passion," neither could Mr. Granat's novel. And it is pleasant to see how the spiritual—accepting all the ambiguities of that term—can still move us, once we stop "clinging to the childishness of our sophistication." We need to be reminded that it is possible "to rise into love as well as to fall into it."

Magniloquence at Magny's

The French have always made a fetish of conversation, unhesitatingly proclaiming themselves masters of this art. Between 1862 and 1872, a number of Paris's greatest *causeurs* met regularly for dinner at Magny's, a small restaurant on the Left Bank. They included Flaubert, the expatriated Turgenev, George Sand, Saint-Beuve, Théophile Gautier, Ernest Renan, Hippolyte Taine and the Goncourt brothers, as well as a number of lesser lights.

Robert Baldick, a writer deservedly known for his works on French literature, had the happy idea of researching these famous evenings and reconstructing six of them from journals, diaries, notebooks, memoirs, letters and actual recorded exchanges. If *Dinner at Magny's* is disappointing, it is not Mr. Baldick's fault. His part of the job is almost a tour de force: It is the principals who have let us down. At one moment, their conversation sounds like locker-room talk after quite a few Scotches at the nineteenth hole; at another, they huff, puff and pontificate like so many old duffers in rockers on a porch.

One of the displeasing things about the book is the way they posture and contort themselves for the sake of a *mot*. They sound as if they were trying to speak exclusively in definitions, or to enunciate epigrams they ghostwrote in advance. (This could be the fault of Mr. Baldick's method, but anyone familiar with their works or their biographies may be more inclined to blame some of the characters themselves.) Their speech rhythms are laden with a consciousness of their positions and strike our Cavett-conditioned ears as terribly slow.

Exclusively made conversations tend to make the speakers sound as if they were each fifty pounds heavier and hung-over as well. Grunts, wheezes, belches, hawkings are all decked out in impeccable diction, but women are needed—if only as a *digestif*—to keep the verbal gourmandizing to a decent level.

Gautier, who is still in his fifties, boasts that he makes love only once a year. The Goncourt brothers, being younger, share a mistress once a week. Balzac, who is not present, is mentioned as practicing coitus interruptus in order to conserve his creative powers. Flaubert is both better and worse, getting up to do a little dance in front of the mirror after each time. Only Turgenev sounds even remotely moved in a way we can empathize into: he says that, after love-making, he is reunited with nature, things look real once more. Saint-Beuve, the reigning critic of the time, has never spent a whole night with a woman: his work schedule won't allow it.

Wisecracks abound, but they are positively architectural, built stone on stone like forts. The best remarks are all too often quoted from someone else. When speaking of literature, our great men all complain of too much work and too little appreciation. The old saw about new words for a new age is exhumed; the "pure" novel, the formally perfect, is relegated to second-raters, on the assumption that true genius cannot be altogether tamed by art. When the theologian Renan foolishly calls George Sand "the greatest artist of our times and the finest talent," Saint-Beuve gets off one of his better bits of malice: "Madame Sand has a great soul and a perfectly enormous bottom."

On the subject of politics, our celebrities are hardly worth quoting. They are far more interested in prostitution, of which Flaubert says: "A man has missed something if he has never woken up in an anonymous bed beside a face he'll never see again, and if he has never left a brothel at dawn feeling like jumping off a bridge into the river out of sheer physical disgust with life." "A glance into its [prostitution's] depths makes you dizzy and teaches you so much. It makes you so sad, and fills you with such dreams of love!" Such hyperbole is more understandable if we remind ourselves that brothels were different sorts of places in those days.

The siege of Paris during the war with Prussia finds our gourmets dining on dog and rat meat, stuffed donkey's head and elephant steak or consommé derived from the two former favorites of the Paris zoo. Turgenev complains that he can't make love any more; Gautier is attracted only to chic, freaky, "modern" types; one of the Goncourts has died of syphilis and the other's talk is a "litany of laments."

Paris, like every great city in the last hundred years, is changing for the worse: You have to buy your books standing up now. Magny's is overshadowed by a flashier place that offers a view of the boulevard and bad food. The new place is patronized by businessmen, politicians and military types. One wonders, irreverently, whether the conversations were better or worse.

Contemplating Sexual Suicide

The women's liberation movement has turned into one of those bitter marital spats in which neither partner will ever have the last word. As far as I'm concerned, though, it can end, for the time being, with George Gilder's *Sexual Suicide*, because I don't think anyone is going to improve on his book for quite a while. With the possible exception of Midge Decter, he is one of the first writers to discuss this subject with any attempt at objectivity. Of course, he has his biases too, but he supports them with reasons rather than rhetoric. Though it is men who are generally supposed to be pigheaded and temperamentally aggressive, Mr. Gilder is positively courtly compared to the vituperations of Germaine Greer, Kate Millett, Susan Brownmiller and other feminists. He is cool enough to be not only objective, but witty —which, of course, will condemn him in some quarters, where humorlessness and wanton disregard of hard facts have become the index of "involvement."

Like many another man who is interested, both by circumstance and by choice, in the evolution of women's attitudes, I was first alarmed, then curious, then sympathetic, then finally alienated by the female chauvinism of the feminists I met. When I tried to talk, not argue, with them, they shouted me down, or disqualified me per se from conversation because I am the enemy, a man. When I occasionally tried to agree with them, I was told that my agreement was presumptuous as well as irrelevant. My entire sex, in fact, had suddenly become irrelevant in what was supposed to be a "dialogue" between the sexes. Female "militants" are now bypassing us and addressing themselves directly to what they consider to be the proper authorities. In other words, they are talking to themselves.

Of course, like all mistreated minorities, they have a right to be angry, but this is an attitude that certain minorities seem determined to perpetuate as if it were an art form. No revolution ever succeeded by looking backward only, and it's time the women's movement admitted that it takes two to raise our consciousness, which is a very heavy object. Despite what some of the militants say, despite cloning and other forms of artificial insemination, men and women need each other. To paraphrase an old American humorist, men may not be much, but they're the best other sex women have. It may be fun to run away from home for a while, to spend a night out with the girls, but a couple of million years of evolution seem to suggest that they'll have to come home again. As someone said, behind every no, there's a passionate yes. Underneath all the noise, we really love and enjoy each other. There isn't a vibrator or warm-water-filled Barbie doll that can compare with us. This cold war can't put the home fires out.

It goes without saying that Mr. Gilder, like the women on the subject, is not always right—but at least I get the feeling that he is *trying* to get at the truth, that his mind is still open to the appeal of evidence. Also, what he has to say is so life-enhancing, his book offers us such a beautiful view from the Mountain of Venus, that I would admire it even if it were wrong. In the last analysis, it is not unambiguously a case of justice or injustice, because as the Princeton philosopher Walter Kaufmann has pointed out, the idea of justice, in our time, is often used as a red herring which can "blind a moral agent to the full range of his choices." Owing to the infinite variables in each individual situation, he contends, we can never hope to achieve full "justice for all." Instead of the sweeping generalizations that characterize so much of feminist literature—the lumping together of *all* men and *all* women—it might be more sensible to look for flexible solutions adapted to the needs of individual couples, as Norman Mailer suggested in his generally underrated book *The Prisoner of Sex*.

Many women's books on the sexual revolution remind me of that television commercial in which an unattractive woman wearing men's clothes scrubs a stubborn stain from an "old" sink. Men are the stain: "Out, out, damned spot!" The revolution is the "cleanser"; it has more ammonia and a host of secret ingredients, all which are fatal if taken internally.

Mr. Gilder writes more in regret than in anger. He, too, was originally a sympathizer who after several years' immersion in feminist literature found it contrary to his experience and to the conclusions of the best authorities he could find on the subject. And though his references are imposing, he generally uses them only as a second line of defense behind his own thinking. Many of the social scientists he quotes are women, as if he knew that his own or other men's reasoning would be dismissed as mere penis propaganda. For all its multiple ramifications, his fundamental theme can be stated in a few words. He feels that love, marriage and procreation seduce men into the "long horizons of female sexuality," which in turn incline them to continuity and commitment in their jobs, in their social behavior and in their conception of themselves.

Without love, sex is a hit-and-run affair in which not only women but men are often injured. Copulation is a "now" trip. In a social and psychological sense, there is no future in "free love." Anyway, nothing in this life is really free—it all has to be paid for in one way or another. The so-called paragons of freedom, the swinging bachelors pursuing a *Playboy* philosophy of polymorphous pleasure, are "by every measure the most afflicted Americans." They "comprise between 80 and 90 percent of most of the categories of social pathology," and their potency is such that "on the average they make less money than any other group in the society—yes, less than single women or married women." According to insurance actuarial records, "single men are also less responsible about their bills, their driving, and other personal conduct."

Most men, if they are not "socialized" and "refined" by women, by parenthood, or a similarly compelling structure, will tend to revert to the predatory nomadic hunter satisfying only his most primitive needs. Anyone who has been in the army can tell you what sort of effect the absence of women has on men. The danger now, Mr. Gilder feels, is that the more militant feminists are using the unsocialized male as a model for the liberated woman. Soon, perhaps, *she* will be able to boast of being "the most afflicted American." He is afraid too that she may succumb to the social hysterectomy recommended by the sexual revolution, so that she will no longer be a woman but a "human being"— that genderless Frankenstein monster of sentimental psychology.

When Germaine Greer advises women to forget about love

and go out and get laid, she forgets that the mind is at least as important as the genitals in sex, that men and women are animals who literally need symbols to make their behavior meaningful to them. At one time, they made love not in a stranger's bed, but in a king-sized cosmology, cheered on by God, society, and the philosophers and poets of the age. "This Extasie doth unperplex," as John Donne said. It is not at all the same as shacking up. If all the world loves a lover, only Germaine Greer loves a layer.

The biologist Desmond Morris, in his *Intimate Behavior*, says that we make love as much to fertilize a relationship as an egg. Rollo May, in *Power and Innocence*, observes that if the old symbols of love and sex seem dead, they should be mourned rather than denied. The feminists have so far refused all male offers of cooperation. They are resolved to be self-made women. But if they succeed in isolating their essences by a remorseless process of elimination, what will follow this starvation diet? What will they do with this long-sought self? So far, as Mr. Gilder points out, there has been very little said on this subject. Even Nora Ephron admits that "It is a great mystery to all of us." There is some question, too, whether sex without love can support women in the manner to which they have become accustomed.

According to the author, many women are already feeling the heavy burden of their new liberty and wondering whether they weren't a bit hasty in burning their bras and bridges behind them. Mr. Gilder agrees with Midge Decter's theory that the feminist movement may be not only a cause of women's increased power and freedom, but an effect of it as well, an attempt to deal with anxieties arising out of an earlier sense of their changing situation. In my own opinion, the movement may be trading away passion for "justice," which could be a Pyrrhic victory, for, though passion is perhaps our greatest luxury, justice is more in the nature of a utility. At any rate, you can't kiss it. Mr. Gilder would like to see women moving toward a greater humanity rather than a "metaphysical humanism," and I would too. I believe Hans Castorp touched on the heart of the matter when he said in *The Magic Mountain* that humanism, in a sense, was "disrespectful of life." The lyrical, at least, has never been its strong point, and it has inspired very few great poems, paintings, or other monuments of the spirit.

If the "free" man is to be set up as an ideal for the "enslaved" woman, it is very likely that she will exchange her "long horizons" for his short one. In the darkness of his "pad," it is easy to mistake discontinuity for freedom, and this, the author warns, can only lead to social disarray or disintegration. Civilization could easily deteriorate to a post-coitum tristis.

A woman, according to *Sexual Suicide*, lacks the innate sexual insecurity of a man. Her sexual identity is "unimpeachable" —verified by her potential for procreation—while a man's is only a creation of culture. If he is not confirmed in his maleness by providing for and protecting his family, his anxiety about his role will reduce him to reenacting it at the lowest common denominator of random copulation.

When Mr. Gilder adds that women control the economy of eros and that "a woman can grant to the man a sexual affirmation that he needs more than she does," I'm inclined to have some reservations. "I want to feel like a woman!" is an anguished cry that most men have heard some time in their lives. And it's my impression that men take more pride and comfort in their visible and dramatically responsive genitalia than the author allows for.

I think too that he underestimates the male role in parenthood when he says "there is no way that early nurture of children will be sexually affirmative for males." If he is correct in maintaining that the love that confirms man's masculinity originates in his anticipation of progeny, then it would follow that intimate contact with his children would further enrich his sexual identity. Mr. Gilder is correct, though, when he observes that feminists expect men to adopt the very characteristics they are discarding as "degrading": an interest in the home, a nurturing character toward children, an attitude of receptivity, passivity, tenderness and delicacy.

The author is very good at exposing the dilettante or distorted anthropology of some of the "stars" of the sexual revolution. Among many solid authorities who are closer to his camp, he cites Margaret Mead, who writes that "If any human society . . . is to survive, it must have a pattern of sexual life that comes to terms with the differences between the sexes." "Differences" is the key word here. To the author, "open marriage" is synonymous with sexual suicide. He sees it as, essentially, an elimination or perversion of all those conditions that marriage connotes. In communes and other strongholds of the counter-culture, open marriage is not conspicuously successful in keeping Daddy in the geodesic dome. I remember an example from Robert Houriet's *Getting Back Together* in which a pregnant girl is abandoned by the father of her baby because he feels that he has to "go and climb a mountain—alone." Even dropouts find that open marriages don't give them enough to do, and they tend to wander off in search of new metaphors. Mr. Gilder is not favorably impressed by the "sincerity" of the "increasing numbers of young people who clutter up their marriage ceremonies with commitments to 'growth,' 'synergy' and 'feedback.' These rebels begin their lives together by reaching for the most honest and sacred language they know, and it turns out to be the idiom of a conglomerate board meeting."

Though day-care centers may benefit some mothers, the author agrees with Dr. John Bowlby, who maintains that "children thrive better in bad homes than in good institutions." Ivan Illich goes a step further in his *Deschooling Society*, when he states that we have never succeeded in designing a good institution of any sort. As Mr. Gilder sees it, day-care centers are already being used to coerce mothers into working whether they want to or not. Because well-educated, middle-class women often get the best jobs, the average woman's "career," with its "inspiring challenges" and "broadening vistas"—as the feminists will have it—may mean a typewriter, a switchboard, a salesgirl's daily dissimulations, or even a mop and pail. Questioning the claim that the home is "less edifying than any remunerative job," the author refers to a demographic sampling of six hundred Chicago housewives, which revealed that they led "more challenging and varied lives" than their husbands. The grass is always greener on the other side.

In his assessment of androgyny, Mr. Gilder strikes me as missing the point. Excessive polarization has stultified both sexes to a degree, and I believe this does more harm than the encouragement of homosexuality that the author sees in androgyny. I think he overestimates the "hospitability" of American society to "passive and effeminate males." Tolerance or condescension would be a better description than "hospitable," and "passive and effeminate" do not do justice to the androgynous ideal, which might better be characterized as an attitude of creative comparison shopping by both sexes in the contemporary supermarkets of male and female ingredients. His conception of the homosexual world is extremely "judgmental," to use a dreadful new coinage that currently "resonates" through our classrooms. And the alternative to the unstable homosexual world—the all-too-stable apathy of many heterosexual households—seems to be urged on us by the author more in the spirit of a pious psychophysical pep talk than a pleasurable prospect.

Mr. Gilder feels that androgyny, and the sexual revolution in general, represent a dangerous tampering with human nature, a reduction of what Robin Fox and Lionel Tiger call the "biogrammar" of the species to "behavioral gibberish." In their book, *The Imperial Animal,* these authors argue that to oppose our instinctual programming is to invite what Yeats felt when he wrote that "mere anarchy is loosed upon the world . . . and everywhere the ceremony of innocence is drowned."

As I have already remarked, Mr. Gilder is not always right, but he is more often right than wrong. And, in either case, his heart is usually in the right place, stoutly beating for love, family and the future of society. It is an ironical comment on that society to reflect that *Sexual Suicide* might be seen as a contemporary equivalent of the love poems of the Metaphysicals—those ardent, brilliant and witty syllogisms with which Donne, Marvell and Herrick celebrated their mistresses. Though Marvell was merely teasing when he described a man and woman as parallel lines that can never meet, certain feminists seem to take him literally.

Yet, Mr. Gilder insists, "love is optimistic." In someone else's definition—I can't remember whose—it is defined as "constructive energy." If we can remain optimistic, constructive, energetic and loving, we may yet reconcile the sexes to each other and put to good personal and social use the anatomical peculiarities with which Nature has so mischievously endowed us. There are hints here and there that we may be destined to go even further than either the author or the feminists have so far envisioned. As the husband says to his wife in Joy Williams's novel *State of Grace*, "What can be beyond love? I want to get there. With you." Perhaps there is a beatitude—beyond sexual adventure, beyond raised consciousness—that we have not yet divined. I remember a remark made by a schizophrenic girl I knew long ago: Two people making love, she said, are like one drowned person resuscitating the other. That's how I see the sexes today —washed up together on some bleak ontological beach, trying to catch their breath while wondering what to do next.

Being vs. Doing in Fiction

The short story today seems to be caught up in a competition of subtlety. Who can weave a web of the thinnest materials? Who is most cunning in avoiding the vulgarity of action? Even the characters, the uneliminable element in stories, are muted down to the point where they are just barely there. In fact, one might call such stories existential or ontological, for it is the characters' "being there"—the *Dasein* of Heidegger—that is their sole drama. For the existentialist, "being there" is the essence of man's condition, and there are authors who are content to illustrate this.

Some of them have worked out a very ingenious way of doing it. Their technique is so smooth, so unobtrusive, that their characters are evoked before your eyes with a hardly perceptible stir. They appear on such crafty cat feet that they are there before you have had a chance to develop any feelings or expectations about them. It's a conjuring trick: the author produces the character so mysteriously that he never "arrives." And since you haven't seen him coming, you don't expect him to go anywhere.

That, in fact, may be the object of this genre: simply to *confront* you with someone. Just as some graphic artists will seize upon a found object and by putting it up on the wall of a gallery transform it into an art object, so these authors make fiction out of "found" people. Since they have no history and no discernible goals, you have no choice but to focus on them right now—on the themness of them.

We are so alert to ourselves as unique animals born into an unprecedented tangle of psychophysical predicaments that—if we want to create a "story"—it is almost enough merely to look at ourselves in a mirror. When we glance back through our recent history, we are not encouraged to believe in the value of meliorative action, so that, if we are not to surrender to the notion of futility, our best strategy is to fall back on our "thereness."

And it's quite tempting in its own right, for human existence today is an equilibrium more complex—more loaded with texture, frozen movement, overlapping planes, point and counterpoint, promise, threat, tension, tragedy and comedy—than most works of art. Our drama as a species threatens to render any further drama redundant.

In *The Devastating Boys,* more than half of Elizabeth Taylor's stories are about "being there." The title piece shows a staid, middle-aged English couple taking two little West Indian boys into their country home for a two-week holiday. Although the boys are busy the whole time, nothing really happens. The point of the story is that when they leave, the middle-aged couple are more aware of their own "thereness." "Tall Boy" is another West Indian, a young adult, all alone in England. It is his birthday, and because he feels the precariousness of his *Dasein* he sends himself a card. In "Praises," a venerable store is closing its doors and Miss Smythe, one of its most faithful employes, is forced to transfer her attention from her job to herself, from doing to being.

"Flesh" deals with two people who meet on a holiday. They are attracted to each other, and after some unsatisfactory necking in a car, they make elaborate plans to spend a night together. But on that very night—their last chance—he has a crippling attack of gout and all she can do for him is prop pillows under his foot. The fact that they don't make love makes us so much more aware of them—and them of themselves. Instead of following what they do, we ponder what they are. And that is the story. They have made their bed—in every sense of the word— and we watch them just lying there in it.

In "Crêpes Flambées," a couple return to North Africa in a sentimental attempt to relive their honeymoon. But their favorite café and its lively proprietor, Habib, have disappeared. When they do finally run into Habib, he is no longer the jovial patron, drawing them together, but an evasive and pathetically boastful liar who exposes the fallacy of the place and leaves them with the cold facts of themselves and each other.

As if she is out of practice in rendering action, Miss Taylor does not do terribly well with it. Three of the stories end in what is commonly known as an "O. Henry twist," and this must be a measure of the author's desperation, that she can create movement only by wrenching things around and contradicting the character of her people. These stories might well be discounted as mistakes by definition.

What is more disturbing is the story of the first sort, which doesn't come off, in which the characters somehow miss their bid for ontological radiance. Poor condemned souls, they drop away into the nothingness that is always breathing down the neck of being. And the failed story becomes one more reflection of the risks we all run, every day.

Opening the Gilded Cage

Martha Graham emancipated both women and dance from the tyranny of prettiness. Just as she reintroduced the law of gravity into dance—by bringing it down to earth—so she brought out the gravity of her sex as well. If women soared in ballet, they bore down in Graham. Her work was a flatfooted confrontation with the anatomy of femininity. While ballet embellished women —even in dying, they were graceful as swans—Miss Graham investigated their anguish. Her choreography was as realistic as ballet was artificial.

The world, of course, was not ready for Miss Graham. It is almost never ready for anything truly radical. Some found her dances ugly, and sometimes, I suppose, they may well have been, for beauty is only one among many of women's options. There is no denying the fact that the obligation to be beautiful is extremely confining. Anyone who sits through a poorly balanced program of ballet—as I sometimes have—will recognize this. I think modern art uses the ugly at least as much as the beautiful and it is necessary to remember that both these words are highly imprecise. Miss Graham transcends both definitions by playing them off against each other.

I remember seeing her years ago at a theater where Katherine Dunham, the primitive dancer, had appeared the week before. Two smart-looking women sitting in front of me had apparently attended the other program too, for after a long, particularly agonized solo by Miss Graham, one of them turned to the other and said: "Well, my dear, Dunham did fertility and here's Martha with menopause." Like any witticism the remark may be unfair, but it raises an interesting question: Why shouldn't Miss Graham do a dance about menopause? The end of fertility is almost as dramatic in the life of a woman as it's beginning—and if anyone could choreograph this, she could. For all I know, I may in fact have seen her do it, under the guise of Greek tragedy.

As Don McDonagh observes in his much-needed critical biography, *Martha Graham*, she left very few female emotions unchoreographed. She has always been the most militant feminist who ever lived and the most talented. In both ballet and society, woman had been "only a bird in a gilded cage." When Miss Graham opened the cage, the bird became a bat out of hell, among other things. She sweated, stamped her feet in defiance, panted instead of pirouetted, brought the heavy burden of her body, soul, and situation onto the stage. Many of Miss Graham's dances might justly be called vivisections. Here was a striptease with a vengeance, as she tore off veil after veil to show us facets of femininity that many men—and not a few women—might have preferred to keep under cover.

The ambivalence she provoked in some dance critics was interesting. While conceding her artistic integrity, one said of her works that "they were morbidly fascinating, like watching a mother in labor or an unfortunate doubled up with acute appendicitis on a curb, writhing wretchedly in anticipation of the arrival of an ambulance . . ." Other critics wrote that "her performance leaves one exhausted rather than entertained," or that "It is impressive but not designed for enjoyment." Though Mr. McDonagh, who is a dance critic for *The New York Times*, tends to regard such reactions as a failure to understand Miss Graham's work, this is not necessarily the case. While these comments may not do full justice to her, they are not altogether undeserved either.

Mr. McDonagh traces Miss Graham's evolution as she gropes for her vocabulary, finds and refines it. He shows us how she used contraction and release as a connective device and the torso as a source of motor energy. Her movements, he says, always grew out from inside, like an organic form seeking its proper shape. They arose out of dramatic necessity, never expediency. He follows her from her early percussive and transitionless intransigeance to the lyrical elegance and sleek sinuosity she created when her fight was won and she knew she could afford it. Interviewing friends, associates and members of her company, painstakingly researching the fifty years of her career, he tells us about her feelings, her thinking, her reading, her relationships, her approach to choreography and training.

Though he must have been hampered by the dissension that has haunted the Graham Company for at least a decade, by Miss Graham's own unwillingness to cooperate, by the silence imposed on those who wished to stay in her favor, Mr. McDonagh has given us a commendably detailed picture.

Since Miss Graham is such an intense subject, he has kept his own tone under discreet control. Realizing that no words can convey the *experience* of her dancing, he resists this rhetorical temptation and does a good job of *describing* her work. He is particularly adept at relating Miss Graham's themes to her life, taking the tension between her puritan background and her thrust toward freedom as the source of her early American pieces, and her hauteur, her increasingly "cosmic" pose, as the impulse behind her later absorption in Greek drama and mythology.

He does not hesitate to say of Miss Graham that "she was interested in herself and the present." Anything she could not dominate as a performer she tended to dismiss. Originally, she admitted men into her company only because she needed them as props or pylons around which she could career. Though she fell in love more than once, we get the impression that she merely "used" men in what women would call a "sexist" way. She showed little interest in choreographing *their* problems, beyond casting them, as Mr. McDonagh puts it, as "ringmaster" and "acrobat," apt evocations of Erick Hawkins and Merce Cunningham.

In referring to her imperiousness and her oracular pose, Mr. McDonagh reminds us that, before she became famous, these may have been the only forces holding her company together. Remarking that, in the last decade, "she had become the hostage of her own fame," he is generous enough to see this not only as a punishment she brought on herself, but also as the isolation that always threatens genius.

When Miss Graham said that she invented nothing, only rediscovered what the human body could do, it was perhaps her one moment of modesty. But even if we accepted this understatement, it would still place her among those few who have carried our image of ourselves beyond our wildest imagining— and who did it, for the most part, against our own stubborn wills.

A Hug for the Antiheroine

The antihero has been hanging around in fiction for quite a while, but the antiheroine is just now making her debut. As one of the fringe benefits of their liberation, women are beginning to realize that they have fully as much right to disappoint the world's expectations as men do. They have become exhilaratingly aware that they are our equals not only in achievement but also in failure. And it is impossible to exaggerate the importance of this discovery. It may turn out to be one of the most far-reaching of all the momentous insights they have gained in the last decade.

Probably the greatest of all antiheroes is Dostoyevsky's protagonist in *Notes from the Underground*. The book opens with these lines: "I'm a sick man. I'm a spiteful man. I'm an unattractive man. I think there's something wrong with my liver." But Dostoyevsky's character is positively benign next to Iris Owen's antiheroine Harriet. Harriet, by the way, is the perfect name for her: she is, above all, a harrier, like that breed of dog that is trained to wear down its prey.

Though Harriet's sexuality is virtually prehensile, her conversation conjures up castration. She plays at bitching as her mother plays canasta. Her intelligence is a St. Vitus's dance of vituperation, and she wears her injuries like pornographic underwear. As if the much-maligned Jewish mother had turned bohemian mistress, Harriet cries Communicate! instead of Eat! But communication—the other consummation of all loving couples—is, for her, essentially an opportunity to exercise her inalienable right to be wrong. In an America where Jewishness has lost most of its stigma, her insistent ethnicity leaves her a rebel without a cause. As part of her personal charm, she has a compulsion to point out everyone's deepest insecurities as if she were merely plucking a thread off their sleeves.

When Harriet goes to bed with a man, she always takes her wet blanket with her. She is a sexual crusader, determined to establish woman as an outrageous but necessary inconvenience. Her life is a lie-in, a protest against the fact that to be female is to be at the mercy of a double irrationality: her own and men's. The impact of her personality is staggering. It reminds one of Paul Valéry's definition of a poet as someone who assembles, bit by bit, a tremendously complicated piece of machinery, and then shoves it off a rooftop onto the head of the unsuspecting passer-by.

Harriet has just come back from a five-year stay in Paris, where she must have soaked herself in the work of that incomparable grievance collector, Louis-Ferdinand Céline. In spite of her disenchantment with France and the French, we find her living in New York with Claude, a Parisian. Or perhaps it is *because* of her feelings about France—perhaps she is avenging herself on that country in the person of Claude.

Claude is here to produce documentary films on the American way of life for French television. As Harriet describes them, they are "riot commercials. Student riots, antiwar riots, gay liberation riots, convention riots, ghetto riots; in short, Democracy at work. The only faces he filmed were covered with blood or gas masks." To hear Harriet tell it, she worked so hard at entertaining Claude that she "should be required to apply for a cabaret license." When he complains about the filth in the kitchen, she promises to get it so clean that Claude's dinner guest "could perform an abortion in there." She is a "slave" who works her fingers to the bone reducing her master's life to chaos.

Harriet's jaundiced views are not confined to Claude: she is irritated by everybody. Of her oldest friend she says: "Maxine was under the impression that since we had jumped rope together in Brooklyn, our insults were predicated on love." Maxine, she adds, "had more accents than Peter Ustinov, but unless you punched her in the stomach, you never heard the real one." Every man not drooling over Harriet—or failing to produce the same effect in her—is a "fag." Every other woman is a whore or a nymphomaniac. Watching TV, our antiheroine impatiently fidgets before "a panel of blacks demanding back payment for three hundred years of tap dancing."

When Miss Owens's style works, it has an ammonia-like astringency: it cuts through the grease, so to speak. When Harriet finds a lover—through a newspaper ad—for a frigid friend, she remarks: "I believe his name was Lloyd. I never established if that was his name or the self-effacing manner in which he said hello." No matter what time of day Harriet phones her parents, who have moved to California, she interrupts their "napping tournament," and one or the other struggles up out of unconsciousness to mumble, Who? Oh, yes, the weather's beautiful.

When Claude suggests that she lose some weight, Harriet observes that "to men who are not basically fond of women, every additional ounce of flesh is like a thorn in their side." When Claude finally threatens to throw her out and she attempts to seduce her way back into his affections, the progression is typical of her. She begins by crooning, "Why don't you lie down here next to me and let nature take its course?" When he shows no sign of responding, she reverts to type and says, "To hell with nature. I'll take nature's course."

After Claude does evict Harriet, Miss Owens seems as much at a loss where to go and what to do as her character. It is as though she suddenly looked at Harriet and said—as they once did in Hollywood movies—"This thing is bigger than both of us." The conclusion of *After Claude* is so far below the rest of the book that it seems to have been written by someone else. It may not matter, though. If you can salvage Harriet, you'll find that Miss Owens has created a new kind of monster for your compassion. And isn't that, after all, one of the classical functions of contemporary fiction?

If the Hat Doesn't Fit . . .

How much of a story does an author have to give a reader before asking him to imagine the rest? I think this is one of the crucial questions of contemporary fiction. The best writers tease us into an ever more active empathy by inspiring—not forcing —us to collaborate in completing their works. They create spaces for us to occupy, opportunities for us to own a piece of the experience. You can do it, they say, like a parent to a doubtful child: Come on, jump! And if we accept the challenge and land on our feet, we feel that exhilaration of a risk taken and triumphed over. We know we could not have succeeded without the author's help and encouragement, but to venture beyond ourselves, under any circumstances, is something. It is part of the genius of a good modern writer that he turns his reader into a bit of an artist too. His story is not unlike an act of love. I will give you the stimuli, he says in effect: whether or not you achieve a climax through them is up to you.

To pursue the sexual metaphor just a step further, I would say that the "old-fashioned" writers—even the good ones—*did* prostitute their art, in a sense. They did everything for the reader, supplied his smallest need. And he often tended to become passive under all these ministrations, even sluggish. He was trapped in the author's solicitude, like a weekend guest whose host plans his every moment for fear he will not know what to do with himself.

Reading fiction today is an adventure in a double sense: the adventure of the material and the adventure of the technique. Some readers—not excluding critics—ignore one in favor of the other. The ideal reader knows that they are inseparable, that he has to be "androgynous"—both aggressive and receptive—if he is to follow the work to its furthest limits. I know that when I manage this, I feel a rich, unfolding sense of "wild surmise," a pleasure complexly trembling on the edge of definition, neither frustratingly obscure nor tamely secure. I feel that I am in the presence of possibilities, of structures and harmonies, I haven't experienced before. Though, like poetry, these experiences are unparaphrasable, they are not vague, not hollow or grandiose promises. As Archibald MacLeish said so long ago about poems: a story should not mean, but be.

For some writers, this new form comes naturally—but Bernard Malamud is not one of them. To me, he seems to be a rather literal-minded fellow, of the best sort, the kind of man who is too involved with—too *pained* by—life to be able to shape it at will in his stories. He suffers it to come unto him, rather than the other way around.

But even the ugliest or unhappiest life is "rotten with lyricism," as Zola said, and the strongest part of Malamud's talent has been his ability to recognize this depressed poetry, to find exact and unforgettable images for it, as he did in "The Magic Barrel," "Black Is My Favorite Color," *The Assistant* and parts of *The Tenants*. Like Wallace Stevens's "Man on the Dump," Malamud writes "janitor's poems of every day," vibrating "between that disgust and this." He "sits and beats an old tin can, lard pail . . . among mattresses of the dead."

Working in a conventional mode, Malamud was rarely conventional; he almost always transcended it. But unfortunately, in electing to write "avant-garde" stories, he has fallen into another kind of conventionality: the habit of glib ellipsis, of awkward, *hamish* surrealism, unsatisfying sleight of hand. (In one of his pieces in this collection, he actually pulls a man out of a horse.)

"The Silver Crown" is the story of a skeptical high school biology teacher who goes to a faith healer because the doctors can do nothing for his dying father. In the space of a sentence— a sign of Malamud's impatience with either his character or his story—the teacher overcomes a lifelong empirical bias and engages the faith healer. The story becomes progressively more unconvincing—especially the "twist" ending—yet the author's fine eye and ear redeem a good deal of it. Two details—the pulled window shades in the healer's house that "resemble faded maps of ancient lands" and the frosted lily light fixture on the ceiling—show you what a master of incidentals Malamud is.

"The Letter" is a mistake, a mere finger exercise, which doesn't even work on that level. "In Retirement" is a lame billet-doux not worth a pink ribbon. In "My Son the Murderer" and the title story, the reader wades through an unrewarding sequence that seems to be only a ramp of sorts to conduct him to the conclusion. And in each case, the conclusion is one of those cryptic, mystic affairs that mean everything and nothing. Together with several other stories in the book, these two left me feeling, when I had finished them, like someone whose dentist has sent him away with a mouthful of temporary fillings.

I can't resist one more complaint, as long as this is the menu for today. Does Malamud's language *have* to be so homely? I get the impression that he employs it as a guarantee of sincerity, of high seriousness. Behind its gimpy diction, I can almost imagine him saying: There is nothing frivolous about Bernie Malamud. I wouldn't try to talk you into buying. Here we sell nothing but the honest truth. Feel the goods—one hundred percent pure wool.

The author's last book, *The Tenants*, was full of fine things. Let's hope he has already worn out *Rembrandt's Hat*—he looks so much better in his fedora or his homburg.

Everything's on My Mind

Though many have tried, Leon Forrest is one of the few authors who have made an art form out of being black. His voice quavers between praying and playing the dozens, a game that uses the tongue like a switchblade. His book is a voice crying in the wilderness of poverty and race relations. Religion is its core, in the sense of felt inscrutable powers and the absolutely indispensable hope of salvation. His rhythms remind me of the at first deliberate, then glory- or hell-bound hysteria of a storefront church sermon. In his nonstop, nerve-racking eloquence, Mr. Forrest also resembles the street-corner evangelist who sputters "Lord!" as if he thought the devil would catch him if he lagged.

What is his novel about? As one of his characters says, *"Everything's on my mind."* The author has so many things he wants to lay before us, and they are all so overlapped, so flattened and sharpened out of shape, that he can only come at them like a cubist. His approach is as ominous and oblique as the Southern custom of "cutting your eyes" at someone. Many of his staccato alliterations are like a slow-tongued, Southern, stuttering echo of Gerard Manley Hopkins. But for all his eloquence, Mr. Forrest is as unequivocally at home, as down to earth, as a kettle screeching on the kitchen stove. Sometimes, in fact, when his voice reaches its upper registers, it reminds me of a mongrel's shrill yi-yi-yipe! as my own grandmother performed the immemorial Southern ritual of cutting off its tail with a cleaver on the chopping block in the backyard.

In his foreword, Ralph Ellison, black literature's magic Old Man of the Mountain, speaks of Mr. Forrest's "speculations upon the shifting relationships between the American myth of democracy and everyday reality . . . evocations of those dilemmas bred of Christian faith and racial conflict, of social violence, family friction and dreams of a peaceful kingdom." He refers to the author of *There Is a Tree More Ancient Than Eden* as "a black American writer who, having rejected the stance of cultural self-segregation, reveals himself as eager to pit his talent against the achievements of the great masters of the form."

Among the many things in this long wail of a short book, there is a funeral, with a little boy following his mother's hearse in a limousine, which follows in its turn the route of a peddler's wagon down DuSable Street, Black Bottom Street, past Abe Weinstein's dog, Wild Helen, past Douglas Street, "hung over and sunken with cracks like the very cavities in Uncle Dupont's bad wisdom teeth." One of the subtlest tests of a writer's talent, his feel for his material, is the aptness, the inevitability of the names he gives his characters—and Mr. Forrest's choices are the coinages, or the recollections, of someone who has "been there," who has known, loved and sometimes feared these people. Here are Taylor (Warm-Gravy) James, Maxwell (Black-Ball) Southport, Goodwin (Stale-Bread) Winters, Ernest (Come-Humming) James, Constitution (Elbows) Armstrong. Names like these are the folk poetry of the Southern Negro; they have the warp and lilt of the street peddler's cries.

Much of *There Is a Tree More Ancient Than Eden* is a passionate apostrophe to a Lord whose "mysterious ways" perplex the narrator. Why, Lord? he asks, returning again and again to his interrogation, twining theme and variation like a Bach fugue. In the first part, introducing his people, he says, Look at these lives, Lord. Why are they so dark and strange? Then he narrates a nightmare, a wild, howling parody of the Church. Another section called "The Dream" is a furious catechism of things as they are. "The Vision" is the ultimate lynching-crucifixion offered up as an apocalyptic piece of vaudeville-cum-picnic.

I want you to taste Mr. Forrest's style: ". . . in the early autumn of that year, in tones which grieved as they sparked with awe, fear—springing from a deeply indelible moment, as if his uncle had become a new man, purged of his wildness, purged of his violence, purged of his humor, purged of his alcoholic feats, purged of his women, his pork, his blues, his dice, his dance, his clothes, his walk, his talk, his name, his self, in the name of Self . . ." Here's another sample: ". . . coming and going down that short long journey road son, he knows you falling and rising, faith crumbling and backbone slipping; and you kinda calling like a baby, as you trying to catch up and reach out at his hand all day and all night, hoping that he'll walk with you through the woeful trials, in the valley of the shadow; through raining down sorrow; the way he has always walked with us as a people through our river-wide tribulations; yes, and just as he's constantly tested us in the furnace of affliction . . ."

Like any man obsessed with what he's doing, deliberately taking breathless risks, Mr. Forrest makes his share of mistakes. He doesn't always have the time or patience to wait for the *mot juste*; he repeats himself to make sure we heard him; he sprints through his book like a record-breaking track star, while we pant behind him. But most of the time, he speaks to us like a fallen angel, struggling to rise. Most of the time his lines are as right as the lyrics of the spiritual that Aunt Hattie sings:

"I knows my wings gonna fit me well!
Lord! You know I done tried 'em on at the gates of hell!"

Catechizing Secular Man

In reading contemporary sociology, I have noticed that many authors complacently assume that their readers share their basic premises. Quite often, for example, I have found myself gathered up in a generalization that rubs me the wrong way, that does not agree with my feelings about myself and my experience. Fashionable New Left sociology is the worst offender, frequently treating the dissident reader as if he were a crank or anachronism.

In *Unsecular Man*, Andrew Greeley ratifies this reaction of mine by attempting to expose the accepted current view of modern man as a sociological caricature. Or rather two caricatures, for as he puts it: "The first is 'secular' man; that is to say, man who has 'come of age.' He is so confident that he has solved all the mysteries of the universe that he can dispense with a sense of mystery and with all questionings about the ultimate. Secular man can do without the sacred. His first cousin is technological man, who not only understands the universe but dominates it with his scientific knowledge and his technological skills. Such men are able to cut themselves off from the primordial ties of faith, consciousness of kind, and common land which bound men together in the past. The relationships which they enter are determined by the functional requirements of the corporate structures that they have built up to understand and dominate the universe."

Mr. Greeley feels that secular man exists primarily in great universities and that he represents a small but vocal minority. To prove his point, he cites a wealth of survey data to show that people today are far more active in religion than they are, for example, in politics.

Religion, he maintains, has not so much declined as sociologists are fond of alleging: it has changed. It no longer has direct influence on most of the large corporate structures that have emerged in the last four hundred years, such as government, big business, labor, the military and education. Religion has had to relinquish many of its "mysteries" to the explanations of science. Man's increased capacity for abstract thought has made a similar penetration of religion's myths, which are now treated more as metaphors than as absolutes. And, finally, the church doors have been thrown open to free choice, to more explicit or individual formulations than previously.

What have not changed, says the author, are the basic functions of religion: supplying a faith or meaning-system for coping with the questions of the human condition; providing for a feeling of belonging, in the broadest sense; integrating the disturbing forces of sexuality with the rest of our human concerns; offering a form of deep and intimate contact with the real.

Fashionable sociologists are fond of describing these functions today as "residual" or "inauthentic." All primordial or prerational ties are considered unenlightened and reactionary. If a man is religious, he is not to be trusted but mistrusted, as someone living in a superstitious and narrow-minded backwater of social evolution.

The evolutionary theory of society, Mr. Greeley feels, is the cradle of secular man. Here again, with the formidable support of Professor Robert Nisbet, the author holds that such a theory is another one of those unconscious or implicit assumptions that current sociology has never really examined. There are no empirical data, according to Professor Nisbet, to suggest that social change is in any sense an evolution. This notion, which arose out of a biological analogy, Mr. Greeley describes as a totally unwarranted inference. History shows social change to be not evolutionary, but discontinuous, discrete and nondirectional.

According to *Unsecular Man*, many misconceptions arise because of a popular "literary myth": the notion that a society can be accurately described in terms of the ideas generated by its intellectuals and philosophers. Snobbery of this sort is one of the occupational diseases of the intelligentsia. In projecting their own image on the universe, they often ignore the evidence right under their noses. For example, their children, students and intellectual heirs are indulging in religious practices so bizarre as to suggest that their need is not less, but more desperate than ever.

The "necessity" attributed to the organic evolution of society is as much an article of faith as any religion, says Mr. Greeley. It is the dogma of progress, secular man's answer to uncertainty. We might describe it as a religion that refuses to recognize its myths or its prophets. Yet these true believers have not hesitated to adopt a moralistic tone and it is intellectual heresy to disagree with them.

Though I have never concerned myself unduly about religion, I believe that my attitude of "benign neglect" does less harm than a scientific attempt to dismiss the subject. When the secular is too much in the ascendancy, the spirit of the culture—even in a secular sense—appears to decline. The "feel" of things is flatter, cruder, narrower. The absence of mystery leaves us with a "now what?" that nothing seems to assuage and man begins to feel and sound like a tautology.

In the second part of *Unsecular Man*, I get the impression that it is easier to repel attacks on religion than it is to make positive statements about it. Quoting Professor Clifford Geertz, Mr. Greeley says that what happened to us in the Ice Age is that we changed from genetically controlled animals to comparatively free agents whose behavior and experience were organized according to systems of significant symbols. As another writer put it, man began to live in "an information gap" between what his body told him and what he had to know in order to function.

This gap was filled by what came to be called culture, which, as man adapted to his new situation, became a biological and psychological necessity that transformed him into a symbolizing, conceptualizing, meaning-seeking animal. Next, this curious animal was obliged to evolve a religion as a means of ordering his experience and interpreting his world.

Bafflement and the threat of chaos were two of the negative forces urging man on in the search for meaning. In a more positive sense, the author describes religion as the beginning of man's struggle for the real. Quoting Professor Geertz again, he says that at the heart of the religious perspective "is the conviction that the values one holds are grounded in the inherent structure of reality, that between the way one ought to live and the way things really are there is an unbreakable interconnection."

Early man expressed his sense of this interconnection through the elaboration of myth. Myth, according to Alan Watts, is meaning divined rather than defined, implicit rather than explicit, suggested rather than stated. It is "emotional thought," truth told not abstractly but concretely. There are human experiences, the author argues, that can be expressed only in symbolic forms or myths, and these forms are profound to the degree that they capture the specificity of our situation. Now that the myths of religion are being invaded by science, Mr. Greeley fears that they are losing their immediacy. But, he adds, by "hearing again," by reinterpreting our myths on new levels, we can achieve a "second naiveté."

Turning to the conception of the sacred, *Unsecular Man* describes it as "the intrusion of the transcendental—real or imagined—in our ordinary life." When the impulse to the sacred is ignored, it crops up in strange places, particularly among disaffected young people. One of the forms of the sacred is the numinous, the "wholly other," an experience both awe-inspiring and seductively fascinating.

On rare occasions or in certain religions, the numinous is approached through ecstatic experience; more often, it is incorporated into ritual, which is described as a formalized commitment to the "serious" element of existence. With an almost audible sigh, Mr. Greeley admits that the number of numinous objects is undeniably declining.

In his chapter on religion and sex, he describes female fertility and the phenomenon of birth as numinous and says that "sexuality is by its very nature sacred and by its very nature religious"—a conception that he never made clear to me, though I am essentially in sympathy with it. It also seems to me that he has said too little about the numinousness of both tender and passionate love.

In his summing up, Mr. Greeley gives us two concrete examples of what he sees as the need for religion today. Our runaway technology, he says, is the result of the lack of a systematic interpretive scheme of the universe. Only myth, he feels, can meaningfully formulate the relationship between technology and nature. The "generation gap" is his second instance. Denying that it is principally a conflict with older structures of

belief, he characterizes it as an absence of all belief that culmi-
nates in despair. And despair, of course, has immemorially been
the business of religion.

As Mr. Greeley sees it, there are three strategies open to the
Church today: to remain aloof, holding its holy skirts clear of
the debris of modern life; to prostrate itself before the false
gods of "social relevance"; or to reinterpret its myths, advancing
them as neither fact nor false, but an entirely different kind of
truth. Myth, he contends in advocating this third alternative, is
a necessary going beyond scientific or literal truth to "existential
truth." In this sense, myth describes not the experience as such
—which might be better achieved by science—but the *meaning*
of the experience.

Though Mr. Greeley has not, in my opinion, provided an airtight proof of the need for religion, he has certainly amassed a
wealth of appealing arguments and circumstantial evidence in
its favor. Or, to put it another way, I might say that I find him
considerably less *un*convincing than the supporters of secular
man.

A Nostalgia for Normality

In quite a few recent novels, I've noticed a growing impatience with human nature, a tendency to try to plumb it by way of shortcuts, using the sort of ellipsis that certain drugs are supposed to encourage. It has become a common thing for an author to push his characters to their extremist limits without passing through the gradations of behavior that would enable them to arrive there with a degree of credibility. You might call this new style a literature of ontological leaps. Every character a kangaroo. Just as few people walk these days if they can ride, so few authors wish to be seen slogging from here to there. Cinematic cuts and shorthand psyches are all the rage. Like the biscuits mother used to bake, the old-fashioned, full-blown, homemade personality is becoming a thing of the past.

Perhaps this is why novels now tend to be brief, running to less than 200 small pages. Instead of mining the particularity of his characters until he reaches bedrock, many a "modern" author simply *imposes* qualities on them whenever he feels the need. This often has the effect, if you take his people seriously, of making them appear insane—in the sense that the sources of their behavior are beyond conjecture.

It may not be unreasonable that, after a run of such books, I feel a nostalgia for normality. The great novelists have always known that even the most ordinary man is more interesting than a surprise-stuffed schizophrenic. At least he offers the possibility of drama, as opposed to the attempt at diagnosis, which has become one of the additional burdens of literary criticism. You can see the same impatience with the slow progressions of personality in current schools of psychotherapy, where case histories are anathema and the emphasis is all in the direction of accelerating the stripping of the psyche, or even bypassing it. Though our age refers with ever greater piety to man's infinite complexity, his "excellent differences" get the bum's rush more and more often in fiction.

In *Ninety-two in the Shade*, Thomas McGuane has made his

people interesting and attractive to a degree, but when we reach for them we come up empty-handed because they are essentially inscrutable. And though such inscrutability is probably deliberate, the result of some sophisticated form of romanticism, it just frustrates me. I can't think of anything more boring or unromantic than someone I can't make out at all. True romanticism, it seems to me, is closer to a voracious curiosity, a wanting to know *everything*.

Thomas Skelton, Mr. McGuane's hero, is one of that immense army of existential drifters who have settled on our country like an epidemic of moral mononucleosis. He lives in Key West, in an abandoned airplane fuselage, naturally, next-door to a flophouse, where an alcoholic former sergeant drills a squad of drunken winos in the yard. Skelton's father has been in bed for seven months. He is not ill, however: he is only attempting, he finally confesses, to create a situation of mystery by artificial means. Artificial is the correct word. Skelton's mother, the sanest person in the book, was formerly a prostitute, naturally, in his father's whorehouse. We discover that Skelton senior has been slipping out at night—more mystery—wrapped in a sheet.

When Skelton, poor fellow, goes to see his girl, Miranda, who is a schoolteacher, she calls out from the bedroom: "I'm making love. Wait out there till I'm through." Though he is a bit cast down by the experience, she says firmly: "You'll have to think of another kind of innocence." Since, by his own admission, Skelton makes love to Miranda seven times in eight hours and five times in one afternoon, her infidelity can only be regarded as doctrinaire. Or perhaps she is avenging herself on him for applying the word "slot" to the part of her body in question.

Skelton's grandfather cavorts on a trampoline with his hefty, middle-aged mistress before he makes love. When you lose interest in the mainsprings of human behavior, you have to fall back on things like trampolines. Nichol Dance, a skiff guide with a violent history, threatens to shoot Skelton if he muscles in on his stretch of ocean, but instead of being put off, Skelton welcomes this "reminder of his mortality." He finds that he functions better under the gun, so to speak. A promising character, Dance disappears into his threat and we lose sight of him.

Though Mr. McGuane writes very good book reviews in which

he shows a rich awareness of the reach of fiction, as well as an extraordinary flair for phrasing, his novels seem to issue from some more "spontaneous" part of his personality. After *The Sporting Club* and *The Bushwhacked Piano*—which I regarded as shake-down flights for his unmistakable talent—it was natural to assume that by now he had found the handle. I felt sure that *Ninety-two in the Shade* would see him more mature, more confidently in control of his material. On the evidence, though, his fiction is still in its adolescence.

One of his troubles is language, for which he has a terrible sweet tooth. Grandiloquence keeps squirming to the surface like worms after rain. We find "poinciana trees that grew with vivid mystery," and on the very next page we collide with "a shy delivery boy of eternity's loops." Stone crabs display "bellicose Pentagonian idiocy." "A silent man wastes his own swerve of molecules." An airplane has "vulvate" exhausts and the roar of its engines is "draconic." "The dream of simultaneous orgasm is just a herring dying on a mirror." And aphorisms like this last one occur like hiccups all through the book.

Inevitably, Skelton is killed, in order, I suppose, to meld the book in a white-hot blaze of intensity. Only it doesn't work that way; in fact, it has just the opposite impact. Skelton is a sacrifice without a religion behind it. Tragedy in art is like a form of religion, but there is no tragedy here—only a desultory trying-on of effects. You might say that, these days, we waste lives almost as wantonly in our novels as we do in our politics.

Author and Title Index

About the Author

ANATOLE BROYARD has been a daily book critic for *The New York Times* since 1971. Before that he published stories and articles in *The New Yorker, Partisan Review, Hudson Review, Commentary, New World Writing, Modern Writing, Life, The New Republic, The New Leader* and various anthologies. He teaches short-story and novel writing at the New School and lectures on literature at New York University. He is now working on a novel.